Use Your Head

AARON LEVENSTEIN

Use Your Head

THE NEW SCIENCE OF PERSONAL

PROBLEM-SOLVING

THE MACMILLAN COMPANY, NEW YORK

COLLIER-MACMILLAN LIMITED, LONDON

160
L657w

To Pearl

in memoriam

CONTENTS

PREFACE

From a *Saturday Evening Post* article, "Never Make An Audience Think!" quoting movie producer Joe Pasternak: "I should blow $2,000,000 to send a message? Western Union is cheaper!"

From a letter of Julius Caesar to Cicero: "It is a nobler thing to enlarge the boundaries of the human intelligence than those of the Roman Empire."

THIS BOOK is a result of my experience in problem-solving. In my professional career, I have seen experts go to work on the problems of businessmen—legal, economic, fiscal, tax, sales, human relations, production, and so on through every major aspect of enterprise.

As a lawyer, I was constantly confronted by the difficulties in which human beings become involved. Extricating them from their problems required more than legal knowledge; equally important was a systematic way of thinking.

At the Research Institute of America, I spent 21 years exploring the facts about labor relations and human relations, preparing material for the guidance of executives, supervisors, and employees. Throughout, I was concerned with the daily problems of people trying to work together for common goals. In recent years, as a college professor, I have had an opportunity to systematize my experience for presentation to young people preparing to meet the practical problems that await them in earning a living.

I believe that the same scientific methods used by economists, accountants, statisticians, legal analysts, psychologists, and sociologists are applicable to the ordinary problems of individuals. This book attempts to translate the research principles and techniques of the specialist into the language and setting of everyday life.

To illustrate those concepts, I have drawn from a variety of different sources. Wherever problems have been solved, there you will find case histories. If the reader is struck by the fact that I make many references to the life of Abraham Lincoln, it is because the Great Emancipator seems to me the finest problem-solver America has ever produced. For the data I have used, I am indebted to Carl Sandburg, Benjamin Thomas, and Fletcher Pratt.

For other historical material, I found it convenient to use the works of Will Durant and Arnold Toynbee as reference sources. Both are treasuries of knowledge, and I have used them liberally. I must also mention here the important service to my own thinking that was rendered by Herbert J. Muller's *The Uses of the Past*—a book that taught me how to utilize yesterday in the interest of today and tomorrow.

For the more topical illustrations—the episodes drawn from the lives of thoughtful though sometimes obscure individuals —I have relied on my own contacts in business and social organizations, plus those of my former colleagues in the Development Division of the Research Institute: Phyllis Brown, Victor I. Bumagin, Ruth Burger, Donald Colen, Raymond Concannon, David A. Emery, Mortimer R. Feinberg, John Livingston, and Auren Uris; I am particularly grateful to the members of the Field Research Staff—Harry Tapper, William Shepherd, and Robert Dobbins—whose reports on their interviews with executives are a gold mine that Solomon the wise could envy. I look back with great pleasure to the joint adventure we conducted over the years.

In the area of theory, I am too hopelessly indebted to be able to list my creditors, much less make adequate payment. Their names are sprinkled through the book: Morris Raphael Cohen, John Dewey, Sidney Hook, Bertrand Russell, Alfred Korzybski, Karl Duncker—an endless list reaching back into the past to the anonymous authors of the Bible.

I must make special acknowledgment of my debt to Leo

Cherne, executive director of the Research Institute, for the years of association during which I could observe the cutting edge of his keen mind. Despite our many differences of opinion—perhaps because of them—I have profited immeasurably from my contact with him.

Two others, each at opposite poles of activity, have taught me much. One is Peter F. Drucker, the noted business commentator, whose original ways of thought I have been able to study at close range in a variety of settings. The other is Norman Thomas, whose nonconformist approach to national problems has been "the leaven in the lump" for an America groping toward new solutions. Among his many achievements is his success in teaching his fellow citizens the importance of courage in exploring new ideas.

In writing this book, I have thought of each chapter as a field in which it was necessary, first, to plough and prepare the soil and, second, to plant the seed. The first task involved the discussion of *principles* and their illustration; the second task was to enunciate *techniques*. *Principle* tells us what to do and why we should do it; *technique* tells us how to do it. Principle without technique is idle dreaming; technique without principle is a fruitless game.

You will notice that the principles are stated in declarative sentences; techniques are usually presented in the form of questions to be addressed to your problem. These questions are broadly stated for the sake of universal applicability, but they must always be reformulated if they are to fit the specific elements in a given problem.

Two pitfalls confront the author of a book on this subject. One is the temptation to reduce thinking to a series of steps or procedures. But it is the very essence of the intellectual adventure of problem-solving that there are no mechanical methods. To suppose that there are would be in effect to give the explorer a complete map with full directions as he sets out upon the journey; if he is going into completely mapped territory, however, he is not an explorer but merely a tourist. What can be done for the explorer is to give him the incomplete maps that others have made, to provision him for the voyage, and to describe what others did to find *their* way (which, in reality, is not his) and what perils others succeeded in avoiding.

This book is not intended to present "six ways to be a genius" or "five basic steps in thinking" that will make thought unnecessary. Nor does it—consciously—fall into the error of treating thought and problem-solving as an exercise in abstract theorizing. General principles are important and must not be ignored. Though such concepts open up no "steps" or "methods," they nevertheless provide an understanding of how our minds operate. William I. B. Beveridge has said: "It is more important to have a clear understanding of general principles, without thinking of them as fixed laws, than to load the mind with a mass of detailed technical information. . . . For creative thinking, it is more important to see the wood than the trees. . . ."

Without a comprehension of mental processes, intellectual effectiveness is bound to be reduced. I think that no psychologist has yet adequately explained why the man who "knows theory" functions more efficiently than the man who does not. Yet the superiority of the first man has been demonstrated. Professor C. H. Judd showed, for example, that the ability to hit a target under water was substantially increased if the marksman has received instruction in the theory of refraction.

To the extent that I have developed here any systematic approach to practical problem-solving, it has come out of an examination of how people have actually solved their problems, whether political, personal, or economic. In effect, my method has been to collect cases of successful problem-solving, and then to reconstruct the mental process involved. More specifically, my method has been to ask: "How did X think his way through to the solution?" Out of the answers I have obtained to this question, it seems to me, a suggestive pattern has emerged.

I do not suppose that the thinker in each case consciously

broke down his problem into the elements as I dissect them. Reasoning is often so fast that we don't perceive it in process. A figurative slow-motion camera can show us phases in the thought. Even if this were not so, to recognize after the event that the thought could have passed through definable theoretical steps is instructive. In the same way, the physicist is helped in understanding true-to-life motion by presupposing frictionless motion.

My decision to work from experience to conclusions rather than from logical systems to practical applications was influenced by an interesting comment in Elton Mayo's *The Social Problems of an Industrial Civilization.* "Speaking historically," he says, "I think it can be asserted that a science has generally come into being as a product of well-developed technical skill in a given area of activity. Someone, some skilled worker, has in a reflective moment attempted to make explicit the assumptions that are implicit in the skill itself. . . . The assumptions once made explicit can be logically developed; the development leads to experimental changes of practice and so to the beginning of a science."

I begin my discussion of problem-solving by examining its nature, distinguishing between a thoughtful and a purely emotional attack on the difficulties that confront us. This leads me then to discuss the importance of defining the problem in terms of the purposes we seek to accomplish and the realities of our situation. Next I turn to the interrogatory character of problem-solving—the need to formulate appropriate questions. Such questions elicit facts, but the facts must be dealt with thoughtfully. This requires that we work efficiently within a frame of reference until we have exhausted its potential, after which it may be necessary to alter or abandon it. That can be done only if we make disciplined use of generalizations and are capable of understanding relationships.

Because problem-solving often presents us with abstractions, we must explore the art of visualization and the manipulation of symbols, both of them tools of conceptual thought.

This paves the way for an examination of types of solutions: (1) choosing among a panorama of alternatives, (2) the method of classification, (3) the critical-factor solution, (4) the method of innovation by bursting the frame of reference, and (5) the solution by adaptation.

One effect of this approach is that we start with the simple and go to the more complex—itself an important aspect of handling any problem. The rhythm of movement is therefore from the more tangible to the more abstract, with a corresponding increase in the complexity of the illustrations used. Our first case histories are based on situations involving limited alternatives; we shall find ourselves eventually exploring how Einstein probed the mystery of relativity and ultimately resolved it by achieving a masterful simplification of the difficulties. And we shall see that simplification is itself a major tool of problem-solving.

I have tried to avoid any assumption that the reader is starting from scratch and knows nothing about the nature of reasoning his way through to a solution. I have also attempted to avoid any suggestion that there is only one method of solving problems or that there is a single system. Fortunately, Man is constantly discovering new ways of tackling his problems. It is this quality in ourselves that gives hope for the future despite the giant problem that hydrogenates over our heads these days.

AARON LEVENSTEIN

Use Your Head

[1]

INTRODUCTION: TWO AGAINST THE SEA

MAN'S FIRST problems arose from nature. His first triumphs were those he achieved against nature.

He was cold. He mastered the power of fire.

He was hungry. He learned to hunt and plant.

He was lonely. He discovered love.

But he has not always given the right answer, and nature has had the last word. There is nothing more depressing, say the explorers, than to come across the ruins of an Inca city in the jungles of South America: where man once built his beautiful towers, vine and weed have reclaimed the earth.

Basically, man has used only two methods in his struggle with nature. They can be illustrated by the experiences of a Persian king and a Dutch boy.

When Xerxes stood on the shore with his army and looked across the Hellespont, he asked himself: "How can I get my men across?" He commanded his generals to build him a bridge of boats and they obeyed. But a storm came up and smashed his bridge into driftwood. In a towering rage, he ordered his slaves to administer 300 lashes to the sea.

He did not cross over. We smile at the absurdity, but it seems much less quaint when we read that he ordered the execution of the overseeers who had directed the work.

That was one man against the sea. He failed miserably.

Now consider the little Dutch boy who triumphed over the sea. Sidney Hook, the philosopher, has said that anybody could become a hero like that boy: all you need is to be present when the dike springs a leak, and have your finger with you. Actually, something more is needed, another piece of equipment that is not always readily at hand—the ability to think. It takes presence of mind as well as presence of thumb.

Xerxes met his problem with passion. It kept him from understanding the nature of his difficulties. Clearly, he was in no mood to look at relationships. But the Dutch boy could see the relationship between his finger and the hole in the dike. *He could put different facts together in a form that made them useful for his purposes.* In short, he was successful because he brought to the situation problem-solving ability.

In one form or another, day in and day out, we are all of us fighting nature. Some of us use the method of Xerxes, others the method of the Dutch boy.

Toward What End?

Let us be sure, first, that we mean the same thing when we use the term "success." Some people think success is making money or beating their neighbor to the draw. If that were so, then Rembrandt was a failure. For his famous "Aristotle Contemplating the Bust of Homer" he received only 500 florins, or $7,800, whereas a recent owner of the painting got $2,300,000 from the Metropolitan Museum of Art for it. Who was the better man? Many of the people who have pioneered on the frontiers of the intellect have been "failures." During their lifetime, some of them were called gutter-names, but when they were dead, streets were named after them.

The real test of success is *whether you solve the problems that are challenges to you.* The challenge varies with each of us, depending on the tasks we have chosen to perform or that life has thrust upon us. To Einstein, the problem is an enigma that lies in the heart of the universe; to the blacksmith, the challenge is in a piece of metal between the hammer and the anvil. For one man, the problem is to compress a sweeping thought into the fourteen lines of a sonnet; for another, it is the equally difficult challenge to obtain the resources that will see his son through college. Each is engaged in a work of creation, and each confronts a problem.

Arnold Toynbee has said that the moving force behind the adventures of mankind is the principle of challenge and response. The needs we feel, the pressures of our environment upon us, create "a problem." The psychologist sees it as a felt need or a tension seeking to be relieved. We are compelled to respond to it—with action that we consider "a solution." Thus, human history, according to Bertrand Russell, is the story of man's bout with the problems (1) that nature presents to him, (2) that other men have fashioned for him, or (3) that he has created for himself.

At the outset of this book on problem-solving, let us make one thing very clear: problem-solving is a task you will never complete as long as you live. Your life will continue to be a series of problems, if for no other reason than that every time you solve a problem, your solution creates new problems.

For instance, faced with the problem of a seemingly endless war, we invent an atom bomb as the solution to our immediate difficulty. The result is the development of new problems that, at the moment, we seem to be completely unable to handle. The same is true in various fields of medicine: cortisone can relieve arthritis, but its use may lead to side effects—that is, other disturbances of the patient's health.

Walt Whitman expressed it this way: "It is provided in the essence of things that from any fruition of success, no matter what, shall come forth something to make a greater struggle necessary."

Endless Variety

Most of our problems are not cosmic like Einstein's. Our difficulties exist in lesser areas:

How can we get the boss to give us a raise?

How can we avoid boredom?

How can we keep the car running for another year?

How can we balance our personal budget?

How can we improve our abilities so that we can get a better job or increase the success of our business?

These questions are on the personal level. In addition, we feel some greater problems overhanging our lives. As individuals living in a democracy, we know that we exercise an influence over the destiny of our nation and hence the world.

We may not be sure just how that influence operates, but we are aware that we contribute, knowingly or unknowingly, to the formation of public opinion—by what we say across the fence to our neighbor and the comment we make over the newspaper to our friend in the bus as well as by the vote we cast on election day and the telegram we send our congressman on a piece of legislation. To the extent that we fail to think through our own opinions on the problems of the nation, we are helping to shape an unwise and ill-informed public opinion that may wreak havoc with our country's future. We sense here the really great problem of our time.

Our Equipment

On the whole, the fact that nature has given us a special kind of brain makes us the most successful of animals in problem-solving.

Take, for instance, man's solution to the problem of climate. The dinosaur, more powerful physically than any two-legged human, disappeared because he could not solve that problem. Release a herd of elephants in the Arctic, and they will die. Man, however, has developed the concepts of clothing and shelter and the use of fire as answers to the problem. He has even learned how to live in space, outside the earth's atmosphere.

As human beings, we begin with an initial advantage. Part of the inheritance we received on the day of our birth is the brain that makes it possible for us to size up a problem and go to work on it. In addition, a trust fund of past experience was set up for us to draw upon as needed.

In some matters, we use that legacy without thinking. The hungry baby does not have to reason its way to a solution when it faces the problem of attracting the mother's attention. It uses its lungs, and the mother comes quickly. That's problem-solving on the crudest level. It is a long journey from the crib to the research laboratory, from the bawl of the baby to the lecture of the scientist. How far we each go on that journey depends on how systematically we approach life's basic problem: the problem of problem-solving.

We begin with nature's endowment—equipment that makes it possible for us to seek adjustments to an environment that will leave us most comfortable. The psychologist studies this human mechanism and tells us a great deal about how we can use it effectively. In addition, the logician spells out for us methods of reasoning by which our responses to our problems become less automatic and more studied.

For most of us, however, the basic difficulty is that we do not use the resources of problem-solving already at hand. We waste our assets in unwise expenditure. Like Constantine the Great, who carried off antique bronzes of rare beauty and melted them down for pennies to pay his soldiers, we debase our natural treasure and spend it on worthless goods.

Our Wasted Assets

To be sure, we suffer many limitations. The brain with which we are born is limited in size, for the baby's head has to be small enough to get through the pelvic region of a woman. In recent years, however, we have learned how to magnify this brain by coupling it with electronic computers thousands of times larger than the human cranium.

We do not possess all the possible equipment with which nature might have endowed us. Lesser animals have some physical faculties beyond ours: dogs can hear higher ranges in the world of sound; homing pigeons have an unerring sense of direction that airplane pilots and ships' navigators could well envy.

It has been pointed out that our race of human beings has lost some faculties in the process of evolution. Apparently, the sense of smell was once a valuable instrument of self-preservation for man; today its vestigial descendant gets its greatest work-out by the gourmet in Maxim's. Lack of use leads to a loss of sensitiveness or even atrophy. The invention of the automobile may render the human leg obsolete everywhere but in the Folies Bergère.

More often than not, however, our failure properly to grapple with our difficulties results from inadequate use of equipment rather than lack of it. The Chinese had gunpowder and used it only in firecrackers to frighten away demons. Cortes had gunpowder and used it to capture the untold riches of the Aztec empire; worse, he destroyed a civilization with it.

Archimedes, in ancient Greece, already knew of the resources of power hidden in water, steam, and air pressure, but his age did not apply this knowledge to its problems. Perhaps it did not want to know, because whatever it could derive from the energy in water it could obtain as easily from the sweat of slave labor.

Problems can be solved with many different answers. Sometimes a bad solution is within easy reach; it is readily accepted and the problem is marked "solved." The ancient Romans knew the principle of printing; they could stamp their names with a seal. But slave labor was available as copyists, so why develop printing? The French say that "the good is often the enemy of the best." Progress depends on discarding an acceptable solution in order to apply a better one.

Whether your problem is to get a raise from your boss or to keep your mother-in-law from visiting or to stop Communist aggression in the world, you are seeking solutions. And in most instances, as we shall see, the road to solution is usually paved with the same materials. Every road goes in two different directions and all roads go to many destinations, but the principles of road-building and map-reading (both are essential for successful traveling) remain the same.

Realistic Target

This is a book about thinking, and the first thought that must be kept in mind is that you must not look for miracles. Please do not expect:

1. That you can learn to think without thinking (nobody ever learned to swim without going into the water), or

2. That this book will solve your problems for you (only *you* can solve your problems).

But this book will tell you how you can proceed to attack your problems and thus solve them yourself. Everyone's problem, in the last analysis, is unique, but there is a common approach that can be adapted by all. There are principles of thinking just as there are principles of driving. It makes no difference where you plan to go: you will need the same skills. Your destination may be Miami, and mine may be San Francisco; we will have to consult different roadmaps and follow different routes. But we will both have to use the same basic equipment and the same skills in handling it. In any event, we will need a vehicle on wheels with a motor.

And now another word of warning: a driving instructor can teach you how to operate an auto but if a neurosis keeps you from going out into traffic, you will not be able to drive. This book will discuss principles of intelligent thinking, but if your problems are neurotic in origin, only a psychiatrist can help you. Do not assume, however, like a lady of my acquaintance, that problems of thinking are all "psychiatric." Thee and I, as the Quaker lady said in her own way, have no neuroses or phobias to interfere with our functioning; yet when we go out on the golf course, we can use the services of a pro. Can we not also use the principles of the professional "thinker"—the concepts evolved by scientists, philosophers, craftsmen, lawyers? Normal or not, we can increase our skill at problem-solving as a housewife improves her menu by using a cookbook.

The purpose of this book, then, is to provide methods of attacking the problems that confront us in our daily experience. Of course, we can always use the trial-and-error method; if good fortune smiles on us, the results will be gratifying. On the whole, trial and error are costly in both time and effort. Unfortunately, we have only limited quantities of both commodities at our disposal.

But there are other methods available to us, products of the whole history of man's intellectual growth. They are called "scientific methods." They are the methods that led our ancestors to abandon the medicine man for the medical doctor, the alchemist for the chemist, the soothsayer for the social scientist, the snakepit for the sanitarium. More important, they led to the substitution of reason for emotion. They taught us to stop worshipping idols as the source of our blessings and to stop appeasing demons as the authors of our frustrations. They made it possible for us to lay hands on our own deficiencies and effect improvement.

Yet even today, many of us, confronted with a problem, are content to lash out figuratively or with our tongues. Cuss words never yet have provided a program for action. But in our political life the institutions that have proved imperfect are given 300 lashes and the architects who built them are executed or defamed. We revert to the futile problem-solving technique of the Persian king. It is completely unscientific and self-defeating.

The Line of Attack

In the following pages you will find methods for making a disciplined attack on your problems, whatever they may be. Instead of being haunted by implacable Fate, you will look for relationships. Instead of cursing the sea or flogging it, you will see the connection between the oncoming tide, the hole in the dike and your own finger.

But as Gilbert Ryle has said, "A soldier does not become a shrewd general merely by endorsing the strategic principles of Clausewitz; he must know how to apply them." It will do you no good to read the suggestions in this book and nod your approval. There is value only in putting the principles to work.

One way of applying the principles is to pick out consciously a particular problem that's bothering you right now —for example, organizing your work on a more efficient basis;

preparing a talk that you are committed to deliver next week; deciding on a plan for raising additional capital needed in your business; developing better relations with the neighbor who has been making a nuisance of himself, or thinks the same of you. Get the problem in mind, and keep focusing on it the light cast by the succeeding chapters of this book.

Remember, it is not what you know but what you do with your knowledge that counts. St. Francis says, *"Tantum homo habet de scientia quantum operatur,"* "a man has only so much knowledge as he puts to work."

The trouble is that most of us get used to living with our problems instead of going to work on them. But, win or lose, you will be a lot happier if you know that you're doing something about the challenges you face in life.

There is no guarantee, of course, that you can solve all your problems. Even when you have the right map and the road is well built, you may still go astray. Mankind as a race has many grim unsolved problems—cancer, war, poverty, and so on. But there is no reason to be discouraged. With the right methods, we have a *chance*—and that's worth taking. There is a famous Greek epitaph for sailors that reads, "This is my tomb, and here I was shipwrecked; but be not frightened, brother mariner, from setting sail, because when my ship went down, others remained afloat."

[2]

PURPOSE COMES FIRST

AN ANCIENT legend tells of the Sphinx who sat by the road-side. Each passing traveler was halted and asked a riddle. If he could not give the right answer, he was devoured.

In a certain sense, every generation of human beings is the traveler. In the eighteenth century, the American colonials were confronted with the question, "How can we win our independence and open the way to development as a great nation?" They escaped from the jaws of the Sphinx by answering the riddle with the act of revolution.

In the same sense, every individual is the traveler. Day after day, we are confronted with problems. They are the riddles of the Sphinx, and we suffer pain if we fail to give the right answer.

The successful traveler has always been the one who understood the question put to him. The unhappy wayfarer has often met his doom, not because the riddle was beyond his capacity, but because he never even heard the question. Confronted by the monster, his mind was captured by fear, and he found it impossible to begin to think. Many a man has fallen victim to his problem because he never knew what it was. Events themselves may have so terrifying an influence that we recoil from them without ever attempting to understand or grapple with the underlying difficulty.

It may seem obvious, but it is the most common cause of failure. When people don't know what their problem is, how can they know where to look for a solution? Aware of difficulty, pain, or frustration, they lose contact with their surroundings. Like a prize fighter stunned by a powerful blow, they don't know where they are.

And that suggests the first question that ought to be asked whenever you confront a problem: *Where am I?* After Adam ate of the forbidden fruit and opened up the world of problems for man, he hid in terror. According to Genesis, God called out, "Adam, where art thou?" Scholars have pondered why God, knowing all things, should have had to ask. The answer they have given is that God knew where Adam was; He wanted Adam to know.

The question *Where am I?* should be asked quite consciously. Otherwise you may not be able to counteract certain psychological factors that go into operation as soon as the Sphinx, the propounder of problems, raises her head at the roadside.

The Challenge

It is the very nature of problems that their first impact is to make us feel lost. They create fear and release the primitive instinct to run away. When primeval man suddenly found himself facing a monster in the jungle, he went through a series of reactions: his heart began to pound, his blood raced, his bowels and bladder emptied. All these were helpful physical preparations for flight.

Today, in situations that do not involve physical danger, we may experience the same bodily sensations of fear, the same preparations for running. Unfortunately, reactions that nature made available for our defense in time of physical danger are not appropriate for solving the nonphysical dangers that are common in our age. In fact, the effect is to increase our peril, because those reactions handicap us in doing the necessary tasks before us.

Take, for example, the young executive at a staff meeting. The company president, without advance notice, has suddenly asked him to report on the excellent job just completed by his department. He knows all the facts, has a wonderful story to tell, but the prospect of delivering a speech releases a cloud of fear in his mind. Now his blood races through his veins, his heart sounds louder in his ears than his own voice, his breath comes faster through his lungs—reactions that are helpful if he intends to run but ruinous in delivering a speech.

The Executive Who Ran

This tendency to run away from difficulty, rather than face it, is one of the first snares in problem-solving. Some people think they can evade consequences by acting as if the problem did not exist.

I recall a conference of business executives that I conducted in Erie, Pennsylvania. The participants had been listing a series of current problems in the area of employee relations. One of them said he had encountered difficulty filling a job opening to which any one of four men could have been promoted.

"To avoid trouble," he said, "I promoted none of them but hired an outsider."

The result, he admitted, was trouble.

A member of the conference group spoke up rather brusquely. "Bill, why don't you follow the principle of promoting from within the organization?"

"But the other men who don't get the job become dissatisfied," was the answer.

"Well, this way four of them are."

"Wait a minute," interrupted a third member of the group. "Bill, what did you say to your men at the time you hired the outsider?"

"Not a thing. It only would have made more trouble. I figured it was best to ignore the whole situation and just go ahead and do what I thought was right."

Half a dozen voices spoke up at once, and when I had restored order, they all made the same point: the worst possible course is to try to solve a problem by pretending it doesn't exist. It just won't go away.

In this instance, the group agreed that the problem became

serious largely because it was ignored. Most people, they said, can understand the simple mathematics involved: if there's just one job, four people can't be promoted to it. What riles employees is the feeling that they were never considered, that objective standards were not used, that favoritism might have been shown.

The executives then worked out on the blackboard a series of four basic steps that could be used to solve such a problem:

1. Give everybody who's interested a chance to apply for the opening. This can be done by word of mouth or by posting on the bulletin board.

2. When you have reached a decision, announce it to everybody who showed an interest in the job. This lets each of them know that he was given consideration.

3. State the basis on which you arrived at the decision—ability, length of service, experience, initiative, etc. You should demonstrate that your judgment was based on a set of standards, and you should explain the standards you used to rate your people.

4. In individual interviews, point out to the unsuccessful candidates the deficiencies they have to correct for future promotion.

At this point, we will not stop to analyze the mental processes by which the group arrived at their solutions of the problem other than to say that they started out by asking the question: *"What results do we want to accomplish?"* Once they had decided that their purpose was twofold—to get the best man in the job *and* to do something actively to keep the good will of each applicant—solutions began to suggest themselves. But Bill could never attain that happy result so long as he persisted in ignoring the problem and remaining silent with his men.

The first phase of meeting a problem is to accept the challenge. You cannot, in most cases, turn your back and expect the problem to solve itself. Confront it—with your guard up and your eyes wide open. And don't be too dismayed because your first sensation on seeing the problem is a feeling of numbness. The initial effect is always damaging—we wouldn't recognize the existence of the problem if it didn't threaten us. Pain is nature's way of calling illness to our attention so that we can treat it. The discomfort caused by a problem is a fire alarm sounding in the night. It startles and frightens, and it points to the need for action.

With most problems you can afford a little time for recovery from the first shock. Then proceed systematically to *state the problem.*

Problem Defined

To state your problem effectively, you will find it useful to keep in mind the meaning of the term *problem.* Professor Karl Duncker, who has done considerable research in the psychology of problem-solving, gives us his conclusion in these words: "A problem arises when a living creature has a goal but does not know how this goal is to be reached. Whenever one cannot go from the given situation to the desired situation simply by action, then there has to be recourse to thinking."

Logic, as a systematic way of thinking, was born from the necessity to think when observation proved to be incomplete or inadequate. We must use logic when direct experience is denied to us, when some of the facts are missing or when we are afraid to experience them directly. The conclusion we reach by logic is never really conclusive; we must often take the step of setting up an experiment to confirm the logic before we dare to believe it.

For example, before getting into a bath, I want to know if the water is too hot for me. I can use a logical method. Heat causes a column of mercury to expand; I therefore insert a calibrated tube of mercury into the water. I observe the column rise to 100° F. and deduce that it is not too hot. But if I have any reason to believe that the thermometer is inaccurate, or if I have no thermometer, I must test the water gingerly with my toe before I get into the tub. In most cases I let direct experience confirm the method of logic.

On the basis of Duncker's definition, a problem is the distance between where you are and where you want to be, when there is apparently no visible means of transportation. But thought can carry us when it is a matter of getting from A to Z without knowing what letters are in between.

Stating your problem then, involves at least two elements:

A. Where you are.

Z. Where you want to be.

More often than not, it is the second element, which I have labeled Z, that is lacking. People may have a vague understanding of their present position but they cannot make up their minds where they want to go. They live out their lives without a philosophy. They do not succeed in reaching any goal, because they have never set one up.

John Dewey, in his book *How We Think*, says that every problem begins with a "felt need" or a tension that one finds it necessary to relieve. We start on the road to solution when we intellectualize "the difficulty or perplexity that has been *felt* (directly experienced) into a problem to be solved, a question for which the answer must be sought."

Of course, many people never move from the "felt need" to the "intellectualization." For instance, almost everybody feels the need to be liked. We want the approval of our neighbors, our fellow employees, our lodge brothers. But some of us never get beyond *feeling*, never learn that we must translate our emotional need into a mental problem: "How do I get from A to Z—from my present state to a condition where I will enjoy the esteem of others?"

Certainly, we cannot hope to find the answer without asking the question. Many a young woman allows her most attractive years to slip by because she does not realize that she herself must take some action to traverse the gap between her single status and the achievement of a happy marriage. She waits, alone with her felt need; she does nothing because she does not see that her condition is a problem for her to resolve.

Sometimes the problem consists not merely of a failure to see the road between A and Z but is due to the existence of visible obstacles that bar the way. Thus, a primitive man on a journey may find himself on the shore of a river, his way barred by his inability to swim or the absence of a bridge. But modern man uses his problem-solving ability to transform the barrier itself into an advantage, into a means of travel. He builds his largest cities on the shores of streams because he knows that they are the easiest avenues of transportation. But first he has had to learn the principle of floating objects and to contrive rafts and then boats. And of course he would not make such an effort if he had no desire to get across the water.

Problems and Purposes

In the absence of a goal to be achieved, you have no standard for judging whether you are getting anywhere. One good reason for defining your goal clearly is that it gives you a fixed point by which you can determine whether you are on course. I once took my children to the Hayden Planetarium in New York. We spent an interesting hour as a lecturer raced through a demonstration of various heavenly phenomena, but I was quite embarrassed when we were outdoors and the youngsters asked me to point out some of the stars that had been discussed. I looked at the sky, and it seemed a miracle to me that anybody could ever identify anything up there among the millions and millions of pinpoints. How could they ever be distinguished one from the other?

Then I bought a little book on astronomy. I read the first few pages. They contained a diagram of the Big Dipper, which was said to be located in the northern skies. I went out on the back lawn and looked, and, wonder to behold, I found the Dipper. According to the book, the two stars that form the far side of the cup, those opposite the handle, are called the Pointers. Follow their direction and you will find the North Star. Now go back and follow the handle for about thirty degrees; there is Arcturus.

From then on, I had no problem. According to the author, the Big Dipper is "the yardstick of the sky." By referring to it, I could identify one constellation after another and then, by referring to them in turn, I could identify still others. The Dipper made the difference.

The mariner at sea depends on the same principle:

A. He "shoots the stars" in order to find out where he is in relation to his point of reference in the sky.

Z. He makes his reading with reference to his ultimate destination.

Just consider how useless the sea captain's sextant would be if he didn't know for what port he was sailing. And consider the benefits of fixing your sights even on an unattainable goal. Carl Schurz said: "Ideals are like stars—you will not succeed in touching them with your hands; but like the seafaring man of the desert of waters you choose them as your guides and, following them, you reach your destiny."

Purpose Must Be Specific

Much of our difficulty in problem-solving comes from being vague about our purpose. If our objective is too loosely defined, we will not be able to uncover concrete ways of getting to it.

Here, again, the analogy of the roadmap is useful. You will do much better in laying out your course if you know the exact point to which you want to go. If your destination is California, you are presented with so many alternative routes that you will have great difficulty in deciding which is best; but if your destination is Los Angeles, fewer roads are relevant.

Specificity of purpose, then, makes the problem more solvable because it focuses our thoughts on the concrete and is more suggestive of direct routes.

Many people would like to be artists, but such a purpose is not enough. A Leonardo da Vinci, for example, does not undertake his artistic journey with so vague a purpose. He does not start out to "make a great painting." Instead, he defines his goal concretely: "Make figures with such action as may suffice to show what the figure has in mind."

Now he has a standard by which to judge means, methods, and materials: Will they help to illuminate the moods and character of his subject? If he is painting a landscape, he defines for himself first what feeling he wants to convey. This gives him a basis for selectivity. He can judge which elements in the scene are of value to his purpose, which are not:

"See to it, O painter, that when you go into the fields you give your attention to the various objects, looking carefully in turn first at one object, then at another, making a bundle of different things selected among those of less value."

Da Vinci also provides us with an illustration of how the mind of the inventor works. For centuries, the world has marveled at his mechanical ingenuity. Here, too, his success was based on his ability to focus his mind on concrete purposes. He did not set out just to "make inventions" but to solve clearly defined problems which others had failed to define before him.

Thus, he could conceive a parachute long before our own times: "If a man had a tent made of linen, of which the apertures have all been stopped up, and it be twelve cubits across and twelve in depth, he will be able to throw himself down from any great height without sustaining any injury."

Even though most of his inventions remained mere drawings in his notebooks, later generations have actually made them work. In the cafeteria of the Thomas J. Watson Research Center at Yorktown, New York, I spent several interesting hours exploring a series of working models built by IBM engineers from his drawings.

The genius of the man, both in art and invention, lay in his power to see things in the concrete and to avoid the trap of vagueness. The degree to which he was able to think in specific terms is illustrated in the famous letter he sent to Lodovico, the regent of Milan, who was looking for four men to add to his retinue—an engineer, an architect, a sculptor, and a painter. Leonardo offered to fill all four posts, in this description of his achievements which I have excerpted from his letter of application:

Most Illustrious Lord, having now sufficiently seen and considered the proofs of all those who count themselves masters and inventors of instruments of war, and finding that their invention and use of the said instruments does not differ in any respect from those in common practice, I am emboldened without prejudice to anyone else to put myself in communication with your Excellency, in order to acquaint you with my secrets, thereafter offering myself at your pleasure effectually to demonstrate at any convenient time all those matters which are in part briefly recorded below.

1. I have plans for bridges, very light and strong and suitable for carrying very easily. . . .
2. When a place is besieged I know how to cut off water from the trenches, and how to construct an infinite number of . . . scaling ladders and instruments. . . .
4. I have plans for making cannon, very convenient and easy of transport, with which to hurl small stones in the manner almost of hail . . .
5. And if it should happen that the engagement is at sea, I have plans for constructing many engines most suitable for attack or defense, and ships which can resist the fire of all the heaviest cannon, and powder and smoke . . .
7. Also I can make covered cars, safe and unassailable, which will enter the serried ranks of the enemy with artillery . . . And behind these the infantry will be able to follow quite unharmed and without any opposition. . . .
10. In time of peace I believe that I can give you as complete satisfaction as anyone else in architecture, in the construction of buildings both public and private, and in conducting water from one place to another.

Also I can execute sculpture in marble, bronze or clay, and also painting. . . .

And if any of the aforesaid things should seem impossible or impracticable to anyone, I offer myself as ready to make trial of them in your park or in whatever place shall please your Excellency, to whom I commend myself with all possible humility.

Note the particularity with which Leonardo addressed himself to the problems of military engineering: bridges that are light and strong and portable, cannon that have mobility, covered cars as precursors of the modern tank—in construction even the problem of running water.

Breadth of Purpose

It is necessary to think both narrowly and broadly. In recent years, the need for redefining objectives in breadth and depth has become a matter of great urgency for business organizations. Many a company, threatened with extinction, has been compelled to rethink its basic purpose and to re-articulate it with a particularity that has resulted in enlarging its operations.

The railroad industry is an outstanding example. Years ago, a father could have rendered no better financial service to his children than to leave them a sheaf of railroad stocks. Today, the railroads have lost their blue-chip status and are deeply in the red. The reason is that they have tried to do their problem-solving with a wrongly defined purpose.

Originally, railroad executives thought in very narrow terms: "The purpose of a railroad is to move passengers and freight in cars along steel tracks." Actually, as they learned quite painfully, they are not in the business of just moving trains from place to place. They are in the business of transportation, no matter what its form; they are in any business that competes with them. In short, they are in the same field as the carriers who use the highways and the airlanes and the waterways.

Once they understood this—that is to say, redefined their

business in new, broader, and yet concrete terms—they realized they were in a better position to compete. Their new definition has led them to see that they are also in the trucking business. It has produced the "piggy-back" and "flexivan" techniques which use special flat-bed cars to transport truck trailers. Result: each year after this discovery, there has been an increase in the amount of freight carried by the railroads.

The oil industry has gone through a similar experience several times. When oil was first discovered, its basic use was to provide kerosene, fuel for lighting purposes. Within the scope of such a purpose, John D. Rockefeller conceived the brilliant idea of sending kerosene lamps without charge to China, expecting to be the source of "oil for the lamps of China."

But a time came when the narrow purpose of providing fuel for lighting would have made the industry as obsolete as buggy manufacture. Edison's invention of the electric bulb would have been the death-knell of oil production. Fortunately, the industry was able to revise its thinking, and set itself a new purpose: providing fuel for whatever purpose could be served. Oil ceased to depend on lighting and began to be used for heating. The invention of the automobile, powered by gasoline, provided an additional purpose for oil, today a major one.

Yet such is the limitation of vision when purpose is too narrowly stated that the same industry lost a great opportunity because it became fixated on the liquid character of its product, just as the railroads had become fixated on steel tracks. Even though the oil industry knew that its purpose included the heating of homes, it refused to recognize that it was in the business of natural gas, located at the very source of the oil wells. While the industry was "burning off" the gas, some of the executives saw that its distribution was a logical part of the oil business, but they could not persuade the decision-makers. They had to break away and form their own companies. Today, after having built a network of pipelines from the Southwest all across the country, they are taking a deep bite out of oil profits with a competitive fuel for home heating.

Apparently, the oil business has learned its lesson. Now it is spending millions of dollars on research and development, in the knowledge that technological advances may ultimately destroy the automobile market. Cars powered by storage batteries or by atomic energy must eventually eliminate the gas station. This time the industry expects to be ready; it is already building a market for petrochemicals, plastics, and other solid products.

Peter F. Drucker, the noted business analyst and commentator, says in his book, *The Practice of Management*:

> It is, then, the first responsibility of top management to ask the question "what is our business?" and to make sure that it is carefully studied and correctly answered . . .
> That the question is so rarely asked—at least in a clear and sharp form—and so rarely given adequate study and thought, is perhaps the most important single cause of business failure. Conversely, wherever we find an outstandingly successful business we will almost always find . . . that its success rests to a large extent on raising the question clearly and deliberately, and on answering it thoughtfully and thoroughly.

The value of such a concentration on the objectives of the company, as Drucker points out, is that "setting objectives enables a business to get where it should be going [Z] rather than be the plaything of weather, wind and accidents."

The same principle applies in every field of human endeavor—politics, science, personal life. The greatest triumphs in history are recorded by those who had the character to set their basic goals and steer for them despite wind and current. "The secret of success," said Disraeli, "is constancy to purpose."

A Classical Case of Constancy

The outstanding example in American history of such "constancy to purpose" is Abraham Lincoln. Almost every step of the way he encountered new tragedies, but he did not swerve from his course. He succeeded in solving his problems because his objectives were as vivid in his mind as if Rubens had painted them.

From the very day that Fort Sumter was fired on, Lincoln knew where he wanted to go. Preservation of the Union was his major target, but he did not stop with this generalization. He saw clearly that this goal consisted of *a series of subgoals*: keeping the support of all factions that believed in the Union; avoiding any measures that would drive the border states into the camp of the South. "I hope God is on my side," he said on one occasion, "but I must have Kentucky."

Despite the conflicting counsels of his Cabinet, Lincoln kept clearly in mind the ultimate objective, the point to which he was going. Lesser men might forget it. When General Frémont issued his own Emancipation Proclamation in the West, Lincoln ordered that it be rescinded; when Frémont persisted, the President removed him from his command under circumstances that threatened military insubordination by a high-ranking officer in the midst of war. Lincoln never forgot that the border states must be kept in the Union and postponed the Emancipation Proclamation until this subgoal had been attained and the border states were safely bedded down in the Union.

It was more important to Lincoln that he accomplish his goal of preserving the Union than that his own personal feelings be assuaged. He was insulted by General McClellan, but as long as Lincoln felt the General was needed by the Union cause, he took no action. On one occasion he waited at McClellan's home to speak to him about the conduct of the war, and the General had the audacity to go off to bed, sending word down that he was too busy to see the President. Completely aware of what had happened, Lincoln said simply, "I would hold General McClellan's horse if that would help us win the war." On another occasion, he remarked: "Statesmanship is the art of exploiting individual meannesses for the general good." At all times, Lincoln kept in view that "general good."

How successfully Lincoln did this can be demonstrated by

contrasting him with the brilliant Horace Greeley. The latter is quoted as saying, "The President is an honest man and a well meaning man; but he lacks the statesmanship requisite to appreciate and use events during a national crisis like this." But read the comment of Alphonse B. Miller who gives the verdict of most historians on both men: "Greeley's heart was just as sound [as Lincoln's] and his intentions equally good. But his judgment was all too often at fault. For a man of such wide experience he was frequently quixotic, gullible and capricious. . . . Consequently, Greeley was one of the most imposing failures in our history, while Lincoln is almost certainly its outstanding success."

As against Lincoln, who charted his course by the preservation of the Union, Greeley the radical abolitionist said to the South, "Erring sisters, depart in peace." He had no conception that matched Lincoln's sense of purpose. Without knowing his objective, Lincoln too might have confused goals and means. He would have been in danger of accepting means that might have defeated his goal. The Emancipation Proclamation, if issued in 1861, would have wrecked the pro-Union coalition and driven the border states into the Confederacy. In 1862, however, the situation had changed; the North had won the Battle of Antietam and the Proclamation not only was consistent with Northern unity but promised a hold over the border states. Then Lincoln could say to his friend Blair: "Slavery is the lever by which the secessionists maintain a hold on the border states. That lever I shall break in their faces." And, at the same time, the Proclamation promised benefits in Lincoln's hard-pressed foreign policy: as Lord Charnwood said, the freeing of the slaves made it morally impossible for any British Cabinet to go to the aid of the South.

Goals and Means

Only when ultimate goals are kept in mind can the means fall into place. The carpenter cannot select his tools before he knows what he wants to build.

Many men go stumbling about in a frenzy of unproductive activity because they cannot differentiate between goals and means, because they cannot see that ends have a prior claim to our loyalty as compared with means. The Communist who believes that "ends justify the means" fails to recognize that the ends must govern the means or, in the last analysis, the violent means will shape the ends.

Here is a situation I witnessed in a society of which I am a member. The Board of Directors had just voted to purchase a building. Another piece of property had been acquired some time before with the idea of putting up a structure. Now, if a customer could be found, the land was to be sold.

"Who has the deed to the property?" asked one of the board members, a rather prominent teacher with a Ph.D. in languages. In response to his question, it became apparent that the deed was lost.

"Don't worry about it," said another member of the board, an attorney. "For two dollars we can get a copy."

"Well," said the Ph.D. "I move that we obtain a safe deposit box in the local bank to keep our documents." His motion was unanimously approved. "Now I move," he went on, "that our attorney be authorized to spend two dollars to get a copy of the deed and that it be placed in the safe deposit box."

"That isn't necessary," said the lawyer. "When we have a customer, we can get a copy of the deed. Why bother now?"

"Oh," said the Ph.D. with triumphant logic. "If we don't get a copy of the deed, what will we have to put in the safe deposit box?"

"I move," said the lawyer, "that we put the two dollars in the safe deposit box."

This confusion in which means became ends was of course unimportant even in the affairs of a small organization. But the same thing happens on a much larger scale—in the affairs of nations, for example. Consider the kind of argument that Lincoln faced in connection with the appointment of Grant as head of the Union armies. Some people protested that Grant drank too much, but Lincoln knew the purpose in se-

lecting a general is not to set an example of virtue but to win battles. The President merely suggested that he would like to send the same brand of whiskey to all his generals.

Foolish men continually get lost between means and ends. An Irish bull tells of the traveler who is stopped by a highwayman with the command: "Your money or your life." Answers the traveler: "Here, take my life. I need my money for my old age."

Suggestive Power of Purpose

There is a second reason for setting up a clear-cut definition of your goal. The mere fact of doing so is itself a stimulus for action toward achieving it.

But, in addition to this phychological benefit, there is a logical value in clearly defined purpose. The seed of solution is planted in the soil of purpose. Before you can hope to solve a problem, you must have some idea of what a solution would look like. To find the city of Samarkand you must have a general idea of its appearance—the domes and mosques and people. Otherwise, you might pass it by on your way.

"I find the great thing in this world is not so much where we stand, as in what direction we are moving," said Oliver Wendell Holmes. In other words, there can be no starting out on your journey without, at least, a general idea of the destination. The captain of the ship may never have been in the particular port designated in the ship's papers. But he knows something about the port: where it lies on the map, its latitude and longitude, the kind of coast he will be approaching, the existence of some inlet or protective curvature of the shore.

In general, you must know the outlines of the terrain, the setting in which your problem exists. This is provided by the definition of your purpose. The question is, *What will be the general characteristics of an appropriate solution when I have found it?*

Now in confronting a real life problem, you must usually

start out with some knowledge of the attributes that your solution will ultimately have. And this knowledge derives from your understanding of your purpose. If your purpose is to invent a horseless carriage, you will immediately have a vision of a vehicle; you will think of wheels; you will entertain the idea of some source of energy to replace that of the horse.

Anthropologists have been intrigued by the fact that races of men who have never had contact with each other have nevertheless invented the same kind of tools. The pygmy in the Congo uses the same weapon, bow and arrow, as the North American Indian. How did they arrive at the same solution?

The answer is that they shared the same purpose: to create an instrument capable of moving speedily and with force towards a target. The purpose itself suggested the form in which a solution could be found. They had all had the experience of seeing a flexible branch bend under the human grasp and then snap forward with enormous force when released. They probably could not understand the principle of a spring or the idea that the energy they had put into the bow as they drew the string would be suddenly released in one cumulative burst. But the almost universal use of the bow and arrow is a revelation of how the same purpose can suggest the same solution even in the absence of theory.

The Pointing Finger of Purpose

The suggestive power of purpose is also illustrated by the way the Japanese solved a major postwar problem. Their recovery from the devastation of the war required an increase in foreign trade. But Japanese commerce for years had carried the stigma of shoddy production. The government therefore decided that the key problem was to establish a reputation for quality.

Such a definition of immediate purpose pointed clearly in

one direction: steps must be taken on a large scale to improve products. The authorities cast about for an existing facility that could be used to achieve this end and found a doddering organization that had been set up in 1928, the Industrial Arts Institute. The government proceeded to sponsor and finance its laboratory. But the purpose itself required that the laboratory not only assess the quality of products but redesign them and eliminate the flaws. Today its findings are made available to manufacturers generally.

But notice the consistency to purpose. All patents are retained by the government and are not licensed to any company suspected of producing substandard goods. And to assure that the fine quality will be identified with Japanese manufacture, the Institute works into its plans clean Japanese-looking lines—even in such household items as candlesticks, salt cellars and cigarette boxes. Regarding furniture, the Institute's laboratory is meticulous about the least detail—testing the holding power of glues used on chair-rungs and even X-raying joints to see how well they resist temperature and moisture. It finishes the job by studying the best packaging and crating methods to protect the quality in transit.

By consciously focusing attention on quality, the purpose clearly foreshadowed what the solution would look like—a public laboratory devoted to testing and product improvement.

To take an illustration closer to home, consider the plight of shoemakers in certain large cities. Their customers were moving into suburban areas where rentals were much too high for small shoe repair shops. An enterprising firm defined its purpose: to reach suburbanites in their own villages.

The purpose obviously pointed in the direction of a system of transportation that would allow for pick-up and delivery. But trucks were too expensive because of the initial cost, upkeep and gas. Well, what would be the cheapest method of transportation? The answer was, "Scooters."

A fleet was acquired, a light, shoe-shaped plastic body was slung over the scooter—and the Shoemobile repair service was on its way to keep suburbanites from going barefoot. In St. Louis, for example, the number of shoemaker shops dropped from 800 in 1950 to about 350 in 1962. But 20 Shoemobiles now deliver about 1,000 pairs a day to a central factory where eight men are enough to do the work.

Just knowing what your problem is gives you the broad outlines of the solution to look for. Then imagination can go to work to fill in the details.

But there is another reason for knowing where you want to go. Without a destination, your journey will not only be aimless—it will be unsatisfying. It may create in you a sense of boredom that will defeat your effort to solve the problem. You will find yourself at one and the same time without a destination and without any awareness of where you are. In short, the basic element of a problem—the gap between starting point and destination—may lead you only to frustration.

Let us examine some of the effects of this gap between being at one point and desiring to be somewhere else. It is illustrated most clearly in boredom, which is itself a problem. In analyzing it and finding some solutions for it, we will discover the importance of purpose in problem-solving.

A Problem in Purpose: Boredom

Actually, it's not the routine, which so many of us blame, that is responsible for boring us. It's the endlessness of the task, the fact that we never seem to approach any ultimate destination. The Greeks knew this long before modern psychology tested and proved it in the laboratory. Among the worst penalties in their version of hell was the fate of Sysiphus, doomed forever to push a stone uphill, only to have it roll back whenever he neared the top. The frustration of never seeing the job completed, of never seeing a purpose achieved, is one of the hardest burdens life can impose on a man.

In the psychological laboratory, scientists have succeeded

in isolating the consequences of purposelessness. They have watched it in action by setting people to making meaningless marks on a never-ending roll of paper and have measured the almost complete paralysis of mind and muscle that results. They have taken volunteers through the horrible experience of repeating the same poem over and over again, leading their victims to the point of meaningless babble and ultimate speechlessness in a few minutes. With dramatic suddenness, they have ended both the paralysis of hand and tongue by simply assigning a different task that does seem to have purpose.

Try this experiment yourself the next time you are scheduled to take a long, tedious automobile trip. Before you start, mark off on the roadmap the points at which you will have covered a quarter of the distance, half the distance, and three-quarters. You'll find the time moves more quickly, the problem of overcoming the journey's boredom draws much nearer solution, as you shoot for each of your milestones. The reason is that you are witnessing in measurable terms the narrowing of the gap that Dr. Duncker says constitutes the problem.

Take this experience of an efficiency expert who noticed that his company's workers were losing time by making several trips a day to the supply bins for more material. The logical thing seemed to be to move the bins closer to the operators' machines. It was done, and the expert was shocked by the result. Production dropped sharply, despite the savings in time and motion. Not until most of the bins were removed from sight did production climb back to normal.

The explanation was simple. Just seeing the mass of raw material suggested the endlessness of their jobs to the workers. "You just don't seem to get anywhere," is the way workers often describe their reason for quitting. There is no sense of progress because there is no defined goal that an individual can use as a yardstick, as a point of reference, to mark the ground he has traversed from A toward Z.

Nowadays industrial psychologists advise management to

do everything possible to break down the stream of work into visible, attainable units. As parts are finished, they go into boxes or trays of ten, fifty, or a hundred—whatever number is convenient. The result is a constantly repeated feeling of "mission completed" and a fresh start on a new effort toward another specific goal.

The Urge to Complete

I have quoted John Dewey's statement that a problem starts with a *felt need*. We feel that something not now in our possession is necessary; without it we are incomplete. The fact is that every human being has a sense of incompleteness. The motor that keeps us on the go, that makes us try to get from A to Z, is the desire for completion.

On one end of the scale of human activity, it leads to acquisition and saving; at the other end, it leads to learning and research. In our contacts with other human beings, we look for friends because they will add to our lives and provide elements we feel we lack.

Even love is part of this search for completeness. Plato dramatized it with the legend that Jupiter, to punish an offense committed by mortal man, had cut "human beings in half, as people cut eggs before they salt them." In such mythological terms, he explained the function of sex: "Every one of us is thus the half of what may be properly termed a man, and like a flatfish cut in two, is the imperfect portion of an entire whole, perpetually necessitated to seek the half belonging to him."

Psychologically, Plato was right. This drive to restore our original unity, to achieve what he called the "completion of felicity," has been demonstrated by modern psychologists. They have taken groups of children and assigned various tasks to them—modeling clay, painting, and so on. Before the work could be completed, however, the children were ordered to put it aside, with strict instructions to proceed to something else. Then the experimenters left the room.

Through a peephole they observed what followed. The children promptly went back to their tasks but concealed their finished work before the experimenters returned.

What had happened? A problem had been created for the children. They had been started on the road from A to Z, but midway a barrier was suddenly erected. As soon as that obstacle was removed by the absence of the experimenters, they rushed back to work surreptitiously and then hid their products. It was the need for completion that compelled their behavior.

Similar experiments have been conducted with adults. The German psychologist Zeigarnik gave his subjects a number of tasks to carry out, some of which were interrupted. Some time later, when the people were asked to recall the assignments, they could give more details about the unfinished tasks than about the completed ones.

As a result of such research, psychologists have come to the conclusion that there is a "persisting task-tension." Any unfinished job tends to haunt us. Unless we relieve the tension, we suffer discomfort. This may well be the most valuable part of the human mechanism. It is certainly one of the distinguishing marks between us and other forms of animal life.

We find it hard to abandon our uncompleted tasks because we cannot forget them. This keeps us working at our problems until solution is achieved. Generation after generation wrestled with smallpox and could not turn away from the unsolved problem. Down the ages marched a horde with pock-marked faces, a procession brought to an end by the work of Dr. Edward Jenner.

One need not have the stamp of genius to feel this horror of incompleteness. We become annoyed at interruptions because they frustrate our need for completion and leave us in a state of tension. We hate to start a new piece of work toward the end of the workday because we don't want the irritation of an unfinished job in the background of our minds.

This same unconscious fear of incompleteness accounts for

our being late on many occasions. Many a husband comes up from his power tools in the cellar to explain to his exasperated wife over the cold soup, "I just had to finish up." The wise mother is aware of the need for completion in individuals and uses it in the proper handling of her child. She doesn't call from the doorway, "Johnny, come in at once; dinner is ready." Instead, she lets the boy know a few minutes in advance: "Better start finishing up, Johnny. Dinner will be ready in five minutes." In this way the child is not forced to suffer the shock of sudden interruption and the abandonment of purpose.

This need for completion comes from a need for *purpose fulfilled*. It worries our adult lives by creating many problems for us. But it can also be put to work to help us solve such problems as boredom. We can fight off the poisons of routine by giving ourselves added opportunities to enjoy the feeling of completion. We do it by applying the roadmap technique. Just as we marked off a set of intermediate destinations in our auto trip, we can set up a variety of subgoals within the framework of the larger goal. As each of the subgoals is reached, satisfaction occurs. The journey is shorter when you find you are a quarter-way, then half-way, there.

Goals and Subgoals

We have set it down as a general rule that all problem-solving must begin with a knowledge of purpose—the Z to which you want to go. Set it down also that you must know the subgoals on the route. In taking the first major step toward solving a problem, be sure you include not only a statement of your ultimate goal but also the subgoals involved in it.

This principle has been demonstrated for a whole new era of problems opened up in recent years. With the launching of the United Nations and the American foreign aid program, many experts have been tackling the specific problems of raising the standard of living in underdeveloped countries.

Studies of the problems encountered were collected from different experts by Professor Edward H. Spicer and published by the Russell Sage Foundation under the title of *Human Problems in Technological Change.* In its pages, we meet typical social scientists—anthropologists, economists, agricultural experts, human relations specialists—wrestling, for example, with the consequences of introducing a steel axe into the life of a primitive, stone-age Australian tribe; winning adoption of a more fruitful hydrid corn among Spanish-American farmers; and so on.

Commenting on the results of all this research, Dr. Alexander H. Leighton, the American sociologist, points out that very often *problems remain unsolved because people think only of the main goal, and ignore the subgoals that are involved.* It's as if we were trying to eat a pie without taking separate bites. In dealing with efforts to improve conditions in primitive communities, says Dr. Leighton, the failure to fix subgoals endangers solution. "Although the people of a society may want to be free of disease, they may have to be led to appreciate many subgoals, such as cleanliness in the house, which are not in their original perception related to the main problem."

We shall see later on how problem-solving requires that you continually change your view of the problem. One of the most effective ways of doing it is by looking for, or at, subgoals instead of keeping your gaze fixed only on the main goal at all times.

I have a feeling that our problem-solving capacity in the United States has been injured by the philosophy preached in our Hollywood movies. They teach us that problems are solved in one sudden denouement, by one unexpected dramatic act. Actually, in most cases we can reach our major goal only by moving from subgoal to subgoal. Usually we must go through a tedious, slow unraveling of difficulties.

Setting up subgoals is, in effect, the creation of specific smaller projects within the main undertaking. By dissecting it into smaller elements you become capable of initiating action. Perhaps even more important, you create a psychological atmosphere in which the problem itself begins to pay off in satisfactions even before it is solved. The sense of accomplishment is enriched as a result. "I'm half-way there" is an achievement already experienced before the task is done. You don't have to wait until the very end to reap a reward. That's why authors write in chapters and baseball is played in innings.

Most of the tasks that loom impossibly large at the outset are susceptible to this kind of treatment. You can spend a week end—a very long week end—putting up your storm windows by just plodding around the house. But the task will seem shorter, and therefore be easier, if you consciously divide your problem into a series of units—putting up the storm windows on the first floor before lunch time; putting up the storm windows on the second floor by dinner; and so on.

Look for the natural landmarks that suggest the existence of units in your problem. The housewife who plans her work—breakfast dishes, dusting, laundry, etc.—does more than avoid the losses of scattered or duplicated effort. She is staking out the boundaries of her problem and dividing them into manageable units. Her satisfactions are similar to those of the football player who hasn't scored a touchdown but who has made a first down. A visible, measurable milestone has been passed on the way to the goal.

It is purpose, then, which serves as your springboard in attacking any problem. Without it, you are like Cymon, that "fool of nature" of whom Dryden wrote:

> He trudg'd along, unknowing what he sought,
> And whistled as he went, for want of thought.

But coming on Iphigenia, the sleeping beauty in the forest, he acquired a new purpose in life, his love for the beautiful girl:

> That sense of want prepared the future way
> To knowledge, and disclosed the promise of a day.

[3]

THE QUESTIONS YOU ASK

IN THE EARLY DAYS of the wireless telegraph, messages were sent by shooting an electric current across a spark gap in dots and dashes. Between the two electrodes you could see and hear a flashing crackle. To the radio amateurs who played with it, there was a fascination about this homemade lightning that all your modern microphones can hardly match. As the current jumped across two poles, we had the feeling we were conquering space and time, effecting a meeting of minds across the miles.

Problem-solving involves the bridging of just such a gap— between where we are (A) and where we want to be (Z). Our problem is not solved until the lightning of thought crackles betwen the two and the link is established. But before we can throw our lightning between the two electrodes, we have to generate a sufficiently high voltage. The generator is our capacity to *ask questions that are related to both A and Z.*

First of all, notice the distinction between A and Z. One deals with something outside ourselves—objective facts about where we are. The other relates to something inside our-selves—something we want. The first element is a matter of observing and reporting facts; the second involves a decision about our own desires and intentions. We bridge the gap between them when we succeed in asking and answering questions that tie the two together.

For example, the human race is asking itself this question: "How can we move from the present condition of interna-tional friction to the peaceful state we desire?" When we have answered enough questions that concern both present inter-national friction and an ultimate peaceful state, we will have the information we need to end war. But before the answers must come the questions.

Obviously nobody can hope to solve the problem of war without first exploring conditions as they really exist in the world today. In short, we must first get the facts.

But you can't gather facts by dropping a fishnet in the sea and hauling in whatever happens to float your way. You will not come up with *useful* facts about A without consulting Z, your objective. Unless you know where you want to go, the farmer at the crossroads can tell you all about the highways in all four directions, but you're not likely to make progress. *Your objective tells you what kind of facts you have to collect.*

But what of the scientist who devotes himself to the study of various phenomena with no thought of their ultimate use? Is he not a man looking for facts without an objective? He is not!

When Wallace Carothers explored the structure of substances of high molecular weight, his purpose was not to glorify the feminine leg in a sheath of nylon, though that was what DuPont finally did with his findings. The scientist had his own purpose as a guide—the purpose of all pure scientists, which is to create a system of order among the facts of human experience. That purpose is more fruitful of sound questions than any of the lesser purposes of individual comfort or invention.

Unused Material

One year after the Constitution of the United States was adopted, a German chemist named Martin Heinrich Klaproth discovered an element which he named uranium. But human beings do not necessarily use a material just because it is available. Not until 1945 did uranium achieve its climactic use—as a result of the specific, destructive purpose of war.

It may seem startling that most of the newly discovered materials we use to achieve technological progress have always been available to the human race. During the Stone Age, iron ore was at hand but primitive man ignored it. Water power that we now convert into electricity poured down the Niagara gorge and spent itself for eons without any effort by man to harness its energy. Even after Faraday put together his magnet and his piece of wire to make the first electric motor, men didn't realize that a giant slave was waiting to serve them. When Faraday showed his invention to William Gladstone, the great British statesman wanted to know what the toy could be used for. With some heat and literal truth, the scientist told him, "Some day you'll be able to tax this"—a standard of value that any politician can recognize.

Why do we pass by the raw materials that are waiting for our use? It is because we fail to ask of nature the question that will invite her confidence and lead her to reveal a secret. When we do ask the right question, she speaks with a full tongue. As John taught his disciples: "Ask, and it shall be given you; seek, and ye shall find; knock, and it shall be opened unto you." It is the ability to ask questions that turns the lock and makes the door yield to our push.

Emerson mentioned, but did not explain, an interesting fact of human history. "Hudson and Behring," he says, "accomplished so much in their fishing boats as to astonish Parry and Franklin, whose equipment exhausted the resources of science and art. Galileo, with an opera-glass, discovered a more splendid series of celestial phenomena than any one since. Columbus found the New World in an undecked boat."

What was it that compensated for their lack of equipment? Nothing less than a unique, intelligent curiosity that raised profound questions about their world and drove them to press for answers. There is magic to open up continents and move mountains in the power to ask a question.

Leverage in a Question-Mark

Auren Uris, the expert on foremanship in industry, told me of a man who made a fortune as a business consultant by helping companies save millions. All he has to sell, in reality, is a little question of five words. They are: "How can we shorten it?"

Like most good ideas, it is quite simple and can be universally applied. Here are some of the problems that were solved in quite different situations because that specific question was asked:

A New York tabloid newspaper, instead of running the date at the top of each page as newspapers have always done, moved it into the left hand margin. That made it possible to shorten the printed page without reducing the amount of copy. The value of the paper saved runs into thousands of dollars. Another New York newspaper, the *Herald-Tribune*, reduced its column width from 12 picas to 11.3 picas. That made it possible to cut the width of the page *one inch*, leading to a saving of $300,000 a year.

Asking the same question, Arthur O. England of the Personnel Planning Office of the Air Materiel Command at Dayton, Ohio, came up with this information for his Air Force superiors: "It costs $24,160 if our employees spend only ten minutes of their working time reading a four-page directive. This is a modest estimate. It takes ten minutes to read and understand even one page of some of our gobble-de-gook writing. Obviously, if the message in the publication is not understood, then our national defense money is not being spent wisely." This inquiry led to the preparation of AMC Manual 11-1, entitled "Gobble-de-gook or Plain Talk?" which cut a great deal of the waste.

These savings resulted from asking, "How can we shorten it?" I mentioned this question in a talk to a group of sales managers and was hard put to answer when one gentleman said, "But what have we sales managers got to shorten?" A member of the group said: "I'll tell you what we can shorten—our sales presentations!" Sometime later I received a grateful letter from my heckler who wrote that he had shortened his standard sales presentation by eight minutes. This had enabled each of his men to make an additional sales call every day, leading to increased income. No thanks were due me; it was his fellow sales manager who had successfully asked the question in terms of his knowledge of the sales facts of life.

Solutions to your current problems can be found if you raise the question that focuses your attention on the basic facts of your situation in terms of the objective you want to attain. A mere knowledge of the facts will not suffice. Only when you have organized facts *in a form dictated by an intelligent question* will you get an answer.

Go back to the case of the pure scientist. It is true that he is looking for facts even before he has ascertained the use to which they will be put. Pierre Curie was studying the properties of radium before he and his wife knew that their discoveries would write a new chapter in the history of medicine. Yet, in the clearest sense, theirs was not just a pursuit of aimless data. They were interested, as is every pure scientist, in the organization of facts into a system of knowledge. They knew that only systematized knowledge of the physical world can give us the power to predict nature's behavior—and ultimately give us control over our environment.

If we know that water will create energy when it turns to steam, we can predict the consequences of boiling water. The next step, then, is to adjust our position to the predictable circumstances on terms that will satisfy our needs. Because we have learned what steam will do when confined in a boiler, we can create a steam engine.

Notice that four steps are involved:

1. The asking of purposeful questions
2. The assembling of relevant data, which may lead to other questions yielding further data
3. Predictability
4. The exercise of control

Each is a prerequisite for the step that follows. The process can be diagrammed in this form:

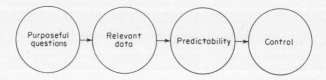

Purposeful questions → Relevant data → Predictability → Control

Viewed in another way, this means that the path from A to Z carries us from questions (inspired by our purpose) to facts (knowledge), to relationships (predictions of resulting behavior), and to control (achievement of our ultimate purpose).

At this point, however, I want to emphasize that the be-beginning of the process is the asking of those questions that will produce the appropriate facts. Scientists have discovered that when they are armed with a purposeful question, which they often put in the form of a hypothesis, they are in a better position to discover facts and the relationships between facts.

But questions can be good or bad, depending on whether they guide us to what is relevant or steer us away from it. Actually, every question does both: it forces some facts across our attention and excludes others from consideration. A man who is asking, "How can I have a good time tonight?" is not likely to see facts that answer how the United States can balance its budget. On the other hand, a man attending the theater who is thinking about the unfinished blueprints on his desk may not notice the third girl from the left in the second row of the chorus.

Relevancy

The question you bring to the facts will influence how you see them and the way you use them in solving your problems. I was discussing this point with Dr. Laszlo Schwartz, who has been directing a team of scientists in a major research project at Columbia-Presbyterian Medical Center in New York for the past few years. From his knowledge of medical history, Dr. Schwartz told me this incident:

One evening in 1844, a dentist named Horace Wells, of Hartford, went out for an entertaining evening. For a long time his mind had been preoccupied with the basic problem of his profession: "How can we reduce the pain of our patients so that we can work effectively on their teeth?" That night he attended a performance arranged by P. T. Barnum. The billing read: "The entertainment is *scientific* for those who make it *scientific*."

Most people in the audience were amused as they saw the effects of "laughing gas" on the volunteers who mounted the platform at the invitation of the performer. But Dr. Wells saw something more; in fact he "made it scientific." He saw that laughing gas, or nitrous oxide, could be used to solve the problem that had concerned dentists for centuries. And so dental anesthesia was born—in a place of public amusement.

The truth is that the man who is always aware of the Z element of his problem will tend to see more facts that are relevant to him. He is constantly asking himself—consciously or unconsciously: "Does this have anything to do with my problem?" Most of the great discoveries are made by what we call "dedicated men." Devoted to an objective, they are constantly associating their experience—the facts they en-counter—with their purpose. They are saying: "This A element that I am looking at right now—does it perchance relate to the Z element, the objective I am trying to attain?" Newton, though sitting under a tree and relaxing, is unconsciously asking questions about his problem: "Does my experience of the moment, which happens to be a falling apple, relate to my objective, which is to explain why the spheres in the heaven remain faithful to their appointed orbits?"

But notice the opposite side of this coin. If Newton thinks only of his objective and does not look at the facts, he will not see the apple. And if he looks only at the facts and con-centrates only on the apple without having in mind his objective, he will not see the principle of gravitation in the apple's fall.

Both elements must be present. The ancient Greek myth pictured Antaeus as invulnerable so long as his feet touched Mother Earth; once off the ground he was a toy in Hercules' hands. So you too are strong as long as you keep one foot solidly rooted in the facts and the other in your objective. Remove either foot—and you're "up in the air" and lost in the clouds.

It is amazing how easily we can lose our bearings and break contact with the Mother Earth of facts. There have been whole periods of history and whole phases of human culture in which facts were deliberately ignored as a matter of philosophy or because of worship of the past. Will Durant, in *The Age of Faith*, repeats a story originally told by Giraldus Cambrensis which illustrates man's capacity for self-imposed blindness to fact. After five years of study in Paris, a young student returns to his home, convinced that all wisdom is his. At the family meal, he undertakes to persuade his father that the six eggs on the table are really 12; whereupon the father eats the six eggs and tells the son to enjoy the rest.

It is part of the genius of man that he can defy obvious fact. Eventually, however, the fact catches up with him, and he goes hungry.

As Aldous Huxley has said, "Facts do not cease to exist because they are ignored." They punish us for our contemptuous treatment of them. "Facts that are not frankly faced have a habit of stabbing us in the back," says Harold Bowden.

A classical instance is the occasion when Rufus Choate and Daniel Webster, two titans of the American bar, faced each other before a jury. The issue hung on the difference between two wagonwheels. Choate had spun out an hour-long oration on "fixation of points" and other esoteric distinctions. Webster rose to reply, and in ten words destroyed the argument of his eloquent opponent. Pointing to the two wheels, he said: "Gentlemen of the jury, there they are—look at 'em!"

That simple sentence deserves a place in your mental briefcase; it's well worth carrying with you wherever you go. If it's facts you're talking about, "look at 'em!"

Digging for Facts

The tool you use to get facts is oddly shaped. It looks like this: ?

The way a question is asked will determine the kind of answer you get. Opinion poll experts can give you statistics from here to there showing that you can get answers to suit your taste, depending on how you word the question. Lawyers who have mastered the art of cross-examination know the importance of the way a question is put.

There is a charming story of a young priest who was very fond of smoking. It was a great burden to him to interrupt his only physical pleasure in order to recite his prayers. One day, he addressed a question to his superiors: "Is one permitted to smoke while praying?" Back came the reply, "Of course not!"

The following day he mentioned his disappointment to an older priest, a Jesuit. "Oh, no, my friend," said the latter. "Instead of asking, 'Is one permitted to smoke while praying?' you should have asked, 'Is one permitted to pray while smoking?' You would have received the answer you wanted."

A great deal depends on how you put the question. Skill in manipulating words is important in problem-solving. As Benjamin Lee Whorf says, "A change in language can transform our appreciation of the cosmos."

A famous example among scientists is the way the U.S. Army defeated yellow fever in Cuba during the Spanish-American War. At that time more American soldiers were dying of the dread disease than were being killed or injured in combat. The Army doctors were ordered into action. Their assumption, which proved true, was that yellow jack was caused by a germ. The researchers stated their question in this fashion: "How can we kill the germ that has invaded the patient's blood-stream?"

Though the story of yellow fever is a familiar one, most people do not know that this question was left unanswered for many decades. In fact, the answer is quite recent. Not until 1951 did Dr. Max Theiler, a South African, finally make possible the mass production of a vaccine that kills the germ; he received the Nobel Prize for it.

Yet the world did not have to wait half a century for a solution to the basic problem because the U.S. Army doctors found a new way to ask the question. It was Dr. Walter Reed who formulated another version of stating the issue.

Instead of asking, "How can we kill the germ in the patient's blood stream?" he asked: "How can we keep the germ from *getting into* the patient's blood stream?" That question led to another: "How does the germ get into the blood stream?" And this produced an answer—the mosquito. On February 27, 1901, Major W. C. Gorgas led his troops against the breeding places of the insects in Havana. After January, 1902, no more cases of yellow fever originated in that city.

The way you ask your basic question, then, is of prime importance. Your formulation of the problem tells you where you will go to look for your answer. Moreover, the character of your question usually foreshadows the nature of the answer. The story is told of two unsophisticates in an expensive restaurant who were given finger bowls at the end of their meal. They exchanged puzzled guesses about the function of these devices, until one plucked up enough courage to ask the waiter. "Oh, that's to wash your fingers," said the waiter. The other man turned to his friend, shrugged his shoulders and whispered, "You see, a foolish question deserves a foolish answer."

On a more sophisticated level, the same point is made by the distinguished philosopher, Alfred North Whitehead, who said of mathematics: "If you ask it a damn fool question, it will give you a damn fool answer, but if you ask it an intelligent question you will get a good answer." Charles Steinmetz, on the other hand, used to say, "There are no foolish questions and no man becomes a fool until he has stopped asking questions." Better more questions than fewer.

Meaningful Questions

Hans Reichenbach recalls the adage that a fool can ask more questions than a wise man can answer—because the fool asks meaningless questions. But what is a *meaningful* question? Says Reichenbach: "A question is meaningful only if it is so asked that before we can give the true answer we at least can tell how a possible answer would look."

Let us dwell for a moment on Reichenbach's test of a

meaningful question. Many people fail to solve their problems because they ask questions that have no possible answer. For example, John Jones finds himself burdened with debt. Depending on his circumstances, he may be tempted to ask himself these questions—check for yourself which are meaningful (that is, suggest "how a possible answer would look") and which are meaningless (that is, don't look like anything in Jones's environment):

1. "How can I get a better-paying job?"
2. "Who will lend me the money without asking me to pay it back?"
3. "How can I cut expenses and save to pay off my debts gradually?"
4. "Which of my relatives will die and leave me a fortune?"
5. "How can I improve my skill and make myself more valuable to my employer?"
6. "How can I figure out a sure-fire system of playing the horses?"

There are many John Joneses who do not realize that only the odd-numbered questions above are meaningful in the kind of world most of us inhabit.

In politics, it is quite common to find people asking the wrong question because they put the issue on the wrong premises. For instance, Senator Everett Dirksen asked Secretary of State John Foster Dulles during testimony on the powers of the President in foreign affairs: "Which is more important—the power of the national government or the power of the people?" Mr. Dulles's answer quite properly suggested that the question was meaningless because it supposed something that wasn't true—namely, that the power of the national government automatically conflicts with the power of the people. As Mr. Dulles pointed out, the only way to protect the power of the people was to have a strong national government that could resist Communist aggression.

You have to be careful of such meaningless questions. W. P. D. Wightman concludes his weighty history of *The*

Growth of Scientific Ideas with this lesson: "If the history of science teaches us anything it is that only to those who ask the right questions are any answers vouchsafed."

As water cannot rise above the level of its source, the quality of your knowledge cannot rise above the questions that elicit it. Your question is like the cone cast by a searchlight. It shows you the way, but you cannot peer beyond its outline into the surrounding darkness. The premises on which your question is based will govern the conclusions you draw.

The problem will go through many transformations while you grapple with it. Odysseus wrestles with the everchanging Proteus but must hold on to him through all the metamorphoses if victory is to be won.

[4]

HOW TO TREAT A FACT

WHEN YOU ARE LOOKING for a solution to a problem, you are like a stranger in town. You know where you want to go, but you don't know how to get there. The only solution is to stop somebody and ask. Of course, if you don't have the address, you'll get nowhere no matter whom you ask.

If you can't speak the language, you're in bad shape, too. I have asked my way around some of the capitals of Europe. In Lisbon, Madrid and Rome, for example, my French saw me through; but the closer I got to Paris, the less people seemed to understand French—as I was taught it.

In addition, I had at my command the little vocabulary books which tell tourists how to ask almost every conceivable question in connection with their physical wants. Thus in Italy, among the first phrases I learned was the invaluable: "Dovè il gabinetto?" If I received the answer "Adestra," I knew that I would find the lavatory on the right; if "Sinistra" it would be on the left.

But life is more than black and white, right and left. I recall the monastery in the little village of Grottaferrata. There the bearded monk who received me responded to my "Dovè?" with a rush of words and gestures that matched the architectural intricacies of the monastery; only his courteous hospitality, that led him to take me by the hand, saved me from disaster.

In dealing with a problem, it is not enough to ask a meaningful question; we must be in a position to understand the answer. And the answer is valuable because it gives us facts. What Carlyle once said contemptuously of students can be said respectfully of questions: they are "like buckets waiting to be filled with facts." It is the purpose of a question to elicit factual material.

Problem-solving has its own etiquette and teaches us how to behave in the presence of a fact. Most people who are asked for directions by a stranger will give him helpful information. But there are occasions when the informant misunderstands the question because it is not well stated. On your second time round, the local resident says, "Oh, I thought you wanted Quaker Ridge, not Quaker Bridge." There are cases when the cocksure native is ashamed to admit that he's never been over to Chimney Corners himself, but he's darn sure he knows how to get there. And there's always the possibility of running into the character who thinks he has something to gain by sending you the long way round. You have to know how to appraise the facts that are offered to you.

In this chapter, I suggest certain basic rules of good manners on being introduced to a fact. Be courteous, respectful, considerate—but watch your step.

You must treat a fact as if it were a potential wife. Follow these rules:

1. No hasty marriage!
2. Meet the relatives!
3. Ask about the dowry!

1. No Hasty Marriage!

It's easy to get involved with a fact and then find you can't disentangle yourself even when you learn she's not quite the lady she pretended to be. Before you form any permanent alliance or even an infatuation, you'd better examine the background.

Philosophy and science have both demonstrated the limitations on our powers of observation. "Seeing is believing," we say as if seeing were knowing. The perceptual experiments conducted at Hanover demonstrate that we must be cautious even about believing what we see. Under conditions created in a specially constructed room, a child looks like a giant and a tall adult like a midget.

Most people recognize the importance of re-evaluating their personal objectives, but they fail to realize that they must also re-evaluate what they believe to be the facts.

There was a young man who wished to become a Talmudic scholar and asked the learned Rabbi to accept him as a student. The sage, after a brief conversation, decided that the youth did not possess the keenness of intellect required by such profound study. But the young man persisted and begged the Rabbi at least to test him. "Very well," said the Rabbi, "answer this problem: Two men go up on the roof to fix the chimney; they fall down through the chimney to the floor below; one man's face is clean and the other man's face is dirty—which man washes his face?"

The would-be student answered: "Naturally, the man with the dirty face."

"No," said the Rabbi, "it was the man with the clean face." He explained: "The man with the dirty face saw the other man's face was clean, so he thought his own face was clean; the man with the clean face saw the other's was dirty and thought his face was dirty, too, so he washed it."

The youth recognized that he had erred, but begged for another opportunity. The Rabbi argued that it was hopeless. "Ask me another question," pleaded the young man until the Rabbi yielded. "Very well," said the Rabbi, and propounded the same question: "Two men went up on the roof, etc., etc., . . . which one washed his face?"

Now the student answered, "The man whose face was clean."

"No," said the Rabbi, "the man with the dirty face. You see, the man with the clean face said to the man with the dirty face, 'Your face is dirty,' so he went and washed it."

Persistent, the young man pleaded for one final chance and the Rabbi yielded again, but said: "This is final. If you fail on this question, you must go away and leave me in peace. Now here's your problem: Two men go up on the roof to fix the chimney; they fall down to the floor below; one man's face is clean and the other man's face is dirty—which one washes his face?"

At this point, the young man gave up and conceded that he was not eligible for a Talmudic career. "But tell me, Rabbi, what is the answer?"

Impatiently the Rabbi concluded: "Look. Two men go up on the roof to fix the chimney; they fall through the chimney to the floor below; one man's face is dirty and the other man's face is clean. I ask you, is this possible?"

Take Your Time

One reason we go wrong in our factual assumptions is that we make them too quickly. Just as soon as a situation registers on our physical senses, we assume we have grasped the objective facts. Yet it is very difficult to get a grip on the world around us.

Here's the way Albert Einstein and his associate Leopold Infeld describe the limitations of our powers of observation in their book, *The Evolution of Physics*:

> In our endeavor to understand reality we are somewhat like a man trying to understand the mechanism of a closed watch. He sees the face and the moving hands, even hears its ticking, but he has no way of opening the case. If he is ingenious he may form some picture of a mechanism which could be responsible for all the things he observes, but he may never be quite sure his picture is the only one which could explain his observations. He will never be able to compare his picture with the real mechanism and he cannot even imagine the possibility or the meaning of such a comparison. But he certainly believes that, as his knowledge increases, his picture of reality will become simpler and will explain a wider and wider range of his sensuous impressions.

Is this a pessimistic picture? If you think so, just remember that men like Einstein and Infeld who are most critical of their own power to peer into matter have increased our power to control the physical universe. In fact, they have been so successful in teaching us how to control nature that we must now learn how to control ourselves.

No, far from discouraging us, the self-criticism of the scientist should teach us to follow his practice. We must be content to move slowly, even in our observation of facts. Perhaps the temper of our times makes this part of problem-solving very difficult. This is an age of speed. Only Heaven knows where we are going, but we are in a terrible hurry to get there. It is a dangerous tendency in our culture to think we can find quick, dramatic solutions—like a drawing-room detective on whom the light bursts with sudden revelation.

The semanticists make a great contribution to problem-solving when they urge us to develop the habit of the "delayed reaction." We are altogether too quick on the trigger; we shoot from the hip and our bullets miss the mark. By the time we really spot the quarry and finally draw a bead on it, we are out of ammunition.

A Good Look

As a boy in religious school, it seemed to me that one of the saddest stories in the Bible was the account of Jacob slaving seven years to earn the hand of Laban's beautiful daughter Rachel. When the years of servitude were over, the wedding ceremony was held; not until the following morning did Jacob see the unveiled face of the woman he had taken to his nuptial tent. Laban had tricked him into marrying Leah, the older sister, and Jacob could only begin another seven years of labor to win his Rachel. At the end of the 14 years, Jacob understood the importance of taking nothing for granted. Always turn on the light and lift the veil.

It's a commonplace that we go wrong because we're too quick to act. That tendency keeps us from solving problems; often it creates problems. In Long Beach, California, the police received a frantic call from an excited lady one day; her car had been stolen. In a short time, it was found—parked in front of the lady's home. She explained, "I didn't recognize it; I guess the rain washed it."

All too often the results are serious instead of funny. The pilot in Korea who bombed his own troops right after they had fought their way to the top of an enemy-held ridge was himself the victim of what psychologists call "over-readiness to react." Wendell Johnson says: "One matures as a person by responding differently today from the ways in which one responded yesterday." But the quicker and more automatic your response, the more likely is it to resemble yesterday's. Only by delaying your reaction can you give yourself a chance to think up a different reaction.

Physiologists have an explanation for this. In effect, they say, we have two nervous systems. One of them directly involves the brain: messages travel through the body to the brain which makes a decision and sends back instructions to the limbs on how to behave. For instance, you're walking down the street and are about to cross. An auto is speeding along. Your eye reports the facts—the distance between you and the car, the speed of your pace—and your brain weighs all the data. It decides, and notifies your legs to stop or to move faster.

But if you're lighting a cigarette and the match burns your finger, you don't have to wait for the message to travel up to your head and for a reply to come back to your hand. Too much time would be lost. You respond with a reflex action. You pull your hand away with less loss of time because the fire alarm need go only to the spine, which has sufficient delegated authority to order withdrawal.

Whenever we settle a question without really thinking it over, we are not "making up our minds," as we say; we are "making up our spine." We are not using the full equipment nature has given us.

There are some situations where surgeons will literally cut off part of a man's brain and destroy its link to the rest of the nervous system. The operation is called a "prefrontal lobotomy," and it is used only on those who are hopelessly ill. The doctors have discovered that it helps to reduce emotional disturbance; the patient recovers the use of part of his brain and his general condition is improved. But a price is paid in terms of intelligence and problem-solving ability.

The patient who has had such an operation can react correctly to simple situations and simple problems. If he enters a dark room, he can handle the elementary problem of turning on the light by pushing the switch. But complicate the problem by putting a sleeping person in the room. The normal individual will delay putting on the light until he has thought through the possible effect on the sleeper; he may decide to leave the room dark. But the man who has lost the use of his prefrontal lobes cannot postpone his reaction and allow judgment to go to work. He proceeds immediately to turn on the light.

When we refuse to give the brain time enough to decide, we are performing a self-lobotomy and cutting off part of our mental machinery. To be sure, there are emergencies when we must gamble on a quick decision because a thought-out decision would arrive too late for use. In certain instances, we have to rely on the "wisdom of the spinal cord." But to do it when there is enough time to consult the brain is to take unnecessary risks.

A New Look

It is frequently recommended that you take a second look. It's not a second look but a new look that's needed. So long as your problem has not yet been solved, you must repeatedly take a fresh look at the facts.

In 1492, Columbus got his first look at the islands of the Western Hemisphere and thought he was in the Indies; he came back the next year and still thought he had reached the fabulous land of spice and frankincense; not until he had come back a third time did he comprehend the fullness of his discovery.

Why was it that after the first and second look Columbus was still mistaken about the nature of his achievement? The reason was that on both occasions he viewed the facts from the same vantage point—the islands we now call the West Indies.

But on a third trip, he found the truth. Cruising westward from the islands, he feared that he would run out of water. He ordered his crew to steer southwest and spotted the three hilltops of the island he named Trinidad after the Trinity; continuing a short distance beyond it, he beheld the endless sweep of the South American continent. Only then, on August 1, 1498, did he realize that he had discovered a vast New World.

To make each repeated examination of the same fact more useful, it is necessary to view it from a different direction. Always seeing it from the same angle will not add anything to your information; in many instances, it may lead to the loss of data. "If you look at your father long enough you will swear he is someone you have never seen before," says Wendell Johnson. Familiarity often destroys knowledge instead of helping it. Yes, take several looks, but let each one be different.

Your first look may be automatic—a mere registering of impressions on your mind with no active effort to sift the data. In a sense, the first look is nothing that you do but something that happens to you. In a simple problem, it may tell you all you need to know. For example, if you want to open a locked cabinet and you see two keys lying on it, your first look will suggest that one of them is probably your answer.

How much your first look will tell you depends to a large extent on the past experience which has shaped both your thinking and your feelings. A primitive tribesman who is unfamiliar with our culture and who has never seen a lock would not know that there was any relationship between the keys and opening the cabinet. After a while, he might deduce from the shape of the key and the shape of the keyhole that the two are related. But he would need more than one look.

The way we see things, then, is influenced by our conditioning. During World War II there were many apocryphal stories about the country lads who went to work in industrial plants and had to learn from the ground up. For example, a farmer fresh from the plow was put to work near a large bell with a sign reading: "Ring this bell in case of emergency." About a week later, the bell sounded and workers came running from every direction. "What's the emergency?" they asked. "My suspenders broke," said the ex-farmer.

Salesmen, particularly, realize the importance of the first glance at the facts. That first impression sets things up in terms that linger on. Intelligent supervisors use the same psychological truth in their dealings with employees. A new plant superintendent who came to work in a small job-shop was warned by his predecessor: "Don't ever ask any of the men to put in overtime. They'll turn you down cold."

Two weeks later, the new supervisor was running behind on the linotyping of a special order because a great deal of tabular matter was involved. On Monday morning, he knew that the only way he could deliver the job on schedule would be to go into overtime on Wednesday night. Knowing the importance of letting the men take their first look at the facts in the proper light, he followed this schedule:

Monday noon. In the lavatory during wash-up, he said casually to a group of the men: "Think we'll get that Registry out by Wednesday afternoon? We pay a forfeit if it's not delivered on time." The answers were vague, but he knew the men would talk about it at lunch.

Monday, 5 p.m. "Sid, don't lock up. I'll be staying late."

Tuesday, 9 a.m. "Fellows, the front office called me to ask how we were getting on with the Registry. I said we'd make it. What do you think?"

Tuesday, 4 p.m. "We're getting close to the deadline. Could any of you fellows stay tonight for a couple of hours, or would it be more convenient if you planned to work tomorrow night?"

Wednesday night. A full crew of volunteers.

The importance of the first approach to a set of facts has been demonstrated by psychologists in formal tests. At Ohio State University, two groups of students were shown a series of simple pictures flashed on a screen. Group A saw them projected in clear sharp focus; Group B first saw them out of focus, then in sharp focus. Both groups were asked to list what they saw.

The result: Group B scored badly in describing the pictures. The errors caused by seeing the pictures out of focus were not automatically corrected by having them clearly projected the second time. Instead, the mistaken ideas formed at first glance influenced what the mind finally saw. For example, individuals in Group B, even after a clear projection, believed that the picture of a rose was an arrangement of flowers, birds in a nest, the face of an Arab, etc.

How to Take a New Look

Since the first inadequate or distorted look influences the second, it's important that we try to correct the initial impression before we go on to formulate our second opinion of the fact.

The secret of a successful second look is to follow the example of Columbus on his third voyage: *shift your ground and look at the facts from a different vantage point.* In the case of the great explorer, it was a physical change that gave him the fresh, new look.

Many people follow the practice of carrying their problem into a different physical site and examining the same facts in new surroundings. They go for a walk, or take the problem home with them from the job. "I'll sleep on it and let you know tomorrow," they say.

Don't minimize the value of this method of taking a fresh look. New civilizations have been built because of it. Europeans who brought their problems to Columbus's New World came up with different solutions and new political and economic forms because they were looking at the old problems in a new setting. "New ground is apt to be fruitful," says Toynbee, because of "its freedom from the incubus of ineradicable and no longer profitable traditions and memories."

By shifting to a new location, you break the fixed association of ideas. Archimedes in the public baths literally got a fresh, clean look at his problem in hydrostatics; the sudden revelation sent him running home naked through the streets in a fit of excitement. A new environment stimulates newer thinking. That is why many companies conduct staff conferences anywhere but in their own offices, and executives sometimes do rush back to their desks figuratively screaming "Eureka!"

Take your problem, then, to a new setting—the city sidewalk, the wooded trail, the sand dune, or the hilltop. Generations wrestled with problems of morality in home and field and workshop, but Moses received his Ten Commandments on Sinai and Jesus preached his sermon on the mount. In striving to see the facts of your problem in a new light, repair to the mountain and you will gain new vision.

Through Another's Eyes

A second method of getting a new look is to ask yourself how the facts look to somebody else, whether or not he is involved in the problem. If the person is directly concerned, you will want his point of view because he is part of the problem and his point of view may itself be a fact of your problem. That would be particularly true in employee relations or personal relations problems. If he is not involved, you can often benefit from his objectivity. If, for some reason, it's impossible to ask, you must use your imagination and project yourself into his position.

Take the case of the father working at his hobby. Says his son: "Daddy, can I help you fix the table?" One look at the teeth of the saw and the tiny hand of his child, and the father sees the fact of danger. If he contents himself with the first look, his answer is a simple rejection of the child's offer to help.

But he must take a second look to see the same situation through the child's eyes. For the son, the fact is merely that he wants to be like his father. From the child's point of view, the nub of the situation is his identification with the father.

If the father has now looked through the son's eyes he is well on the way to reading the facts in a new light. By combining the data derived from the two looks, the father sees both the danger he fears for his child and the child's desire to be identified with him. This leads him to restate and reexamine his problem. He no longer asks: "How can I keep my son out of danger?" He asks, "How can I keep my son out of danger while letting him satisfy his desire to be like me?" And the answer comes: "Of course, you can help me, Johnny. I'll do the sawing and hammering, and you help me by handing me the nails."

2. *Meet the Relatives*

The preceding paragraphs have emphasized that you must not rush into wedlock with any fact that comes along. It is very important for you to check on the lady's family and the company she keeps. The kind of facts with which she associates can tell you a great deal about her.

Whenever scientists analyze their own mental processes, they always point out that a fact by itself is meaningless. Dr. James B. Conant, formerly President of Harvard University and later U. S. Ambassador to West Germany, warns about the limited usefulness of isolated facts: "Facts speak for themselves, we are often told. Anyone who is familiar with the course of scientific research and development knows this is nonsense." Two centuries before, Voltaire had expressed his biting contempt for "the man who can think no deeper than a fact."

A fact is valuable not for itself but because it can be put to work. All facts are related to other facts—and *it's the relationships that count*. Says Professor Anatol Rapoport, "Meaning in its most basic form is the association of one experience with another." Make a fact talk about a relationship, make it reveal a pattern, and it will have value for you.

Gerald Kersh, the novelist, used to play stud poker with other war correspondents during World War II and always lost. He never knew why. Years later Leonard Lyons, the columnist, revealed the reason: every time Kersh was bluffing, a vein stood out on his forehead. One of the correspondents had noticed it as a repetitive pattern that always appeared when Kersh was bluffing. After that, it was easy to call his bluff.

Always look for the pattern of which the fact is merely one part. The man who sees only the fact itself—the swelling of the vein—can do nothing with it. The man who thinks deeper than the fact reads the card player's mind and wins.

At the start of one of the early postwar negotiations with the Soviet Union Ernest Bevin, the British foreign minister, told his colleagues that the Russians intended this time to negotiate seriously. "How do you know?" he was asked. His response was to point to a fact: Soviet Minister Molotov had brought with him a staff of a hundred advisers. Bevin concluded that Molotov would not have needed a hundred experts to help him say the usual *Nyet*. As matters turned out, the Russian spokesman in his opening remarks did present serious proposals which, unfortunately, were later abandoned under orders from Stalin.

Many people collect facts the way they fill up their attics. Unusable junk not only fails to help; it gets in the way. For example, General Pope of the Union Army was the kind of person who crippled his problem-solving muscles by condemning himself to carry a load of unconnected facts. "Pope had a passion for detail," writes Fletcher Pratt. "Lee smothered Pope's intelligence by keeping in constant movement—giving him so many details to look at that he could not form them into a connected whole before the kaleidoscope had changed."

In other words, Pope could not see the relationships. But consider the man who defeated Robert E. Lee in turn. General Grant, watching a few prisoners being led to the rear, noticed that their knapsacks were filled with food. "These men are trying to escape," he said. "They have rations for a long march, not a fight." If the Confederate forces did not want to fight, Grant reasoned, this was the time for him to attack. Events proved he was right.

In handling a fact, you have to ask, "Is it related to my purpose?" And for the answer, you have to look at the surrounding circumstances. You can't tell how big a fact is unless you see it next to another fact or against a background. Interior decorators have taught us that a piece of furniture is often large or small, depending on where we place it.

Ask always: *"If this is a fact, then what else is also likely to be a fact?"* This question can trigger a chain reaction for you that will move mountains out of your way and permit you to reach the golden city of solution.

Winston Churchill, another of the great problem-solvers of our time, was always conscious of this power of facts to peel away ever-new layers of truth. He says this awareness was not fully appreciated until the Victorian era when science made lengthy strides forward. Then, as he wrote, "Science had opened the limitless treasure-house of nature. Door after door had been unlocked. One dim mysterious gallery after another had been lighted up, explored, made free for all: and every gallery entered gave access to at least two more."

It is literally true that you can take any single fact and never exhaust the avenues through which it can lead if you are willing to follow.

Dr. L. Susan Stebbing, in her excellent little book, *Thinking to Some Purpose*, says: "We can make use of knowledge we already possess in order to discover something we did not know, but need to know in order to answer our question." A fact can open up new doors for you if you will only insist on cross-examining it. Demand that it tell you all about its relatives.

Start with any simple fact—for example, "It is raining outdoors." Follow the threads of inference and you will find they lead to the possibility of additional knowledge. Ask yourself the key question: "If this is a fact, what else is likely to be a fact? If it is raining outdoors, what else is likely to be true?" The number of possible answers is almost limitless. Here are a few:

Anybody who comes in from out of doors will probably be wet; anything that was left uncovered out of doors will probably be wet; soft ground will probably have become muddy; anybody who walked on the soft ground will probably have mud on his shoes; anybody who has wet outergarments was probably out of doors during the rain; anybody who has mud on his shoes was probably out of doors during or after the rain; and so on.

All this is pretty obvious inference—at least it seems obvious once you've thought about it. But many of us never think that way, and most of us think that way only occasionally. Yet there are people who make a living out of this kind of thinking—not only the detective story writer and the policeman but also the doctor, lawyer, and Indian chief.

The doctor does it this way: "If this patient has a high temperature, he has an infection." In effect, the doctor is spelling out the relationship between temperature and health.

The lawyer does it this way: A witness has testified that he saw Lincoln's client commit a murder at night. With great skill, Lincoln uses one fact to open the door to another until the fact of perjury is revealed. Here is the cross-examination:

Q: And you stood very near to them?
A: No, about twenty feet away.
Q: May it not have been ten feet?
A: No, it was twenty feet or more.
Q: In the open field?
A: No, in the timber.
Q: What kind of timber?

A: Beech timber.

Q: Leaves on it are rather thick in August?

A: Rather.

Q: And you think this pistol was the one used?

A: It looks like it.

Q: You could see the defendant shoot—see how the barrel hung, and all about it?

A: Yes.

Q: How near was this to the meeting place?

A: Three-quarters of a mile away.

Q: Where were the lights?

A: Up by the minister's stand.

Q: Three-quarters of a mile away?

A: Yes,—I answered ye twiste.

Q: Did you not see a candle there, with Lockwood or Grayson?

A: No! What would we want a candle for?

Q: How, then, did you see the shooting?

A: By moonlight! (defiantly).

Q: You saw this shooting at ten at night—in beech timber, three-quarters of a mile from the light—saw the pistol barrel— saw the man fire—saw it twenty feet away—saw it all by moonlight? Saw it nearly a mile from the camp lights?

A: Yes, I told you so before.

"Then," according to Judge Joseph W. Donovan, "the law- yer drew out a blue covered almanac from his side coat pocket—opened it slowly—offered it in evidence—showed it to the jury and the court—read from a page with careful delib- eration that the moon on that night was unseen and only arose at *one* the next morning!"

What Lincoln had done was to ask of one fact that it give him information about another. The witness said it was a fact that he stood in beech timber. Reasoned Lincoln:

If it is a fact that the witness stood at night in beech timber, it being August, then the leaves must have been thick and the light dim.

If it be a fact, as the witness says, that he was three-

quarters of a mile away from the light and there was no
candle on the scene, then it must follow that he could not see
by the light.

If it be a fact that the witness saw by moonlight, as he
says, then it must be a fact that the moon was in a position
to cast a light.

At this point, Lincoln had reached a matter of fact that
could be checked independently of the witness by examining
the data recorded in the almanac. He was thus at the end of
the trail, for he now had an undisputed fact that contradicted
the witness's original assertion.

Lincoln's problem—to prove the testimony false—was solved
because he asked of each asserted fact that it *reveal its associations with other facts.* And as he tracked down each alleged association he ultimately reached the point where
contradiction emerged and the testimony of the witness fell.

The Indian chief uses the same technique: "Ugh, twig
broken. Paleface pass here. Where is my tomahawk?" Actually, the only fact he sees is the broken twig. If the twig is
broken, someone broke it. If someone broke it, he is not an
Indian because Indians are not so careless.

Safeguards Needed

We all make inferences and deductions. The problem is
that we sometimes make too few, sometimes too many. But
you will tend to be better off if you are among those who err
in the direction of making too many tentative inferences,
rather than too few. The reason is that there are safeguards
against too many inferences, whereas there is no remedy for
making too few.

The first safeguard against drawing too many inferences
from a fact is to add a "maybe" to every inference. As you
increase the number of facts from which you are drawing
your inferences, the "maybe" will begin to shrink. *If the same
inference comes out of a series of facts, you are increasing the
chances that you are right.* The one fact of a blonde hair on a

husband's coat will never justify a verdict in a divorce suit,
but the added fact that the man was seen leaving a hotel plus
the fact that the names of "Mr. and Mrs. Jones" appear on
the register in his handwriting reduce the amount of speculation involved in the inference.

I was once the guest of a fairly large firm in a southern
city. One of the executives told me he was troubled by a
problem with one of his employees—a rather able man whom
he wanted to promote to timekeeper for the crew. The man
had refused to accept the job, a fact which the executive considered evidence of hostility to the company. He was so irri-
tated that he said, "If we're ever in a position where we have
to make layoffs, that man will be among the first to go."

"Just on the basis of this one fact—that he won't accept a
job as timekeeper?" I asked.

The executive was embarrassed by my lack of sympathy
for his point of view. He backed away a little by asking me
what I thought was the reason for the man's behavior. I
didn't know, of course, but suggested we look for more facts
in the man's personnel file. (Notice that one of the few facts
I had was that the man was employed with the company;
that fact suggested where I could find other facts because "if
he's an employee of the company, the Personnel Office has
a file on him.")

When we checked the file, we found his job application
form had been typewritten—the answers had been dictated to
a clerk in the office. Usually the answers are handwritten by
the employee himself, except when he says he can't write
well. In this case the man's signature was a semiliterate
scrawl. "I get it," said the executive; "as the time-keeper, he'd
have to keep written records, and that's what he's afraid of."

In considering the fact of the man's refusal to take the promotion, the executive should have *looked for the associated
facts* before arriving at a judgment. The approach I used was
to ask: "If this is a fact, then what else is likely to be a fact?"
Had the executive asked that question, he might have gone
through this process: "If it is a fact that the man refused to

accept a promotion, then it must be due to another fact—namely, that there is something about the promotion that bothers him. I have looked at the fact of the promotion from my point of view; now I must take a look at it from his point of view. What is there about the promotion that makes it unacceptable to him?" This would have led to a list of the job's characteristics, among which would have been "keeping records." That would have opened up the pathway to the real explanation and a sounder reaction on the part of the executive.

The executive, I should add, was a very alert and highly intelligent individual. But he had come close to making a serious error because of his speed in jumping to a conclusion. Curiously, it is the quick, alert mind that is most likely to make this kind of mistake. To be able to leap from a fact to a conclusion is not itself a vice: *the fault lies in the failure to go back after the conclusion is reached and actually establish the chain of facts that is being assumed.*

As Dr. Paul Weiss, Yale professor of philosophy, expresses it: "We are confused because we have not learned how to distinguish inquiry and speculation." Inquiry is a pursuit of further facts; speculation is an impatient chasing after conclusions.

When we fail to insist that the facts should blaze the trail to new facts, we go astray. Then we conceive solutions for problems that do not exist; we invent remedies for diseases that have never yet been contracted. The worst of our error is that we distort accurate diagnosis and prevent the healing action of objective research.

3. *Ask About the Dowry*

The average experienced fact-finder—whether he's a lawyer, detective, newspaperman—knows that the best way to pin facts down is to ask questions. Journalists use a formula requiring that the lead paragraph of the average story answer these six specific questions: *Who?—What?—When?—Where?*

—*Why? How?* Omit any of them, and your story is incomplete.

To assure complete coverage, W. Alec Jordan, when he was editor of *Chemical Week*, used to send instructions to his correspondent on a given scene of action by wiring, for example, "Kipple Monsanto announcement re new plant." He had coined the word *kipple* to summarize Rudyard Kipling's quatrain:

> I keep six honest serving men
> (They taught me all I know);
> Their names are *What* and *Why* and *When*
> And *How* and *Where* and *Who*.

Recall the incident that begins with the telephone ringing in the police station. "A woman is being murdered in the upstairs apartment," says an excited voice.

"I'll be right over," shouts the rookie policeman, hanging up and rushing out. The only thing he forgot was to ask, *Where?*

But there is an additional question that is more often ignored. Whenever you are examining a fact, be sure you ask, "*How much?*" The effect may not be romantic. Nothing is more prosaic than arithmetic, but nothing provides more trustworthy milestones on the road to solution. Unfortunately, the answer to this question is not always available, but how do you know unless you have asked?

Physical scientists feel they don't really understand a subject until they have been able to express it in numbers. This was already recognized in the thirteenth century by Roger Bacon whose inquiring, experimental mind made him the first modern man. Leonardo da Vinci, writing as a scientist, declared that "there is no certainty where one can neither apply any of the mathematical sciences nor any of those that are based upon them." Francis Galton, who like Leonardo seemed boundless in his scientific curiosity, said it very simply: "Whenever you can, count."

In our own time, great progress has been achieved in the

social sciences because an effort is being made to gather figures about human behavior, not just to rely on general impressions. Today universities are offering special courses in mathematics to older sociologists who feel the need for acquiring the benefits of the new, mathematical equipment. Similarly, businessmen are taking courses in statistics, mathematical decision-making and computer equations.

Of course, the social sciences are nowhere near the precision of astronomy, which has such exact mathematical knowledge of its subject that it can predict to a split second when an eclipse of the moon will take place. Space technicians can even aim a rocket at a point in space where the planet Venus will be several months from now. Economists cannot predict the behavior of the national income or the cost of living, except in broad terms. But don't write off the social sciences. The techniques of econometrics and sociometry, made possible by statistical method, offer new hope for more intelligent control of our economic and social life.

The path of progress lies along lines drawn by the mathematician. Today knowledge can often be calibrated. Years ago surgeons would cut open a man's side and remove his appendix on the basis of a series of symptoms: fever, tenderness to the touch, and so on. Now medical science does not rely on guesswork; a literal blood count tells mathematically whether an appendix is pouring poison into the blood stream.

In social psychology, Dr. Kurt Lewin developed his field theory which opened up a new science of group dynamics by making it possible to measure reactions. His genius, in part, consisted of the ability to devise experiments in human relations that lent themselves to mathematical answers. For instance, during World War II the United States Government presented this problem to him and his staff: "How can we change the present eating habits of the nation to counteract the meat shortage?" Dr. Lewin promptly set up "laboratory conditions" that allowed him to examine *mathematically* the effectiveness of different methods.

He subjected some groups to lectures on the wisdom of

switching to new foods; others were merely invited to participate in group discussions and decide for themselves. Some time later, all were interviewed on whether they had actually changed their menus. The results showed that less than 5 per cent among the lecture group were influenced, whereas about 35 per cent responded to the "discussion on group decision" method. Further studies revealed that even individual instruction is less potent in changing behavior than group discussion.

Another situation in which scientific method asked *How much?* and solved a social problem involved the famous American anthropologist Franz Boas. In 1923 he was called upon to testify in a case that stemmed from a now obsolete state law forbidding non-Caucasians to own property. The issue was whether Armenians were Caucasians. Instead of approaching the problem on the basis of theoretical considerations, Boas decided to *measure* the facts.

He examined Armenians born on the other side and Armenians born in the United States and measured their heads with calipers. Until that time people had attempted to draw conclusions about race from the physical proportions of the head. Professor Boas's statistical study showed that Armenians born in the United States did not have their parents' "occipital protrusion" at the back of the head. The reason for the difference was that in Armenia children are tightly swaddled on a cradle board; in the United States they are physically free and consequently their heads grow differently. Boas's testimony established the right of Armenians to own property despite the racial law; but, more important, his "facts and figures" underscored once again how unscientific race prejudice really is.

A great deal of information awaits you on matters relevant to *your* problem if you too will ask *How much?* Consider an ordinary, everyday type of problem. An employer is trying to decide whether to hire a particular job applicant as a stenographer. He might ask himself: "Can Miss Carstairs handle the job?" If that is as far as his thinking goes, he is more likely to hire Miss Carstairs for her appearance than for her skill. To get the really important facts, he has to ask himself: "Can Miss Carstairs take dictation at 90 words per minute and type up correspondence neatly with no more than two typographical errors per page at a speed of 45 words per minute?"

In so doing, he is following the wisdom of Alfred North Whitehead, the philosopher and mathematician: "There is no getting out of it. Through and through the world is infected with quantity. To talk sense, is to talk in quantities. It is no use saying that the nation is large.—How large? It is no use saying that radium is scarce.—How scarce? You cannot evade quantity. You may fly to poetry and to music, and quantity and number will face you in your rhythms and octaves."

But aren't there some things on which you cannot get specific mathematical answers? Suppose our employer is also interested in how much team spirit Miss Carstairs has, how well she will cooperate with the other girls. Nobody knows yet a mathematical way to measure temperament and character; but we do know that personnel officers have achieved good results by using "merit rating scales" that range through some five categories:

Excellent—Good—Average—Below Average—Poor

Just by making the effort to put the individual under one of these headings in respect to distinct qualities that cannot be precisely measured, you learn a great deal you would not otherwise have known. Even when you cannot answer the question *How much?* with a number, the effect of asking it is that you are forced to think more specifically.

Professor Anatol Rapoport, who is a mathematical biologist and naturally stresses the mathematical nature of information, shows the progress of medicine in the following examples.

Before healing became a science, the most that people could do was to look at a fellow tribesman who was sick and say:

Og is sick.
Let us find ways to make Og well.

"Vague statements lead to vague methods, where success is erratic and questionable," says Professor Rapoport of this approach. After Hippocrates, however, the problem could be restated in this form:

Anaxogoras has a fever.
Let us look for ways to rid Anaxagoras of his fever.

Obviously, there is a better chance of success because this statement of the problem reveals more specific information about the patient's condition. Nowadays, since we have had the benefit of Pasteur's problem-solving revelations about germs and Koch's experimentation, a general practitioner reasons like this:

John is infected with tuberculosis bacilli.
I must look for ways to get rid of the bacilli.

Does this seem far removed from mathematics? In Og's case, to be sure, we had no information that was capable of measurement. But in Anaxagoras' case we can take a mathematical reading on a thermometer. And with John, somebody can look through a microscope and spot a rod-shaped parasite, one eight-thousandth of an inch long. Whenever your examination of a fact allows you to measure, the resulting knowledge is more precise and more useful in problem-solving.

The Game of Twenty Questions

You have probably seen people play the game of Twenty Questions. The contestants are given a problem—to "guess" an object that one of the players has in mind. Since some people systematically get better results than others, more is involved than accidental guessing. ("If it is a fact that some people systematically get better results, it is likely that they have a skill.")

Actually, the good player of Twenty Questions is the person who can make one fact put the finger on another. Gregory Bateson, the anthropologist who is also an expert on linguistic communications, gives this illustration: "You think of something. Say you think of 'tomorrow.' All right. Now I ask 'Is it abstract?' and you say 'Yes.' Now from your 'yes' I have got a double bit of information. I know it *is* abstract and I know that it isn't concrete. Or say it this way—from your 'yes' I can *halve* the number of possibilities of what the thing can be."

That's a very dramatic result to achieve from one question —narrowing the number of possibilities by 50 per cent. It is therefore worth while to notice just how the player accomplishes it. Bateson explains that this result is obtained not only by the *nature* of the questions asked in the game but by the *sequence* in which they are asked. "Those questions have to be in a certain order. First the wide general question and then the detailed question. And it's only from the answers to the wide questions that I know which detailed questions to ask."

By using the broad question first, the player gets on the trail of his solution. Eventually, he narrows the scope of his inquiry. But if he began with the finely pointed question, the odds would be overwhelmingly against him. You must start with the broadly conceived question.

Facts Come in Categories

John Dewey once said in another connection, "We take out of our logical package what we have put into it. . . ." If your package contains only isolated, narrow facts, that is all you will have at your disposal. But if you are to succeed in solving the problems with which life confronts you, then you must have at your command certain broad questions—large packages with large ideas that cover a multitude of facts.

It is important to appreciate how the path of progress in problem-solving often moves from the broad question to the narrower one. That is the way the average specialist, whether he be an automobile mechanic or a researcher in cancer, proceeds.

Consider this fairly typical situation: My car will not start. To retain the confidence of my wife and children, I have no choice but to open the hood, stick my head in (which I do as if it were a lion's mouth), and try to spot anything that looks out of the ordinary. It never does—and I then phone Eddie, my mechanic, to rescue me.

Now watch the approach of the true scientist. Eddie's years of training and experience have taught him that there are certain general questions to ask whenever a motor refuses to run. Those questions literally tell him what facts to look for. Eddie says he asks questions like these:

1. Does the trouble lie in the electrical system? If it's in that class of problem, he must check the lights, make sure the ammeter (I have an old car) shows a discharge when the key is turned on, look for loose ignition wires, etc.

2. Is it a problem of fuel supply? In that case, he must check the gas, sniff learnedly at the carburetor, examine the settling glass on the fuel pump. If these are okay, the search for the specific must continue, and Eddie may have to open up the fuel line.

What the problem-solver here has been doing is asking and answering broad questions that gradually narrow down to the specific facts. When one of his broad-then-narrow questions led to the discovery that the fuel supply was blocked, he could fairly quickly focus the problem down to the fact that the fuel pump wasn't working.

Often when you've watched a specialist do his job, you feel you could have done it yourself. The physical part of the job is easy; it's the brainwork that's usually hard.

This was illustrated in a lawsuit that held the spotlight for a long time in England. John Ruskin, the famous critic and essayist, had written of a painting by the artist Whistler: "I have seen and heard much of Cockney impudence before now, but never expected a cockscomb to ask 200 guineas for flinging a pot of paint in the public's face."

Whistler sued for libel, and on the witness stand was asked how long it took him "to knock off that Nocturne." "Two days," answered Whistler.

Said Ruskin's lawyer: "The labor of two days then is that for which you ask 200 guineas?"

"No," retorted the artist, "I ask it for the knowledge of a lifetime."

Whistler won, but the jury awarded him only one farthing for damages, which was enough to make Ruskin resign his art professorship at Oxford.

It is long-accumulated knowledge and experience that make the expert, not the individual facts his eye happens to spot. Whistler's answer on the witness stand might well have been the model for the dentist's reply to a patient who asked how much it would cost to have a tooth pulled. When the fee was mentioned, the man exclaimed: "Ten dollars—for three minutes work!"

"Okay," said the dentist, "if that's the way you want it, I can make it take longer."

The Mystery Woman

In this chapter I have drawn a parallel between the treatment you accord facts and the treatment you give a woman in whom you have a romantic interest. I hope the parallel has not been too extravagant, but I must indicate another similarity between the two. A man can never hope to know all about a woman no matter how long they are married. It is better so. There is no hope for any marriage in which mystery ceases to exist. And in the world of facts, it is ordained that the element of mystery must always be with us. It is not given to the mind of man to know everything about anything.

Back in 1950, I tried an experiment with a group of industrial foremen. That morning the newspaper had carried an employer's description of a man who was on his payroll: ". . . a model worker, an unusual craftsman, extraordinarily punctual. He left his bench only for lunch. He did not join other workmen at the bar. He hurried home at night."

I asked the group if they would hire the man for their own company on the basis of these facts, assuming he was otherwise qualified. All agreed they would. I then revealed to them that this was a description of Oscar Collazo given by his employer. Collazo had attempted the previous day to assassinate the President of the United States.

We can never know all the facts about any person or situation. But that is no reason to abandon the pursuit of detail. Fortunately, we do not always need *all* the facts to obtain a solution. Semmelweiss defeated childbed fever, the terror of motherhood, a disease so widespread in European hospitals, according to Dr. Oliver Wendell Holmes, that it killed women "so fast that they were buried two in a coffin." Yet Semmelweiss knew nothing of bacterial infection!

Lister introduced antiseptic techniques in surgery—and his life-giving boon had to await the insight of Pasteur before the principle could really be understood. Semmelweiss conquered puerperal infection with no conception of surgical infection; Lister conquered surgical infection and ignored contagious infection. Millions of human beings owe years of life to the *incomplete* knowledge of Semmelweiss and Lister. Not until Pasteur had revolutionized all of medicine with his vision could the world understand the meaning of his predecessors' contributions.

The important thing is to be aware that your information is incomplete. It will keep you alert to new facts so that your unsolved problem begins to approach solution, is then partially solved, and is ultimately solved more satisfactorily, even if never completely. Actually, there is no final solution—only good and better solutions.

The semanticists have emphasized the incompleteness of our knowledge and have urged that we use as a regular tool in communications and in problem-solving the symbol *Etc.* So important is this concept to the semanticists that their learned journal carries that name. In working out your problems, you will find on many occasions that it pays to use paper and pencil. You may be listing causes and effects, developing itemized series of facts. Always add *Etc.*, the abbreviation for the Latin words, *Et cetera*, meaning *and others*. It can save you from accepting a wrong solution or from permanently closing the books on an "unsolved case." While it acknowledges the unknown element in your problem, it is a symbol of hope that additional facts may be forthcoming to shed new light.

In listing alternative explanations for any given fact, it is especially important that you add the *Etc.* A very able columnist for the *New York Times*, for example, suggests to psychologists that "excitement stirs human appetite." He bases his observation on the fact that at the World Series games "hot dog men and chocolate bar venders did their briskest business after the stirring action on the field." He may be right. But when I laid the matter before Dr. David A. Emery, the psychologist, he promptly came up with a list of possible alternatives to explain the increase in sales:

1. People who were already hungry were distracted temporarily by the exciting plays and deferred buying.

2. People who might otherwise have purchased refreshments during the excitement were unable to get the attention of the excited venders.

3. The venders themselves, once the excitement was over, burst forth with renewed sales efforts, inspired by the action on the diamond.

4. Fans whose team had scored or made brilliant plays expressed their joy by eating.

5. Fans whose team suffered a setback overcame their frustration by eating.

6. Etc., etc.

Emphasizing his Point 6, Dr. Emery went on to say: "Especially when it's a question of human behavior, it's always wise to earmark conclusions as 'tentative' until you've explored all the conceivable alternatives. Even when the circumstances require immediate action, the knowledge that you can rarely be certain will make your decision more thoughtful. Moreover, when the same type of problem arises in the future, you will be less likely to duplicate previous errors."

The value of knowing that our knowledge is limited is underscored in the story of St. Paul's second mission which brought him to Athens. Standing in the Areopagus, he called the Athenians' attention to their altar dedicated "To the Unknown God." They had erected it as religious insurance; they wanted to be certain they were not overlooking any god whose sensibilities might be offended. "You are too superstitious," said Paul, but welcomed the fact that their superstition had left the door open for his message: that Unknown God, "whom therefore ye ignorantly worship, Him I declare unto you."

So long as men know that their limited knowledge is bounded by a vast shoreline of ignorance, they can continue to learn. Wherever you stand, build an altar to the Unknown Fact.

[5]

YOUR FRAME OF REFERENCE

IN THE FOLKLORE of many peoples you will find the story of
the errant husband who wandered into the woods one day
with his mistress. There he was espied by the town gossip.
He realized at once that he had a problem.

His first thought was, "How can I keep the gossip from
reaching the ear of my wife?" A moment's consideration led
him to the conclusion that there was no answer. Then another thought struck him, and he leaped into action. As fast
as he could, he made his way home, and taking his wife by
the hand, he led her back to the same place where he had
dallied before—and for the same purpose.

Later that day, the gossip put in her expected appearance.
With a smirk she announced, "I saw your husband in the
woods with a woman this morning." But the wife only smiled
strangely, undisturbed by the news.

Let the psychologists explain why this tale is repeated in
so many cultures. Our concern is solely with the technique of
problem-solving used by the protagonist of the story.

Even from the brief account given here, it is clear that the
husband first stated his problem in a form that made it un-
solvable. But then he shifted to a new formulation that allowed solution.

A lesser man would have stayed hopelessly with his first
version of the problem: "I have been seen by the gossip; how
can I keep her from telling my wife?" Had he asked only that
question, exposure would have befallen him. Instead, he had
the wit to phrase a better question: "I have been seen by the
gossip; how can I nullify the effect of her story on my wife?"
Asked in this form, the question could be answered by his
fertile mind.

Reread the two questions, and you will see why one leads

up a blind alley and the other to self-preservation. The first question is the obvious one: "How can I keep the gossip from telling my wife?" But there is no practical answer to that. To find solution, the mind must shift to another statement of the problem that *makes it more manageable because it takes into account more facts.* The additional facts are that there is no way to keep the gossip from conveying her information, that the wife is certain to hear the story. Translated into our basic pattern of A and Z, the original unsatisfactory question amounted to this:

A   The present position of the problem-solver: His behavior is known to the gossip.

Z   Where he wants to be: Keep the gossip from telling his wife.

But notice that the man changed Z in his restatement because second thought made him change A, his statement of the facts:

A   His present position: His behavior is known to the gossip and *there's no way to keep her from telling.*

Z   Where he wants to be: Keep the information, once it has reached the wife, from having any effect.

Facts Need a System

In the preceding chapter I discussed the gathering of facts. But why do we have to go on gathering more facts than we started with? The answer is that we face an unsolved problem only because we don't have enough meaningful facts with which to go from A to Z.

Professor Duncker, you recall, put it this way: "Whenever one cannot go from the given situation to the desired situation simply by action, then there has to be recourse to thinking." The thinking will uncover new facts, we hope, which we can use as girders to bridge the gap. This chapter will discuss how we rivet the new facts into place.

Just as soon as you have uncovered a new piece of information or come to any new conclusion about your factual position, you have to *restate your problem in the light of the additional information*. That's the function of the additional facts.

Simply to heap up more data and do nothing with the new facts would be more foolish than mining gold in Nevada in order to bury it in Kentucky. Actually, of course, the gold in Fort Knox has a great deal more meaning than the unmined ore in Nevada: the former is part of a currency system; paper has been issued against it; transactions are occurring. So, too, with the facts you dig up: they must set in motion a series of new transactions or your effort is wasted.

Let us stop for a moment to visualize what is happening here. Our problem-solver is standing with fact in hand, as if it were a coin. He is about to drop it into one of the slots on a jukebox, and set in motion a complicated mechanical process. Gears will whir, one specific record will drop onto the spindle and the music he wants to hear will blare forth. An intricate apparatus intervenes between the coin and the music; indeed, the apparatus is a pre-established system of communications, and the coin (the fact) is simply a final impulse that will activate the system. At this stage, the fact is poised for action; it is looking for a slot through which it can enter the pre-existing system.

The system, in the case of problem-solving, is *your frame of reference*. And it is usually revealed by the form in which you state your problem, by the *basic* question you ask.

Various students of the thinking process have used different names to designate the frame of reference. Bertrand Russell, for example, sees science, which is high-level problem-solving, as concerned principally with the formulation of frames of reference. "Science, though it starts from observation of the particular, is not concerned essentially with the particular but with the general. A fact, in science is not a mere fact, but an instance." An instance, that is, of a general principle in operation.

Dr. James B. Conant sees science as the process of developing "conceptual schemes." In the next chapter we shall examine the illustrations he offers of how outstanding scientists have developed and used conceptual schemes to meet the challenges of the unknown. There we shall see how a frame of reference uses generalizations, abstractions, and relationships.

No matter what terms we use, we all have many different frames of reference. Some are broad—for example, our theory of human nature, which may range like Freud's through various depths of conscious and unconscious motivations. Others may be as simple as a Mid-Victorian schoolteacher's view that a child is either "good" or "bad." Some frames of reference are quite narrow, like the straying husband's first view of his problem which led him to think originally of controlling the gossip's movements: he had to shift his frame of reference to controlling his wife's movements.

For purposes of this chapter, we can use the term in its loosest sense, to mean no more than *the orientation with which you ask your basic question.*

In succeeding chapters we shall speak of the elements involved in frames of reference—such conceptual tools as generalizations, abstractions, and relationships. These will give us a more refined definition of the term. Before we handle our tools as craftsmen do when they are working on expensive oak and mahogany, we should experiment on cheaper pine. In the end, perhaps, we may achieve the artistry of the cabinet-maker.

Facts and Frame of Reference

Many people who consider themselves hardheaded say they ignore theories and operate solely on the basis of facts. But the truth is that no fact can be used until it has been set in a frame of reference. Thomas Huxley said that "those who refuse to go beyond fact rarely get as far as fact"—that is, they really fail to understand the facts at their disposal.

The meaninglessness of a fact by itself, divorced from a setting, is easily illustrated. Consider the matter of "an error of five minutes." In keeping a social appointment, a five-minute lateness is a fault that can be erased by an apology; but an error of a few seconds is an enormous miscalculation in shooting a rocket to the moon.

Let your mind play with the connotations you derive from the simple sentence, "He picked up the knife." To what conclusions are you automatically led if that is the opening line in a murder mystery? But how different if you encounter it in the biography of a noted surgeon.

In the average setting, a penny has no significance. But shift the locale and the consequences may be tragic. In Santiago, a riot takes place; seven men die; the Chilean Congress is called into emergency session; charges and countercharges of conspiracy are hurled. Why? All because the bus fare has been raised from 1.40 pesos to 1.60—an increase of two-fifths of a cent.

In all these instances, it is clear that the fact is meaningless without a context, a background against which its true dimensions can be seen.

Your Personal Frame

Originally, as a race, our frame of reference viewed man as the center of the universe. It was exploded by Copernicus and Galileo, who proved that the earth is not the center of the solar system; Darwin then scattered the remaining pieces by demonstrating that man was not the center of creation but merely the topmost branch sprouting from the tree trunk of life.

Yet there is psychological truth in the picture of man as the focal figure. Each one of us lives in a world of our own, in which all things radiate from and converge on ourselves. As individuals, every fact we encounter is stamped with some element of our own personality. When we receive facts, we fit them into a framework that is peculiarly our own.

An old device used by policemen in proving guilt relies on

this important psychological truth. A suspect will be given an account of the crime, but some of the details will be omitted. Some time later he is asked to repeat the story he has been told; if he is guilty, he will usually include some of the details that were withheld from him. In the detective melodramas, the hero concludes: "As soon as he said he didn't poison his rich uncle, I knew he was the one. I never told him how the victim was killed!"

This self-betrayal happens because the individual who receives a fact associates it promptly with other facts that he knows and with opinions he already holds. The old and the new merge so quickly that it is almost impossible to dissociate them.

The greatest single value of the frame of reference is its happy faculty of making it unnecessary for us to have *all* the facts. This is important because most of the time we can't have all the facts we need—that's what makes a problem, as Professor Duncker says. A good frame of reference can fill in the empty spaces very neatly. It does so because it gives order to what would otherwise be unrelated, irrelevant facts.

This becomes clear if you examine the kind of results you get from the same series of words put together in completely different frames of reference. What additional facts can your mind's eye fill in when you hear the words: "glass . . . bottle . . . alcohol"? Try it with two different frames of reference:

In the frame of reference of a cocktail lounge, you will add the vision of "lovely ladies . . . gay conversations" and so on.

In the frame of reference of a hospital laboratory, you will add to "glass . . . bottle . . . alcohol" additional items like "test tube . . . bunsen burner . . . microscope."

The Function of the Frame

In effect, your frame of reference organizes the facts for you, gives them order, classifies them, establishes relationships between them. One valuable product of this *capacity to order the facts* is that your frame of reference suggests what gaps exist in your supply of facts.

It was not until the scientists could arrange the elements in an atomic table that they were able to track down the missing element uranium. The same approach applies to the filing clerk. If she knows that the principle (the frame of reference) is alphabetical filing, she can tell at once which file is missing when the P's are gone.

To solve our problems, we have to ask ourselves, "Where are the gaps in our pattern?"

It is only the existence of a pattern of order that makes it possible for us to spot the essential omissions in our knowledge. Fortunately, our frame of reference not only helps to identify the gaps but makes it possible for us to invoke the resources of imagination to fill them in.

I recall my first visit to Rome. My plane had arrived after dark. A friend had met me at the airport and rushed me off to the famous Taverna Ulpia for dinner.

After we had eaten, I suggested that we take a walk. Without a word of warning, my friend led me a distance of a few yards around the corner, and there I was in the midst of the ancient Forum where once the Caesars received the plaudits of the populace. History came alive for me in that sudden revelation of the Roman ruins; yet I must confess that all I saw was a row of cracked columns here and a crumbled slab over there.

The next day an expert guide took me back to that unforgettable scene and named the individual places for me. Then my mind could begin to restore the buildings ravaged by time and weather and war. Now that I knew the row of jagged pillars was the Temple of Venus, the empty spaces were suddenly filled with marble walls. What was lacking to the physical eye, the mind's eye could supply.

The more clearly defined the frame of reference, the more one can see. After eight years of patiently removing the rubble from the ancient Temple of Palestrina, archaeologist Pietro Romanelli looked at the foundation stones and the few broken columns that remained and declared with confidence: "We have unearthed enough to show the broad outlines of the temple at a glance, and to give us so much precise knowledge of its layout that except for a few details we could rebuild it today as it was in its prime."

So too in dealing with the problems of our own existence. A frame of reference gives us a better chance to fill the gaps in the incomplete structure of facts and makes it possible for us to move towards our solution.

This is of critical importance. If we had to wait until every last piece was fitted into the jigsaw puzzle to identify the picture, we would probably kick over the table in a fit of frustration long before we approached completion.

Many people do react that way. The Cassandras of caution have misled them into believing they must not reach a decision until they have "all the facts." A newborn baby doesn't wait to find out where it came from and where it's going before it decides to eat. But many adults suffer from the serious psychological disturbance called abulia—inability to reach decisions. And they are encouraged by those philosophers who caution against taking any action before *all* the evidence is in.

Here the advice of George Santayana is helpful:

It is not necessary to fathom the ground or the structure of everything in order to know what to make of it. Stones do not disconcert a builder because he may not happen to know what they are chemically; and so the unsolved problems of life and nature, and the Babel of society, need not disturb the genial observer, though he may be incapable of unraveling them. He may set these dark spots down in their places, like so many caves or wells in a landscape, without feeling bound to scrutinize their depths simply because their depths are obscure.

Similarly, physicist J. Robert Oppenheimer speaks of scientific knowledge as merely "a lacework of coherence." There are gaps, but we nevertheless have some meaningful pattern.

Do not wait for "all the facts"; *pursue all the facts that are available*. Then you can reach judgment on the basis of how well they dovetail according to your lights—your frame of reference.

The Negative Side

The light shed by a frame of reference can be revealing, or it can blind your eyes. A frame of reference, after all, is usually a theory. The psychologist E. C. Tolman warns that in many cases it "serves as a sort of sacred grating behind which each novice is commanded to kneel in order that he may never see the real world, save through its interstices."

Lord Acton says, "The worst use of theory is to make men insensible to fact."

Unfortunately, when a fact contradicts our theory or frame of reference, we try to retaliate against the fact. For its impertinence, we proceed very systematically to snub it. Some Japanese, for example, go on believing that their Emperor is divine, despite the fact that he lost a war. They push that fact into oblivion by saying that the Emperor was misled by his advisers; but they don't bother to explain how advisers can mislead the All-knowing.

More sophisticated people find it harder to ignore the fact, so they distort it to make it fit their frame of reference. That is true of philosophers and scientists as well as the rest of us. Ernst Cassirer said of some of the profoundest minds of recent times:

Each individual thinker gives us his own picture . . . they would show us the facts and nothing but the facts. But their interpretation of the empirical evidence contains from the very outset an arbitrary assumption—and this arbitrariness becomes more and more obvious as the theory proceeds and takes on a more elaborate and sophisticated aspect. Nietzsche proclaims the will to power, Freud signalizes the sexual instinct, Marx enthrones the economic instinct. Each theory becomes a Procrustean bed on which the empirical facts are stretched to fit a preconceived pattern.

But don't misunderstand the point. Though light can blind us, we must still have it to see. An Indian guide in the north-woods may conceivably mislead us; nevertheless, we must have a guide when we go into the forest. A given frame of reference may keep us from solving a problem. But solution will come when we have finally seen the problem in a better frame of reference.

Let us first illustrate the way a wrong frame of reference operates. For that purpose, try to solve this problem: Here you have a square made up of three rows of equally spaced dots. Using only *four* straight lines, can you connect all *nine*. points without taking your pencil off the page?

```
        .     .     .



        .     .     .



        .     .     .
```

Stop here and try to solve the problem.

On the next page you will find the answer. Turn to it after you have attempted to solve the puzzle. If you succeeded, congratulations. If not, it may be some consolation to know that on the average only one person out of 25 gets it right. Most people fail to find the answer because they think they must draw the four straight lines *within* the nine dots. So long as they see the problem in that frame of reference, they cannot possibly solve it. Once they break out of the bounda-ries they have set for themselves by the way *they* stated the problem, they can come up with the solution.

We all have our frame of reference which sets for us the boundaries within which we allow ourselves room to maneu-ver in looking for a solution. If the frame of reference is how to keep the wife from knowing, then there is no possible course of action short of murdering the gossip. But if the husband can think beyond the boundaries of that too narrow frame, a solution is available.

John W. Livingston, Jr., who has advised thousands of sales executives on their problems, emphasizes the importance of thinking constantly in terms of a new frame of reference. He cites the modern marketing approach, recalling that businessmen used to think within this frame of reference: *How can we sell our product to our customer?* Now they have changed their frame of reference to ask, *How can we determine what our customer needs?*

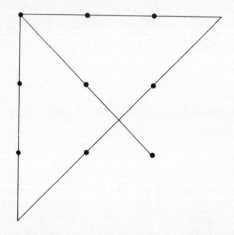

"A good example of how this results in tailor-made products," says Mr. Livingston, "was reported in the newspapers. A British manufacturer of shooting sticks—those walking sticks whose handles unfold into seats for game shooting or for spectator sports—wanted to invade the American market. But he was a little worried whether his product would fit the potential customers. Good thing he was, too. The British trade expert he sent over made an extensive tour, sizing up U.S. sportsmen by the seat of their pants. As a result of his investigations, the manufacturer doubled the seat width of his American model. What he plans for the feminine market apparently didn't quite measure up to publication standards. Anyway, the moral of this story is that you may have to go to extreme ends to satisfy customers."

Many writers on human relations have noted that people often come into conflict because they see problems from a different frame of reference. Consider the story told by Dr. Frederic Loomis, the well-known medical consultant. His patient, a young lady thought to be suffering from a heart condition, undressed for the physical examination. Trying to determine the presence of the characteristic "thrill" of mitral stenosis, he had raised the patient's bare breast and applied his stethoscope. He turned to his nurse who was taking down his findings and said: "No thrill." The young lady jumped up and exclaimed: "Well, isn't that just too bad? Perhaps it's just as well you don't get one. That isn't what I came for."

Of course, Dr. Loomis had been using the word in his medical frame of reference but the young woman was thinking of it in the frame of reference of a back porch or a moonlit beach.

Whenever you cannot make the facts add up right, you may be a victim of your frame of reference. You can consider that you are making progress if each new fact that you get is used not only as another brick to be built into your system but as a potential challenge to your system or frame of reference. Until Einstein, new facts of astronomy and physics were being fitted into Newton's frame of reference; Einstein used those facts as bricks also, but he threw them at Newton's system and arrived at new understanding and new control over the forces of nature.

The importance of the frame of reference has been illustrated by the English psychologist, C. F. Mace, who presents this problem:

Imagine a propaganda campaign through press and radio, say in the interests of fuel economy, to persuade a sleepy public to rise with the lark. Suppose, even, you empowered an army of snoopers to go into every British home and whip the bedclothes off anyone found asleep after seven. It would still be difficult, and would lead to "questions in the House." Approach the matter in a different way, and the solution is childishly simple. When the voice of the cuckoo is first reported in the daily papers, you tell everyone to put their clocks forward an hour. Next day everyone is up bright and early with scarcely the rubbing of an eye. What has happened? You have not changed the intensity of anyone's desire. You have simply changed your sleepy public's "frame of reference."

Understanding the nature of the frame of reference makes it possible to influence the behavior of others. In one of the most famous passages in American literature, Mark Twain's Tom Sawyer solved his problem of whitewashing the fence by giving his friends a new frame of reference: painting a fence was shifted from a "work" frame of reference to one of "fun." Tom, says Mark Twain, had discovered "a great law of human action"—how people will respond to a change in the frame of reference. "*Work* consists of whatever a body is *obliged* to do, and . . . *Play* consists of whatever a body is not obliged to do. And this . . . (is) why constructing artificial flowers or performing on a treadmill is work, while rolling ten-pins or climbing Mont Blanc is only amusement."

Changing somebody else's frame of reference is one of the most fruitful solutions to problems in the field of human relations. *Changing your own frame of reference in the light of new facts* is the most useful step you can take in wrestling with your problems.

Know Your Frame of Reference

Your frame of reference is "the way you see things." It is determined in the first place by the culture in which you are raised. Culture is the anthropologist's word for the mental set, the thinking habits, with which we grow up. Often our culture will dictate whether or not we have a problem. Take, for instance, the various food difficulties confronted by individuals who come out of different cultural backgrounds:

Four hungry men are sitting around a table but none will

eat, though steaming meat is heaped on their plates. One of them is a Roman Catholic, and this is Friday. Another is Jewish, and the meat was not prepared according to Orthodox ritual. The third is a Hindu, for whom the cow and her spouse are sacred animals. The fourth is an Englishman, a follower of George Bernard Shaw and his vegetarianism. All four have a culture which excludes the meat as a solution to their problem.

That table surrounded by four hungry men illustrates the cultural frame of reference. But in our individual experience we also develop a personal way of looking at things. The result is that our thinking is directed into certain fairly limited channels. If I hand you a monkey wrench and ask you to fix a piece of machinery, you proceed automatically to look for a nut that is to be loosened or tightened. You see *monkey wrench* in a frame of reference that calls for working on nuts.

Now suppose I give you another problem. I show you two strings hanging from the ceiling (see the illustration on this page) and give you a monkey wrench with instructions that you may use it to tie the two together. You are thoroughly accustomed to solving certain problems with the aid of the monkey wrench, but your first inclination may be to use it on my head. Nevertheless, you ignore the monkey wrench and me. You calmly take the end of the string and reach for the other, only to discover that the strings are so short that you cannot grasp both at the same time. Yet I assure you that you can use the monkey wrench to tie the two strings together.

Stop here and try to solve the problem.

All right, here is the solution: So long as you think of the monkey wrench in its usual frame of reference—namely, as a *grasping tool*—you will not find the answer. Instead, think of it in another frame of reference—as a *weight*. Now the answer should come to you. Just tie the monkey wrench to the end of one string, start it swinging back and forth in the direction of the other, take hold of the other string and catch the weighted one as it comes toward you. Now you can tie the two together.

The difficulty is that all our past associations with the monkey wrench send our thoughts in the wrong direction. To solve our problem, we must get off the track which has become a rut. *The first step toward changing your frame of reference is to recognize it clearly.*

In the above problem, you would say to yourself, "Now what is this tool in my frame of reference? Well, first of all, it's a grasping tool. How can I use a grasping tool to tie these two strings together? . . . Well, I can't see how the grasping quality of this tool helps. Let me then see if this tool has any other qualities in addition to its character as a grasping tool. It has the quality of toughness; it has a color of gray—but these characteristics don't help. Next, it has weight. Will the quality of weight help me bring the two strings together? Ah, yes. . . ."

There is no guarantee that you will automatically reason this way. The most we can say is that you have a better chance to get the right answer if you first test your traditional frame of reference, then, when it proves unsatisfactory, deliberately undertake to break out of it. In the case of the wrench you try the *grasping* frame of reference first, next you look for others.

The ability to recognize your frame of reference, to try it and then discard it, explains some of the most dramatic dollar-and-cents developments in business. For example, enormous fortunes have been built up out of by-products that were once viewed as waste. One man's frame of reference tells him that wood shavings are "scrap," to be thrown away. But his competitor who has the capacity to shake off that frame of reference makes composition board out of the shavings; another develops insulation material out of sawdust.

It takes almost a stubborn quality in a man to fly in the face of an existing frame of reference. For years everybody has said, "This is waste; this is scrap; this is useless; this is for the garbage heap." But some persons dare to say: "I refuse to consider this as waste; I will look at it as if it has useful qualities."

For example, there was the man who watched a machine tool turning out shimmering, metal, spirally coiled pieces of "waste." But he refused to see them as something merely to be swept off the floor; he looked at them as objects that were (a) bright, (b) light, (c) available in large quantities for mass distribution, (d) fire-proof, (e) inexpensive, (f) etc. He kept describing them in new terms, looking for new ways of saying what they were. He might even have looked up Roget's *Thesaurus* for synonyms and paused over each word: *light, brightness, sheen, shimmer, tinsel*—and he has it! Christmas tree ornaments, of course. And his company proceeded to develop a market in Christmas tree icicles.

You are an engineer in the construction business? Then talcum powder should be of interest to you. If it isn't, that's because you think of it in a frame of reference of bathrooms, babies, etc. But construction people are now using talcum powder to "chalk" marking lines—because somebody thought bigger than his usual frame of reference.

You are in aircraft manufacture? Your usual frame of reference will tell you that female sanitary pads are remote from your interests. But one engineer discovered that they can be used as airfilters in testing flying instruments. What circumstances led him to make the association, we do not know. What matters is that he was able to crack the crust of rigid thinking imposed by the usual frame of reference.

A Limited View

I have indicated before that our frame of reference can give us much information, but it can also limit our view and isolate us from data. William James has explained the psychological factors that are involved: "The human mind has no ... power of universal intuition. Its finiteness obliges it to see but two or three things at a time. If it wishes to take wider sweeps it has to use 'general ideas,' as they were called, and in so doing to drop all concrete truths ... The human mind is essentially partial. It can be efficient at all only by *picking out* what to attend to, and ignoring everything else—by narrowing its point of view. Otherwise, what little strength it has is dispersed, and it loses its way altogether. Man always wants his curiosity gratified for a particular purpose. It is, then, a necessity laid upon us as human beings to limit our view."

Unless we limit our view, we see nothing. And since our view is focused for us by a given frame of reference, we see only a limited number of items and may fall short of all that we need to arrive at a solution. Consequently, when we have explored what our original frame of reference can show us, we must use another. It is as if we had a series of fixed-focus telescopes at our disposal. As we put each one to our eye, we limit ourselves to a certain range and depth. That gives us an efficient examination of a limited area. But to see what we need to know may require that we scan the field with another telescope.

Consider the kind of situation encountered in many industrial plants today as a result of the widespread development of unionization. We can approach that problem with several different frames of reference that will produce widely different results.

One frame of reference through which unionism might be examined by an employer is a simple refusal to recognize the right of the union to act for the employees. That will lead him to resist unionization; his efforts may or may not be successful, but they will assuredly mean hostility between him and the union.

If the union succeeds in organizing the employees, the employer may decide to use the same frame of reference and continue his refusal to recognize the union. Then, either strike action or the national labor law may force him to change his frame of reference, and while still remaining hostile, he will look at the situation in a new light. Instead of, "How can I make it unnecessary to bargain with the union?" he now asks, "How can I bargain successfully with the union to defeat extravagant demands?" A whole new series of facts immediately comes into focus for him—he examines union contract clauses, weighs the effects of proposals, develops counterproposals, and so on.

Most employers today use this second frame of reference, though the first one was fairly common several decades ago. Actually, there is a third possible frame of reference that some employers are using today. They sum it up in the question: "Since the union is here to stay, how can I utilize this relationship to get affirmative benefits for my company?"

That leads to a variety of other facts that the employer examines: advertising the union label as part of his sales appeal to customers; using the grievance machinery to localize petty issues on the foreman-shop steward level; stimulating employee suggestions for cost cutting by setting up an awards panel that includes a union representative; launching a training program for apprentices, with union consultation to assure a future supply of labor; involving the union in safety campaigns; etc.

Two Frames of Reference: FDR vs. Churchill

The relation between your frame of reference and the kind of solution you propose for a problem is illustrated in the wartime differences that arose between the two great allies Winston Churchill and Franklin D. Roosevelt. Though united in the common enterprise of defending the world against Hitler, the two leaders came to the task with different backgrounds and standards of value—in short, with different frames of reference. Let the survivor of this historic partnership tell the story of one of the dramatic clashes of opinion between himself and the American president. As you read it, look for the frame of reference of each of the parties.

> At Washington, [writes Churchill] I had found the extraordinary significance of China in American minds, even at the top, strangely out of proportion. I was conscious of a standard of values which accorded China almost an equal fighting power with the British Empire, and rated the Chinese armies as a factor to be mentioned in the same breath as the armies of Russia. I told the President how much I felt American opinion overestimated the contribution which China could make to the general war. He differed strongly. There were five hundred million people in China. What would happen if this enormous population developed in the same way as Japan had done in the last century and got hold of modern weapons? I replied I was speaking of the present war, which was quite enough to go on with for the time being. I said I would of course always be helpful and polite to the Chinese, whom I admired and liked as a race and pitied for their endless misgovernment, but that he must not expect me to adopt what I felt was a wholly unreal standard of values.

As Churchill describes it in retrospect, it is clear that the two men were looking at the same set of facts from different frames of reference.

Within the frame of reference of a European whose major challenge was the Hitler threat, the facts looked all towards a neglect of China—so much so that the usually urbane prime minister, writing years later, is still unable to conceal a note of asperity.

But the President of the United States, leading a Pacific as well as an Atlantic power, could not help but look toward a future in which China would be a world force. Mr. Roosevelt did not live to see his judgment vindicated as it was when the troops of Mao Tse-tung attacked the army of General MacArthur in Korea. One wonders if Mr. Churchill, who was still alive at that time, was led to change his view and concede the limitations of his own wartime frame of reference.

Incidentally, the converse was also true where Europe was concerned. The American rejected the Englishman's proposal that Europe be invaded through the Balkans; the prime minister in this instance was using a long-range frame of reference, for he had his eye on the postwar role of Soviet Russia.

Relate to Your Frame of Reference

In all the instances I have cited, decision has depended on the way the problem-solver permitted his frame of reference to operate. It can be a serious obstacle to solution or it can make solution possible. It is therefore important for you to know how to use it. A key rule, as we have seen, is first of all to recognize your frame of reference. Next, you must quite consciously align each fact into the frame of reference.

We must consciously strive to see our frame of reference and ask what the relationship is between it and any new fact that arises. That is not easy, but it can be achieved. It is a laborious task to ask of every fact, as we observe it, whether it has a relationship to our problem and how it fits our frame.

For example, Newton, living in his frame of reference, must not assume that a falling apple has nothing to do with his interest. When he was asked how he discovered the law of gravitation he answered: "By thinking about it all the time." In effect, he was always relating his observations to his basic question. When the relevant ones came along, he was ready to welcome them.

The salesman who is waiting to see his customer must not assume that the secretary's idle chatter is irrelevant to his sales frame of reference. When she thoughtlessly says, "Mr. Jones won't give you much time today because he's got a golf appointment," the intelligent salesman recognizes at once how that tidbit of information relates to a goal: it may open a door of mutual interest through which the customer will receive him. Deftly, he weaves into his sales talk such terminology as will identify him too as a devotee of the game, and the illustrations he uses come out of the lexicon of the golfer: his goods are above par; his product will help the customer out of the rough; his company has scored a hole in one as against all competition.

But why can the salesman do it? Because the frame of reference he uses—winning favor with the customer—is immediately related to the new fact given him by the secretary. Quite literally, this problem-solver goes successfully from door to door because he is willing earnestly to ask, "What's Hecuba to him, or he to Hecuba?"

To be able to look at every new fact as having special meaning for you—that is, to assume that it may fit somewhere into your frame of reference—is a golden quality. It makes all past experience, as well as present, grist for your mill. Men who read history and can assert with every page, *De nobis fabula narratur*, will make its content truly a story of themselves, for even if the event did not live in their past it may shape their future. The ancient Haggadah of the Jews commands them to tell their sons at the Passover feast: "This is what the Lord did for me when I went forth from Egypt—for me!"

This identification of one's self with the events of the past is more than a mystic dream that has no consequence. Where men have had no capacity to see their own link to the achievements of others, civilization has stagnated.

Santayana refers to "the Oriental imagination that is able to treat all existence with disdain and to hold it superbly at arm's length." This dissociation of one's self from the environment prevents the solving of problems. It explains why so little material progress has been made in raising the standard of living of the masses in the Far East. Not until men recognize their own involvement in human experience can they draw from it. First we must say, "This story is about me" before we can apply its moral to ourselves.

We must ask, then, "What is this to me?" And the answer to that question can be given from an existing frame of reference or from one that is reorganized to include the new facts. Take the plight of those good wives during the Middle Ages who saw their husbands put up a vain defense against the Swabians during the wars of the Guelphs and the Ghibellines. As an act of mercy, the victors told the vanquished that only the wives would be spared, that they could leave, taking with them only as much property as they could carry. The women solved the problem presented in the terms of the offer by asking, "What is this to me?" And when they had answered it out of their whole life's frame of reference, they had no difficulty in choosing the objects they would rescue. What an impression they must have made on their enemy as they marched out of the doomed city, carrying their husbands on their backs!

Equally dramatic can be the situation in which a single new fact succeeds in changing the basic frame of reference. When the glacier crept down from the north and forced man out of the trees into the grasslands, that one fact changed his whole outlook. From a tree-dweller he became a biped who walked on the ground. He stood erect now, his hands freed from the duty of locomotion, and he could begin to build. His new posture allowed his braincase to grow so that there was room for thought and imagination and inspiration in his skull. All because his hands had been liberated. Helvetius, the French philosopher, has suggested that if horses had hands and men had hooves, we would be pulling the beer wagons and the horses would be drinking the beer.

Language and Frame of Reference

Your frame of reference is fixed by your mental attitudes, but they in turn are often the result of the language you use. Thinking is not independent of the words we use.

In England during the war people complained about the medical care that was given in the emergency "hospitals." When the name was changed to "clinics," the complaints ceased. In the frame of reference suggested by the word "hospital," a whole series of expectations were aroused that never came to mind in the presence of a signboard reading "clinic."

In one very important respect, every science is like every
other: It requires the learning of a new vocabulary. With
words we are capable of manipulating ideas; without them
our minds are limited.

Of course, the mere possession of a large vocabulary does
not mean that a man is rich in ideas. Polysyllabic words are
often found in monosyllabic minds. Winston Churchill once
devastated an opponent on the floor of Parliament with the
remark that the "right honorable gentleman has a facility
for compressing a minimum of thought into a maximum of
words." Indeed there are many people who use the fluent
word as a fig leaf to hide their mental nakedness.

Yet it remains true that a small vocabulary limits the capacity to think. This has been dramatically demonstrated
by a mental disease that involves the loss of language—
aphasia. Ernst Cassirer describes the condition as follows:

> Patients suffering from aphasia or other kindred diseases
> have not only lost the use of words but have undergone
> corresponding changes in personality. Such changes are
> scarcely observable in their outward behavior, for here
> they tend to act in a perfectly normal manner. They can
> perform the tasks of everyday life; some of them even can
> develop considerable skill in all tests of this sort. But
> they are at a complete loss as soon as the solution of the
> problem requires any specific theoretical or reflective ac-
> tivity. They are no longer able to think in general concepts
> or categories. Having lost their grip on universals, they stick
> to the immediate facts, to concrete situations. Such patients
> are unable to perform any task which can be executed
> only by means of a comprehension of the abstract.

Their inability to think in *general concepts or in categories*
means that they can see individual facts but not in a frame
of reference. Consequently, they cannot think their way
through to a solution. To have no frame of reference leaves
one in a hopeless position, for the frame of reference is
usually related to the verbal structure in which a man has
arranged his experience and his view of the world.

But words have their limitations. "Language," says Robert

Louis Stevenson, himself a master of words, "is but a poor bull's eye lantern wherewith to show off the vast cathedral of the world." To discover more of this vast cathedral, you must be ready to change the lantern you use. Be prepared to find new words with which to state the facts of your problem or to ask your questions. "A change in language can transform our appreciation of the cosmos," says Benjamin Lee Whorf.

It is no simple matter to rise above our vocabulary. According to the researchers at the Human Engineering Laboratory in Hoboken, New Jersey, there is a statistical correlation between vocabulary and executive status. After a careful study of "leading hands" (one rung below foremen) and company officials, this conclusion emerged: "As far as the Laboratory can determine by measurements, the leading hand and the official have much the same inherent aptitudes. They differ primarily in vocabulary."

Here is the Laboratory's theory about the significance of words: "Why do large vocabularies characterize executives and possibly outstanding men and women in other fields? The answer seems to be that words are the instruments by means of which men and women grasp the thoughts of others and with which they do much of their own thinking. They are the tools of thought."

Realities and Real Estate

A large vocabulary gives you the ability to word and re-word your view of things and makes it possible for you to develop a more effective frame of reference in tackling your problems. This is as true of the businessman's trade talk as it is of the scientist's technical jargon.

For example, William Zeckendorf of Webb & Knapp refuses to use the frame of reference of typical real estate people. They operate on the basis of acquiring property and holding it until they can find a customer who will buy at a higher price. Zeckendorf uses a different frame of reference for his operations.

Business Week quotes one of his associates in these terms:

> When Bill Zeckendorf looks at a piece of property, he doesn't think of it in terms of its present value, but of its potential. He may be able to increase that value manyfold just by adding an idea, which costs nothing. If he can't see some way to increase its value, if he can't create an increment, create new values, he simply isn't interested.

Increasing the value of the property—that's his basic concept. And as he asks himself the question, "How can I increase the value of the property?" he finds that a series of subquestions help him:

1. "By retenanting?"
2. "By rebuilding?"
3. "By reconception of the use of space?"
4. "By demolishing and new construction?"
5. "By refinancing?"

"Retenanting" might mean shifting from short-term tenants to long-term tenants. As tenants move out of a property, Zeckendorf may refuse to rerent until he has accumulated a large amount of vacant space. Then he knocks out walls and rents the quarters to big firms that are willing to take long-term leases.

Perhaps his most esoteric technique is "reconception of the use of space." Many realtors rejected the Central Park riding academy in New York because there were few customers available for such a property. But Zeckendorf paid $700,000 for it because, as he saw it, he was not buying a stable. When he looked at the open, high-ceilinged arena with its 92 × 200 foot expanse of floor, he saw a television studio. He made a $600,000 profit by selling it to the American Broadcasting Company.

Perhaps his greatest stroke was accomplished by applying the frame of reference of demolition. Here's the way *Business Week* describes what he did:

> For years New York's streets in the East 40's were made unsavory by a group of slaughterhouses lying between First Avenue and the East River. In 1946 a broker ap-

proached Zeckendorf, offered him the entire group as a unit at a price of $17 a square foot of land. Observers may have thought the figure outlandishly high; other property in the neighborhood was going begging at $5 a square foot and even less.

But to Zeckendorf, the $17 figure seemed the greatest bargain he had ever seen. He simply said to himself: "There are no slaughterhouses." And, immediately the land wasn't worth $5 and it wasn't worth $17. It was worth $50—because the existence of slaughterhouses and their stench had been the only thing holding back eastward expansion of the fabulously valuable Grand Central business district.

By buying the property and destroying part of it, Zeckendorf increased its value about three times. Today the eyes of the world are literally focused on those parcels of land; on that site now stand the buildings of the United Nations. John D. Rockefeller, Jr., bought two-thirds of the property from Zeckendorf's company and contributed it to the UN. The price was $8.5 million dollars, and the profit was $2 million, a mere fraction of what Zeckendorf could have obtained if he had proceeded with his original development plans.

Subject to Change

A frame of reference is useful only so long as you are willing to re-examine it. Once you decide, either consciously or unconsciously, that you will cling to it at all costs, you shut off access to possible solutions.

In the last analysis, your present frame of reference is the result of past solutions to problems. When they recur, or when you encounter similar problems, the old frame can still render service. But when you confront the unprecedented problem, the past has to give way. "Change something—even if it's only your vest" was a hard and fast rule on the old two-a-day circuits. In problem-solving, it's usually some aspect of your frame of reference that has to be altered.

The problems we have been describing, and the solutions that ingenious men developed for them, illustrate the importance of being able to handle a frame of reference. Before we proceed, let us summarize useful guides that have emerged so far:

1. You use a frame of reference to understand the facts involved in your problem and to fill in gaps in your knowledge.

2. You draw nearer to a solution if you can develop a new frame of reference that will take into account a greater number of facts and help to produce additional ones.

3. As you acquire more facts, you look for ways to change your frame of reference.

4. To use your frame of reference effectively and to prepare the way for changing or abandoning it, you must be able to recognize it and state it explicitly.

5. The only way to discard your frame of reference is to substitute another for it—in whole or in part.

6. Changing your language will often help you change your frame of reference.

In short, frame of reference is the key to solution. An adequate frame of reference is one that gives you guidance along the road from A to Z. In probing for the answer to your difficulty, it is natural to start by applying your current frame of reference. But if no solution comes and you have exhausted all the possibilities, you must change the frame of reference.

To achieve such a transformation in your thinking, you must clearly understand the components of your frame of reference—generalizations, abstractions, and relationships.

[6]

HOW TO USE GENERALIZATIONS

IN ATTEMPTING TO SOLVE A PROBLEM, you are trying to know the unknown. But no number of known facts by themselves can teach you the unknown facts. Something else is necessary.

That something else is a *generalization.*

When prehistoric man learned how to generalize, he opened up the gates of problem-solving. A triangular piece of chipped flint cut his hand by accident. He watched it bleed, and felt the pain. Some time later, he was angry with a fellow primitive. At that moment, his eye lit on a similar triangular piece of chipped flint. He hurled it at the other man, causing him to bleed.

What was the mental process involved? In his mind he held the fact, perhaps repeated several times in his experience: "Sharp flint injured my hand." But to use that fact in the new unexperienced situation, to know that he could injure someone else, he had to generalize: "Sharp flint injures."

Armed with this generalization, man could now win food more efficiently for his hungry stomach. Because he could generalize from the specific instance—"flint pierces hand"— he concluded that the flint could hunt for him—"Arrowhead on spear will pierce animal." He had moved from the known fact to the unknown, and his pathway was through a generalization.

It has taken me a few sentences to describe what looks like a simple process. It took thousands of years before man made the connection. As soon as he could generalize his experience with the flint, he was able to launch a whole new civilization. The Stone Age was born, and man had become the tool-using animal. But notice that every tool he has since developed came from his use of a key mental tool—the ability to generalize.

Man's capacity to formulate general principles makes it possible for him to use his past experience for present purposes and to plan for future purposes. William Howells, the anthropologist, suggests that it took many generations before human beings began "to keep a stick which seemed to have just the right heft, instead of dropping it and forgetting it after it had been used." The link between present use and future use is something the average child has to relearn from generation to generation, as Mother's aching back so eloquently testifies.

Generalization at Work

Here are three problems. They were solved in each instance only because a generalization was used effectively.

1. A sales manager finds he has exhausted his own thinking and is eager to get the recommendations and suggestions of his salesmen on how they can increase business. He decides to call a meeting at which he will ask for ideas. At the meeting, he sets up a large box, labeled *Suggestions*, and keeps a spotlight turned on it throughout the meeting. Result: a flow of ideas from his people.

2. In India a crisis confronts an elephant driver. His beast has fallen into the quicksand and will surely perish. Obviously, the mahout cannot pull the elephant to safety. He turns to the standard operating procedure in India: he brings up a borrowed female elephant, and his own animal, with a burst of energy, extricates himself from the quicksand.

3. Many American businessmen have not yet awakened to the fact that they are clogging their own communications lines with voluminous memos. The only effect of their inter-office letters is to complicate, not simplify, the flow of information. They could go a long way toward solving their problem if they followed the example of the schoolgirl whose note was intercepted by the teacher. It read: "Dear Herbie,

do you love me? Yes ☐ No ☐. Check one. Dotty." (There *was* a checkmark next to "Yes.")

In each of these cases, the problem was satisfactorily solved because the problem-solver *succeeded in tying his or her situation to a general principle.*

The sales manager used the generalization, "Dramatizing ideas will make people more responsive and will motivate action."

The Indian mahout used the generalization, "Sexual urges can move animals."

The schoolgirl acted on the generalization that many experienced adults ignore, "Simplified, short communications bring more responses than complicated, long ones."

The Process of Generalizing

In each of the cases, whether articulated or not, the problem-solver had gone beyond the facts and had invoked a principle. On the simple level of his own problem, each applied the same lesson that dawned on Charles Darwin suddenly while talking to a geologist in the midst of a gravel pit. "Nothing before had made me thoroughly realize that science consists of grouping facts so that general laws or conclusions may be drawn from them."

To be sure, the sales manager, the mahout, or the schoolgirl is not likely to articulate how his or her mind worked. The process of thought is part of our nature, and in most simple situations we readily, often unconsciously, associate fact and generalization to produce a solution. The electric current of understanding leaps between the poles of fact and generalization, producing instantaneous light.

But in more complicated problems the relationship between the facts and generalizations, particularly where they are numerous and involved, must be laboriously established. It is only when we are equipped with adequate generalizations that we are able to bridge the gap between where we are and where we want to go. And the reason is that a generalization automatically gives us command over a greater number of facts than we started out with.

"Think of heat as motion and whatever is true of motion will be true of heat," says William James, illustrating this point. Once we apply the generalization, "Heat is like motion," we can bring to bear on the situation all the additional facts we know about motion.

The reason a generalization can do this lies in a very important function it performs for the human mind: *it serves to unify a series of facts.* If I ask you to think of a particular man, you will form a definite image of a definite person. That gives you a particular fact. Then suppose I ask you to think of Man—that abstract generalization of all individual men. Now you have in mind the essential qualities, whatever they may be, that you consider characteristic of any and every possible individual man. The generalization *Man* brings to mind the unifying element that runs through our understanding of all the billions of individual men who have walked, and (we hope) will walk, the surface of the earth.

We can all recognize the difference between Man and man. In writing we may symbolize one by using a capital letter and the other by a lower-case m. Generalization is considered one of the major differences between Man and Animal—that is, between all men and all animals. The psychologists call this ability to create generalizations from facts the ability to conceptualize.

Julian Huxley, from his biological background, declares that "the first and most obviously unique characteristic of man is his capacity for conceptual thought." He believes Man has advanced only because of this mental agility that transforms isolated facts into a generalization or a concept. "A brain capable of conceptual thought," he says confidently, "could not have been developed elsewhere than in a human body."

This may be an overstatement. In some slight respects, animals can form conceptions. After conditioning, rats can distinguish, and give different responses to, triangles and circles, can associate one with pain and the other with pleasure. This would be impossible if they could not manipulate some kind of abstract triangle and circle in which they recognize the essential quality of shape that distinguishes one from the other.

Animal psychologists have found, for example, that chimpanzees have some rudimentary powers in problem-solving and must therefore have the ability to think in some kind of abstract form. A chimp will try to jump up in the air for a banana that's out of reach. If he fails, he will turn to another method, unlike a dog, which would in similar circumstances exhaust itself in repeated jumping.

The ape is brighter. He will solve the problem by moving a box into position and piling another on top of it, if necessary. The abstract elements that he is capable of grasping, according to one writer, include "the actually unjumpable gap between him and the banana, and the movability of the box, and the property the box has of serving to fill the gap."

In other words, even a chimpanzee fills the gap between A and Z by using abstract ideas. But his problem-solving abilities are highly limited because he can retain a hold, only briefly, on a very few abstractions at any given moment. Man, on the other hand, has prospered because his potential control over abstract ideas seems constantly to be growing. He can bring to bear in any given situation abstract ideas of right and wrong, the need for preserving human relationships, the desire for social approval, etc., as well as immediate self-interest. (Or, at any rate, he should—because he is capable of doing so. After all, civilization is primarily a system of abstract ideas or generalizations that man has arrived at by logic or has inherited from his culture.)

The process of using generalizations to solve specific problems is illustrated by the case of the housewife sitting in her home. The dog barks outside. "Johnny, go and see who is coming up the walk," she says to her son.

How did she know a visitor would soon be at the door? All she did was to rely on a generalization: "Our dog barks whenever strangers approach." With that generalization available in her mental tool kit she is able to fill in gaps in her knowledge about situations around her.

Hans Reichenbach puts it this way: "The essence of knowledge is *generalization*. That fire can be produced by rubbing wood in a certain way is a knowledge derived by generalization from individual experiences; the statement means that rubbing wood in this way will *always* produce fire. The art of discovery is therefore the art of correct generalization."

When we generalize or conceptualize, whether we do it automatically in small problems or consciously in wrestling with big ones, what is happening? Specifically, we are *looking for the unifying thread that binds the facts together*.

In a figurative sense, we all live in the labyrinth that Theseus conquered. The corridors of our maze, however, are separate facts that we have gathered through our physical senses. The very abundance of facts, like the abundance of corridors, is our undoing. We need the unifying thread to guide us out into the sunlight of understanding.

As Ernst Cassirer puts it, "Our wealth of facts is not necessarily a wealth of thoughts. Unless we succeed in finding a clue of Ariadne to lead us out of this labyrinth, we can have no real insight into the general character of human culture; we shall remain lost in a maze of disconnected and disintegrated data which seem to lack all conceptual unity."

In moving from facts to generalizations, then, we are asking ourselves this problem-solving question: What common pattern ties our separate facts together into an intelligent design? Dr. Conant, the scientist, words his query this way: What is "the most convenient way of ordering these facts?"

The Newsboy Generalizes

At this point, let us look at a homely illustration of the scientific principle at work. I call it the Case of the Conceptualizing Newsboy. It was told to me by an executive in a firm that handles the distribution of newspapers in a metropolitan area.

Every Sunday morning a group of newsboys would be sent out to sell subscriptions for the Sunday editions of all the newspapers. One of the boys surprised the crew manager by coming back regularly after an hour's work with more orders than all the other youngsters could bring in after four hours of canvassing. Almost invariably, his customers had subscribed for two Sunday papers, not just one.

Ultimately he was prevailed upon to reveal his method, which proved to be the height of simplicity. All he did was to station himself near a newsstand, observe the people who bought two newspapers and follow them home. He would then offer to deliver the two papers each week, and the individual almost always signed up immediately.

What was this lad doing that the other newsboys were not? He was conceptualizing; he was generalizing about the facts that were available to him. The other boys had had exactly the same opportunity as he to observe the facts. But he had taken one step beyond observation: he had applied a pattern to tie together the facts he had observed. His dextrous mind was able to conceive and manipulate a number of generalizations—for example:

1. People who buy newspapers at newsstands will buy newspapers at home.

2. People who buy two newspapers have a double value.

In short, he looked beyond the given instance—man-at-newsstand—to the broad concept. He was able to see not only the man at the newsstand but a whole class of men who follow the same pattern of behavior, a pattern consistent with his objective as a problem-solver.

The value of a generalization is its capacity to expose to us more than the isolated facts themselves reveal. We lose detail for a time in order to see the pattern of relationships.

Thus generalizations advance our knowledge by broadening our perception of the problem. Then we are able to "look not at the things which are seen, but at the things which are not seen," as the Bible says. By penetrating behind the surface of the visible we are able to move more surely toward the solution—which remains invisible only so long as we concentrate exclusively on the individual facts.

What we cannot *per*ceive, we have to *con*ceive. What nature withholds from our limited *per*ception, we can nevertheless master with a great *con*ception. And our conceptions or generalizations are the handles by which we take hold on facts and relationships that are beyond the immediate reach of our senses.

Two Kinds of Generalizations

In the case histories given above, we have seen two kinds of generalizations. It will be helpful to spell out the distinction between the two:

1. Look back at our use of the term "Man," which we described as a generalization drawn from our examination of individual men. This kind of generalization I shall call an *abstraction*.

2. But consider this kind of generalization: "Flint pierces hand" or "People who buy newspapers at newsstands will buy newspapers at home." This kind of generalization I shall call a *relationship*, because it is a relationship between abstractions.

Abstractions

An abstraction is a shorthand way of indicating a whole series of separate facts of a similar kind. Its value is that it puts the emphasis on the same characteristic. It is useful because it tells you about those members of a class whom you have not yet seen; when you do see them, you will not be taken by surprise. Traveling through a jungle you encounter a striped, huge cat. If you are familiar with the abstraction *tiger*, you need not investigate the temperament of this particular animal to know what instructions to give your feet.

In the preceding chapter, I quoted William James's remark about the "finiteness" of the human mind. No matter how good we are at juggling, there is a limit to the number of balls we can keep in the air at one time. Similarly, there is a definite limit to the number of facts we can juggle at one time.

The problem is very much the same as the one faced by the average lady who carries at least two dozen items with her wherever she goes—lipstick, house keys, handkerchief, compact, money, car keys, etc., etc. If she had to rely on her hands and fingers to transport these possessions, she would not be able to move. Instead, the lady solves the problem of many-items-to-carry by merging them all into one package—her purse. The result is that the individual items disappear from sight. But she can lay hands (allowing for a brief delay) on any given item when she needs it. The alternative would be to lose some of the items altogether.

Just as the feminine need for manipulating a large number of items led to the invention of the purse, so the mental need for manipulating a large number of facts led to the invention of the abstraction. The abstraction is the handbag into which our mind sweeps a great variety of data. When we need them, they are at our disposal. But we must know how to use the abstraction; otherwise, we will find ourselves in the painful position of the lady who must dump everything out of her purse in order to locate her lipstick.

The first thing to notice about an abstraction is its literal meaning. The word comes from a Latin verb, *to draw out of*. To come up with an abstraction, we have to pick out from a mass certain common qualities about each member of the group.

Two things happen when we are abstracting: (a) we omit some details, and (b) we include and concentrate on the dominant details that are always found in members of the class.

These characteristics of an abstraction are very significant. Thinking would be impossible for us if we had to manipulate relevant *and* irrelevant details at the same time. The abstraction saves us a lot of trouble. Its purpose is to wipe off the slate the figures that are unnecessary for our calculations, just as in most shorthand systems the vowels are dropped for purposes of speed. To be effective, stenography must be transcribed and all the omitted letters must be restored. Similarly, in dealing with abstractions, you must be ready to restore the omissions.

This is the point at which abstractions, whose use is inevitable, may cause us trouble. We think we are seeing the actual objects we are trying to inspect. In reality, we are merely seeing the shadows that approximate their form.

Our abstractions are like X rays. When Roentgen first discovered the value of the rays, it was popularly assumed that he could look into matter. In the United States, bluenoses demanded legislation to forbid the use of X rays in opera glasses for fear that modesty might be violated. Actually, of course, the X rays merely cast shadows on a photographic plate, revealing the outline of material that is more resistant to penetration, thus showing fractured bones or tissue growths.

In the same way, our abstractions permit us to see the form of a mass and to make deductions about the details. In using them, we must always remember that our abstractions are important excerpts from the book of experience and that we are dealing with a substantially abridged version.

We are in danger, however, when we feel that the abstraction is itself the truth. Actually, it is only a device with which we try to grasp reality. Truth is like a glowing coal that you cannot touch without the fireplace tongs. Your abstractions are your tools. Reach for reality without them and you will either lay hands on nothing or burn yourself. But they are useful instruments if you remember they are only tongs.

Most people who handle dynamite are safe so long as they realize what they have in their hands. So too you can be productive in using your abstractions if you know what they are and make it a practice to remind yourself of their basic character. You can do that by frequently asking yourself, particularly when you are not making progress toward a solution, *"What are the facts behind my abstraction?"*

An American Abstraction

Suppose you are the officer of the United States Navy who has been placed in charge of the military occupation on the Pacific island of Truk after World War II. It is your task to maintain civil government and administer law—quite a problem. From time to time, complaints are brought to you, but never by anybody who is aggrieved. Strangely, the gripes come to you only second-hand. Your informant puts it to you that "So-and-So has a problem." But So-and-So never tells you himself.

You are an American, trained to act on certain abstractions, one of which has been inculcated in you and all your fellow citizens: "Hearsay" is unreliable. Our courts will not admit it as evidence; we want to hear the evidence from the man who was there and not from somebody who heard about it. (There is good reason for it: we want him under oath and subject to cross-examination.) So you act on the assumption that you are dealing with complaints and grievances that should not be taken seriously. You decide to take no action unless you get a grievance first-hand. But nobody comes to you—and suddenly you have a virtual revolution on your hands.

This actually happened on the island of Truk, to the damage of American prestige. As a result, for quite some time, the native population considered the U.S. authorities lawless and unjust, wantonly disregarding the elementary duties of fair play and good government. Why? Because our Naval officers had lumped together all the complaints under the heading "Hearsay" and did not bother to go behind the abstraction to the facts which it summarized. The abstraction was an accurate summary; each of the individual facts was indeed a case of "Hearsay."

Eventually, somebody was willing to review the individual cases. When the veil was pierced, another abstraction—that of the natives—was revealed. By their tradition, which is an abstraction from their own historic experience, "Hearsay" is the only proper way to present a grievance. No man would be so ill-mannered and so lacking in human dignity as to press a personal complaint. The abstraction by which the Trukese live requires that a third party present the grievance.

Only when the American was willing to go behind his own abstraction to the facts for which it stood could the difficulties in the situation be resolved. Then a corrected abstraction ("Hearsay" is now perceived as the normal method of presenting grievances) is invoked, and the problem of friction is happily resolved.

Thus, in the end, it is the abstraction, reincarnated and strengthened by the ordeal of decomposition into the facts again, that emerges phoenix-like from its own ashes.

Checking Our Abstractions

Now we have said that, in addition to summarizing facts to omit unnecessary detail, abstractions also perform the function of selecting the most important or dominant characteristics of all the individual cases. The abstraction expresses the cathood of the individual cat.

Unfortunately, this aspect of the abstraction also presents snares for the unwary. Inevitably we must travel the road under the guidance of our abstractions, but the pitfalls are many. For every abstraction rests on an assumption that we have correctly evaluated the dominant characteristics in every member of the group from which we have "abstracted."

Our abstraction tells us distinctive, unifying characteristics that will be found in every given instance of the facts. Every "cat" will have a feline quality. Every "woman" will have a feminine quality. Every "night" will have the quality of darkness.

But when we are loudest in our pontifical orations about

the abstractions we hold dear, experience tugs us by the coat tails and urges us to sit down. Then we are forced to turn back from our abstractions to the facts and ask ourselves, *"Are the qualities alleged to be characteristic of each case really present in all?"*

My generation was given one of the greatest object lessons in abstractions that the human race has ever been taught. The abstraction "Atom" has been revolutionized since I was a boy. My Webster's *Universal Dictionary*, copyright 1936, defines it: "1. In physics, a particle of matter so minute as to admit of no division. . . . 2. In chemistry, a supposed ultimate particle or component part of a body; the smallest particle supposed to result from the division of a body, without decomposition." Any high school boy who repeats that today is certain to flunk physics and chemistry.

What happened to change the abstraction that was thus enshrined in my dictionary? Scientists had gone back to the facts summed up by the abstraction, and had found that the essence of the atom—the characteristic of each and every atom, its indivisibility—was not really the unifying quality to be found in all of them. Fermi and Szilard had taken a very specific kind of atom, U^{235}, and had proved that the abstraction of indivisibility was not to be found in it. The resulting explosion was felt around the world.

Significantly, the result of nuclear fission was not to destroy the abstraction but to revise it. Far from being abandoned, the concept of the Atom is a more vital abstraction today than it was in 1936. So abstract is it now that few laymen pretend to understand it.

Thus the abstraction lives. We come full circle in our mental journey. Beginning with facts, we hasten to develop an abstraction; it seems to fail us; we turn back to the facts from which the abstraction was born; and we find that the result is a stronger abstraction, a newborn Hercules ready to bear the burden of solving more advanced problems.

Abstraction triumphs because it alone can accomplish for us two tasks essential to problem-solving:

1. *It identifies objects for us.* Without the ability to point out objects, we could never develop solutions. Unless the physician can identify the bacillus, he cannot undertake to destroy it. Remember that problem-solving requires a clear understanding of where you are (A) if you are to be able to proceed to the objective you want to attain (Z). That means that identification is an essential step.

2. *It classifies objects.* In a later chapter we shall take up the importance of classifying the problem. At this point it is enough to mention that the physician who has identified his medical problem as involving a specific germ, can attack it with certain weapons if he knows to what class the germ belongs.

To summarize what we mean by the term abstraction (which I have used here to describe the simplest generalization about facts), let me quote Professor W. Edgar Vinacke: "Concepts at the lowest level represent generalized categories of objects. For example, a concept of 'cat' refers to no particular cat but constitutes a general cat in terms of which never-before-seen cats can be identified or recognized."

[7]

SPELLING OUT RELATIONSHIPS

GENERALIZATION does a great deal of work for us, in fact much more work than a mere abstraction. It points out the *relationships between abstractions*.

The abstraction shows us only how a series of facts affect each other. Relationships show us how abstractions relate to each other. The abstraction tells us the common characteristics of individual facts; the relationships tell us how one abstraction interacts with another.

The difference can be illustrated this way: Our thinking is like a brick building. In putting it up, we must manipulate individual bricks (facts). The bricks have to be put together to make walls (abstractions). The walls have to be put together to match the architectural design (the relationships).

In problem-solving, defective bricks used for our facts, inadequate mortar used to hold them together in an abstraction, or unsound draftsmanship in the design of relationships, can lead to collapse of the whole structure.

We can diagram the complexity of the elements in this way:

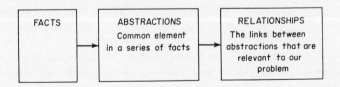

FACTS	ABSTRACTIONS Common element in a series of facts	RELATIONSHIPS The links between abstractions that are relevant to our problem

Suppose I tell you that in the United States there are 15 suicides for every 100,000 people. (That is an abstraction—a summary of a series of cases). You can make a mental note of the figures, but there is very little you can do with them. Now let me give you another abstraction: in Switzerland there are 33 suicides for every 100,000 people. That abstraction, too, may be of little value by itself.

But because you can handle relationships, new understanding is available to you when you have both abstractions. You can form connections between the two, and you can say: "The rate of suicide is more than twice as great in Switzerland as in the United States." You have moved from mere facts to abstractions to relationships.

Galileo's Mistake

With this as a background, let us examine a group of scientists at work on a fairly technical problem that they ultimately succeeded in solving.

In a villa overlooking the beautiful city of Florence, the boldest scientific mind of the Italian Renaissance is at work. It is five years now since he has been released by the Inquisition after having recanted his views on astronomy, but he is still busy attempting to unlock the secrets of nature.

At the moment, Galileo is absorbed in a humble problem called to his attention by local mechanics: Why can't a suction pump lift water more than approximately 32 to 34 feet?

Observation of pumps in action shows this to be the fact. In case after case, pumps in sound working condition fail to raise the water beyond the stated height.

Galileo's mind searches for the solution. His fertile brain has no difficulty handling the facts or the abstractions— "water pumps," "raising water," "distances of 34 feet," etc. He has in mind, too, a generalization that has long been the accepted view since the philosopher-scientists of ancient Greece. Aristotle himself had indicated a relationship that seemed to apply: "Nature abhors a vacuum." Supposedly when the pump pushes air out of the pipe, nature rushes to fill the vacuum by forcing the water into it.

But at one point—and this presents the problem—the explanation breaks down. If nature abhors a vacuum, why does this abhorrence stop at 34 feet?

Galileo's mind does not stand still. He has examined his facts. He has explored the generalizations involved—the abstractions and the relationships. Because he accepts the relationship involved in the generalization "Nature abhors a vacuum," he is looking for another relationship that will give him the answer. He finds it in another generalization: "Suspended copper wires, if they are made long enough, must eventually break of their own weight." (This generalization is what I have called a *relationship*: it spells out the relationship between the weight of a copper wire and its length.) Now he uses this generalization, reasoning that there is a relationship between it and the problem with which he has been wrestling. He concludes from his analogy that the column of water in a pump breaks of its own weight when the height of 34 feet is reached.

There you have the picture of a great scientific mind at work, using facts, abstractions, relationships—in short, generalizations. But Galileo, as further research reveals, is wrong.

Years after he has been buried in the Florentine church of Santa Croce, two of his students, Torricelli and Viviani, finally come up with the right answer. It involves a complete rejection of the vacuum generalization. They learn that the water is raised, not because nature abhors a vacuum, but because air has weight and the water will rise as high as the pressure of the air's weight will push it when a vacuum has been created. It happens that the weight of air is sufficient to create enough pressure to raise water about 34 feet. If you climb a mountain, the pressure of the air lessens, so that the push is reduced and the water will rise only a shorter distance. From this Torricelli went on to invent the barometer which measures the pressure of air on a column of mercury, and he tested it at different points on mountain slopes.

This process took time. Today every elementary science student knows that air has weight—a fact that was not easily come by. But it took intellectual daring to make that suggestion. Charles II, an amateur scientist himself and patron of England's historic Royal Society, laughed at those of its members who were attempting to perform the ridiculous experiment of weighing air.

The odd thing is that Galileo knew that air had weight. Yet he did not succeed in seeing its relationship to the problem of the water pump that couldn't pump more than 34 feet.

The Misuse of Generalizations

Galileo had misused his generalizations, but Torricelli and Viviani had correctly used theirs. Let us see how.

Martha Ornstein, in her book *The Role of Scientific Societies*, describes Galileo's failure in these terms:

> Galileo was strangely conservative on a few points. For instance, he accepted . . . a modified *horror vacui* as an explanation of why a pump could raise water only thirty-two feet. In the *Discorsi e dimostrazioni matematiche,* Galileo says that, as in the case of a suspended coil of wire there is a length at which its own weight breaks it, so it must be with the column of water raised by the pump. Inasmuch as *Galileo knew that air had weight, and had devised a means of weighing it, all this is the more strange,* and in a measure, enhances the historical interest of the man.

Notice the words I have underlined. The key to the correct solution—the weight of air—was within the grasp of the scientist. Why did so great a mind fail to use the objective fact that was readily at hand?

Once again we have proof that the facts by themselves do not give us solutions. Something additional has to be done with the facts. Some alchemy has to be performed on the facts to transmute them into solution. The alchemist is a theory or generalization—or more specifically, the kind of generalization that involves the use of *relationships.*

Dr. Conant offers us an important explanation of Galileo's error:

We can put it down as one of the principles learned from the history of science that a theory is only overthrown by a better theory, never merely by contradictory facts. Attempts are first made to reconcile the contradictory facts to the existing conceptual scheme by some modification of the concept. Only the combination of a new concept with facts contradictory to the old ideas finally brings about a scientific revolution.

It is worth lingering over Dr. Conant's analysis because it may help us escape many of the pitfalls that lie between us and the solution of our problems. Three important ideas are involved in the quotation just given:

First, do not assume that the mere acquisition of additional facts will solve your problem. It is desirable to get more data, but their value depends on what you do with them. In the last analysis, there are only two possible uses: (a) fit them into your existing generalizations and see their relationships with other facts, abstractions, or generalizations; (b) allow them to compel abandonment of your present generalization and substitution of another for it.

Second, no matter how well established your generalizations may be (hundreds of years in Galileo's case), you must ask whether they actually do create order among all the facts and abstractions by describing the relationships that exist among them. We cannot generalize except by knowing such relationships. And for this we need what Whitehead calls "that eye for the whole chessboard, for the bearing of one set of ideas on another."

In establishing relationships, we are asking ourselves what facts go together and in what way they are interdependent. Are the facts and the abstractions joined in a relationship of cause and effect? Or are they all the result of the same or similar causes? In their interrelationship, which elements are more important than the others?

The first function, then, of relationship is to establish order. One scientist, Herbert Dingle, sums up the nature of knowledge this way: "We can no longer say, The World is like this, or the World is like that. We can only say, Our experience up to the present is best represented by a world of this character; I do not know what model will best represent the world of tomorrow, but I do know that it will *coordinate a greater range of experience* than that of today."

But order, apart from its aesthetic appeal, is only a means to a larger end. We want order among the facts and abstractions because such order can point the way toward more facts and abstractions, which can in turn suggest courses of action leading to our goal.

The Process of Rearrangement

The important question you must ask yourself is, How can I rearrange my facts, abstractions and relationships (A) so that they will produce my objective or lead me closer to the place I want to get (Z)?

Return to the boy at the newsstand. He had to be capable of rearranging the data of his experience. He had to be able to see the abstract *people-buying-two-newspapers-at-newsstands* as *people-buying-two-newspapers-at-home*. And that meant bringing into his service generalizations about the attitudes of people toward their own comfort. Conceived in these terms, the newsboy was now ready to rearrange his own behavior; instead of canvassing from door to door, his action was to follow buyers from the newsstands.

But this rearrangement of his behavior was not easy to achieve because it had to be preceded by the even more difficult task of rearranging his thinking, of reordering his understanding of the problem.

We can now summarize the over-all point we have been making: the most important use of a generalization is its ability to help us rearrange all the elements involved in our problem so that they point to the action we can take. On our journey from A to Z, each of the elements must be woven together to make a consistent pattern—a design in which each thread is properly intertwined with the next. The generalization is the loom on which we execute our pattern.

"Increased Significance"

It is time now to formulate what happens when your generalization goes to work on your facts. Simply put, your generalization has to undertake the task of rearranging your materials by *joining them up with additional meanings* and giving them "increased significance," as John Dewey expresses it.

We can illustrate this effect of "increased significance" resulting from new combinations of meanings by taking one of the critical changes in man's history—the transition from the Stone Age to the Bronze Age, one of the longest strides in man's effort to solve problems presented to him by nature.

Let us begin by defining the problem that man faced. He needed tools with which to control the physical world around him. He had already succeeded in shaping stone for knives and hammers, wood for clubs and spears. But in both cases, he was limited by the original form and nature of his material. If only he could have available a material that would take on whatever shape his need required.

For the millions who lived through the Stone Age, and for the Australian aborigines who are still living in the Stone Age, that problem was never solved. But somewhere along the line, probably with the aid of accidental observation that was then purposefully employed, men learned that copper could be melted and shaped in a mold, and that the same could be done with tin. Yet the Bronze Age was not ready to be born—not until men learned that copper and tin could be fused to form a *durable* tool shaped to the human will. Bronze became possible because men could conceive of new combinations—that is to say, new relationships.

A. V. Gordon Childe points out in *Man Makes Himself* that this was a difficult discovery because copper and tin are rare, and are not usually found in the same places. For each of the metals to acquire added significance in the solution of man's tool problem, they must be brought together in a new relationship through the use of many generalizations and abstractions. For example, importation (involving trade and communication), specialization ("the casting of bronze is too difficult a process to be carried out by anyone in the intervals of growing or catching his food or minding her babies"), barter (the bronze-caster must acquire food from his fellows in return for making their tools), etc., etc.

Another anthropologist, Carleton S. Coon, sees the problem complicated by the need for additional concepts or generalizations brought to bear on the two metals: the use of fire to melt the metals in a forced-draft, charcoal-fed furnace; the use of a rotating shaft for the shaping of bronze pottery; even the use of writing to maintain the communications needed to import one or the other of the metals.

The process is one of illuminating the available facts by exposing them to generalizations that give them added meaning by creating fresh relationships.

Adding Meaning to Your Facts

You are a salesman. Your permanent problem is how to increase the amount of goods you sell. Can generalizations—the spelling out of abstractions and relationships—help you solve your problem?

Take the case of Luke Small, a salesman for a large New York distributor of canned goods. This is the Research Institute's description of the way he used his ability to manipulate generalizations and observe new relationships among facts:

By watching the pattern formed by his customers' purchases over a period of time, Luke was able to spot trends as they developed—and then sell to those trends.

In one instance, he was calling on a store located in mid-town Manhattan. He noticed a gradual increase in its orders for precooked foods and more expensive delicacies. Up till then this had been a low-income neighborhood. Luke looked around for the answer.

And since he knew what he was looking for, he was quick to spot it. A few minutes walk from the store, a huge old-fashioned apartment building was undergoing major repairs. And a number of brownstone houses nearby were being remodeled into attractive modern homes.

Luke concluded that soon the neighborhood would consist mostly of young executives and their families. He went to the supermarket manager with a plan for promotion of the costlier merchandise, got quick action and a bigger share of the store's business.

Let us list some of the abstractions he used: "precooked foods"—"more expensive delicacies"—"low-income neighborhood"—"young executives and their families." Notice how each of these terms and phrases summarizes whole groups of objects by extracting the dominant characteristic of each individual item included in the term.

But in addition he was able to spell out the relationships between his abstractions and his facts: "The more expensive delicacies" meant that the income in the neighborhood was rising. The moving in of "young executives" meant an improvement in the living standards of the "low-income neighborhood." The "remodeling of brownstone houses into attractive modern homes" meant new possibilities for "promotion of the costlier merchandise."

The Use of False Generalizations

In most of the cases cited in this chapter, we have assumed that the generalizations being used were true. The outstanding exception was the case of Galileo who built his view of the water pump on the generalization that nature abhors a vacuum. His disciples, Torricelli and Viviani, had also used that generalization, but in the end they abandoned it. And there is good reason to believe that they were able to find the right answer, not in spite of their wrong assumption, but because of it. In other words, they had used the wrong generalization to the fullest possible advantage, and had then abandoned it only after it was no longer useful to them.

This was what Einstein did with Newton's physics. The greatest of our modern scientists did not discover relativity by

ignoring Newton. He used his predecessor's generalizations
to shed all possible light on the factors available. As Einstein
said, he stood on Newton's shoulders and therefore got a
larger view of the universe.

For centuries men believed that the sun rises in the east
and moves across the heavens to set in the west. We know
now that it is not the sun but the earth that moves. Yet this
concept of the sun rising and setting was useful to man
throughout the ages. Though it was astronomically incorrect,
it gave the human being a method of measuring the abstraction *time* on the face of a sundial; it made navigation possible by orienting man to the relationship of east and west,
north and south. Thus, it became man's key to time and
space. It gave him stability in a mysterious world. From it he
derived self-confidence, a belief in the central importance of
his planet in the scheme of things and of himself among the
creatures and races of earth.

In the period when he was beginning to acquire mastery
over nature, these mistaken assumptions encouraged his progress. But eventually he had to correct them. His notion of the
rising and setting sun, linked to the idea of a flat world instead of a round one, had to go. Useful for many human
goals, it had served a purpose; now it was defeating new
human goals—for example, the navigational effort to find a
water route to the east. A new generalization about the world
had to be born, and it came with the realization that the
world was round and that the sun was the center of the solar
system.

In your own affairs you use many generalizations, which
may or may not be true reflections of your world. But they
work, in the sense that they solve the relevant problems. But
when an unsolved problem confronts you, you have to re-
examine your generalizations and modify or abandon them.
Or do you? The truth is that most people don't—because they
treat their generalizations as ends in themselves, instead of
recognizing that their value lies in opening the doors to new
knowledge or solutions.

This understanding of generalizations as means and not ends is most clearly grasped by our advanced scientists. Despite popular misconceptions, most of them do not really struggle over the metaphysical "truth" of their generalizations. Their primary concern is whether a concept or theory or generalization gives them new questions to ask that can be tested by observation or experiment.

In the words of J. J. Thomson, "From the point of view of the physicist, a theory of matter is a policy rather than a creed; its object is to connect or coordinate apparently diverse phenomena and above all to suggest, stimulate, and direct experiment."

The Value of Inconsistency

Modern scientists take this so much for granted that they do not hesitate to work at the same time with inconsistent and even contradictory generalizations. Only philosophers insist on consistency; scientists and poets, being more practical, are willing to accept contradictions, provided they yield results. Philosophers want everything to fit neatly into their "system," as Heine pointed out in his satirical poem:

Life in this world is a muddled existence—
Our German professor will give me assistance.
He knows how to whip the whole thing into order;
He'll make a neat System and keep it in line.
With scraps from his nightcap and dressing-gown's border
He'll fill all the gaps in Creation's design.

You can see the difference between the philosopher and the scientist in the mind of one of our leading modern thinkers, Bertrand Russell. As a philosopher he condemns "the subterfuge of the 'double truth': one sort, based on reason, in philosophy, and another based on revelation, in theology." That's from his *History of Western Philosophy*. But in his book, *Human Knowledge*, he finds it possible to live with the "double truth" in physics.

As he indicates, one can be quite comfortable about accepting two mutually exclusive theories of light—the particle hypothesis and the wave hypothesis. He says that ". . . either may be adopted in any problem as may suit our convenience. But whichever is adopted, it must be adhered to; we must not mix the two hypotheses in one calculation." The reason, as he explains, is that either one, when used, produces the same "verifiable consequences"—that is, both have "the same relation to experience."

In other words, it is perfectly correct to use contradictory generalizations in attacking your problems—*provided* you recognize that your generalizations are to be means and not conclusions; *provided* you use your generalizations not as answers but as methods of discovering questions to be asked. Even a "wrong" generalization can solve a problem if it leads you to ask the question that reveals the crucial facts.

This was what happened in one of the outstanding discoveries achieved by a human intellect—Darwin's theory, or generalization, about evolution. Dr. Conant assures us: "Darwin convinced himself and later the scientific world and later still the educated public of the correctness of the general idea of evolution because of a theory as to the mechanism by which evolution might have occurred. Today, the basic idea of the evolutionary development of higher plants and animals stands without question, but Darwin's mechanism has been so greatly questioned as to have been almost overthrown."

An erroneous concept is often useful because it leads us toward reality. The converse is also true; we may allow a useful concept to lead us up a blind alley. The ancient Babylonians went from astronomy to astrology. The great Kepler, on the other hand, started out by writing astrological almanacs in which he sincerely believed but was then led by these absurd theories to the discovery of the two basic concepts of modern astronomy—the laws of elliptical orbits and of equal areas. It is a far cry from the fortuneteller's theory of planetary influences to Kepler's theory of refraction by lenses, which yielded some of the basic principles in astronomy. The road to many a truth is paved with false generalizations.

But we can arrive at the truth only if we have the courage to sacrifice our own generalizations. Abraham must raise the knife over Isaac's head before the ram will appear in the thicket. "Science, like life, feeds on its own decay," says William James. "New facts burst old rules; then newly divined conceptions bind old and new together into a reconciling law."

But the facts, as we have seen, cannot burst the old rules unless we are willing to doubt our generalizations, to modify them, or to construct new ones. This requires courage, for the abandonment of an old theory is like cutting our moorings and permitting ourselves to float on uncharted waters. When the facts accumulate against your theory, which will you part with? Emerson gives us the answer: "Leave your theory, as Joseph his coat in the hand of the harlot, and flee."

Easily said—but hard to do. Yet there are two instruments at your command. They are visualization and symbolization.

[8]

THE ART OF VISUALIZATION

VISUALIZATION requires that you make an effort to see the abstraction or the relationship as physical images. That may necessitate going back to the elementary facts again so that you can construct a visual image.

By using visualization as a check on the abstractions and the relationships that affect our problem, we stay on the road to Z. The man who says, "Let's include all the details in a thumbnail sketch" is not seeing what he's saying; if he visualized the "thumbnail sketch" as occupying a half-sheet of paper, he would know his absurdity. When a man can't see in his own mind what he's talking about, he is talking about nothing. He is like the Confederate legislators in Richmond during the Civil War who voted nonexistent arms to nonexistent troops in regiments that were facing a very existent enemy.

Visualization and Reality

The more intricate our thinking, of course, the more difficult it is to visualize our ideas. And in some cases, visualization will prove to be impossible. That's because some of our ideas, like the idea of God, are undefinable, which is another way of saying that they cannot be visualized. In the case of religion, we must resort then to the second instrument, symbolism, which is discussed in the next chapter.

It is important to make the distinction between the two because reality may be just as real even though we cannot visualize it. But to lay hold on it, we must first make the effort to visualize.

For example, a soldier who is lying wounded on the field of battle, his life having just been saved by blood plasma poured into his veins, is indebted to science, the abstraction, for having saved his life; but his eyes, though closed, are seeing an image. It is a man in a white coat, in a laboratory, surrounded by test tubes and beakers. He is trying to visualize Dr. Edwin Cohn, the biochemist who had solved the secret of fractionating blood to make mass transfusions possible across continents and oceans.

The soldier will not see the bald head and the white around the temples, nor the lines about the scientist's mouth, nor even know the name of the man to whom he is indebted for his life. But to assure his understanding of his relationship with his benefactor, he must call up the image of a man.

Thus things are made real to us even when we have never seen them. To make the unseen truly understandable, we contrive our own image out of the shreds of past experience that seem relevant.

To transport oxygen, a gas, we find it desirable to liquefy it in a steel tank. To grip an idea with the fingers of the mind, you must contrive some kind of physical image. You have never seen Dr. Cohn? No matter. You can speak of him and think of him because you have no difficulty constructing the figure of a man; in visualizing "a scientist," perhaps you find it necessary to draw a beard on his chin, as children do on the advertising posters, or you may dress him in a laboratory jacket and make him peer into a microscope, as an advertising agency inevitably does.

Whenever you feel lost among the abstractions and relationships that make up the generalizations in your problem, ask yourself, "How can I visualize these terms and the situations they represent?"

The ability to visualize is valuable because it makes possible a reconstruction of past experience that is relevant to our problem and that may guide our action. Here again is a talent that is distinctly human, setting us above the other animals. Writes Dr. W. Grey Walter, the distinguished British neurologist who pioneered in the study of brain waves: "The nearest creature to us, the chimpanzee, cannot retain an image long enough to reflect on it."

But visualization is an important human device for projecting ourselves into the distant past or future. We can perform giant experiments without leaving our armchair—just by letting our minds construct images consistent with our generalizations. We can spell out alternatives without committing ourselves by action to any of them. In choosing among the alternatives, we can make judgments because we can visualize the consequences. We can conjure up a suspension bridge and calculate the costs before we build it and can then decide to build a visualized cantilever instead.

It is visualization that leads us back and forth among our generalizations. James Watt sees the pressure created by steam in a teakettle; he creates a generalization that summarizes the relationship between steam pressure and motion; he visualizes the relationship and sees a piston in a steam engine turning wheels.

Sight-Minded People

Involved, of course, are "imagination, calculation, prediction," as Dr. Walter sums up the qualities on which visualization depends. "We can imagine making one of a number of possible responses, and imagine it so clearly that we can see whether it would be, if we made it, a mistake, without having to commit ourselves to action. We can make our errors in a thought and reject them in another thought, leaving no trace of error in us."

This description of what happens, however, calls for some qualification. We cannot always remain in our armchairs, like the fictional Nero Wolfe who solves crimes without leaving his house. We can never be sure that the objects of our visualization correspond with reality, until we have gone and checked.

Reliance on visualization is not necessarily true of all peoples in the same degree, but it is certainly an outstanding characteristic of our own civilization. Martin Buber, the philosopher, considers this a legacy from the Greek culture, which stressed the visual—hence, the preoccupation with the graphic arts. Because God, the great abstraction, had to be grasped through a visualization, primitive peoples worshipped clay idols; the ancient Hebrews, on the other hand, capable of more abstract thought, forbade the making of graven images. But even the Hebrews gave ascendancy to sight over sound. Job says: "I have heard of Thee by the hearing of the ear; but now mine eye seeth Thee. Wherefore I abhor myself and repent in dust and ashes."

In any case, Western patterns of thought are geared principally to the visual. The sense of sight appears to be the strongest sensory power we possess, the one we use most in our efforts to learn and understand. One psychologist reports that more than 85 per cent of the impressions that reach our brain come through the eyes.

We say, "I'm from Missouri; *show* me." Most of our technical instrumentation is based on transforming data into visual forms. We rarely rely principally on our sense of hearing; we do not judge noise through our ears but through our eyes. In amateur contests where the verdict depends on the volume of applause, we use a meter to measure the decibels. We do not even trust our sense of smell; to prove that odors are eliminated by his deodorant, the man in the TV commercial holds an onion in front of a gauge. The triumph of television over radio, incidentally, is having the effect of reinforcing our dependency on sight.

Dr. Grey suggests a simple test by which you can get some idea of how visual-minded you are:

Shut your eyes. Think of a wooden cube like a child's block. It is painted. Now imagine that you cut it in halves across one side, then cut these halves in halves, and then cut them a third time at right angles. Now, think of the little cubes you have made. How many of their sides will be unpainted?

"Did you work it out or did you 'see' it? Then what else did you see? What colour was the cube? Did you see the sawdust falling as you cut it?

People respond differently. The question about color, for example, leads some to acknowledge that they "saw" none. Perfectly all right, since color is not relevant to the problem. But if their visualizations did not include the cubes separating into halves, as suggested by the instructions, they are not likely to have solved the problem.

Using the electroencephalogram, Dr. Grey has classified people into three types: visualists, with few if any alpha rhythms; nonvisualists, with persistent alpha activity; and mixed types. Some studies have been made to find out how these groups are distributed in the general population. It is interesting to note that science students rank high as visualists according to the evidence of their alpha rhythms.

My interest in this subject led me to raise several related questions with Dr. Simon Biesheuvel, the South African psychologist whom I had the good fortune to meet at the National Institute of Personnel Research in Johannesburg. He has been directing a team of psychologists who go out in the African bush with an electroencephalograph to make comparative studies of the Bantu population.

Dr. Biesheuvel is of the opinion that whatever differences exist between the white man and the African are not inherent but due to environmental factors. He does find an encephalographic difference which, in the African, reflects less reliance on the visual than on the auditory sense. This works a hardship on engineering and medical students, he says, who must learn to read blueprints, charts, and diagrams. But this he considers cultural and, as he points out, changing cultural influences can alter a person's electroencephalogram.

He offers the hypothesis that the environment of the jungle may have led the natives to rely more on the auditory sense than the visual. Survival depended on the ability to hear danger in the underbrush, and natural selection produced a group whose auditory ability was the most efficient among the senses. Hence, the development of a wonderful musical talent. He tells of a group of Africans harmonizing, as they explained, with a female singer who was not even present; they said they could hear how she would be singing if she were present. They were doing on the auditory level what we do on the visual level when we imagine what something would look like.

Some people are said to be highly efficient at abstract thought without having to visualize what they are thinking about. They are able to think about classifications of items—abstractions—without calling up a visual image of the individual items. In *A Study of Thinking*, the psychologists Jerome S. Bruner, Jacqueline J. Goodnow, and George A. Austin say: "Indeed, it is characteristic of highly elaborated cultures that symbolic representations of formal categories and formal category systems are eventually developed without reference to the classes of environmental events that the formal categories 'stand for.' "

But don't overlook the phrase, "symbolic representations." The abstract thinker does his visualizing by using symbols, which are physical representations of abstractions—equations, statistical curves, etc. Dr. Grey, a very successful abstract thinker, manipulates concepts like alpha rhythms and brain waves, terms that have some obvious visual content. It is not accidental that the electroencephalograph itself translates brain waves into visual patterns on a tape.

Undoubtedly one of the greatest abstract thinkers of our time was Albert Einstein. Again, it is revealing that most of us visualize him in front of a blackboard covered with mathematical formulas.

In dealing with our own less cosmic problems, the key is often found in our ability to see images that relate to our problem, or at least run parallel with the relationships involved in our problem. Often, at the heart of a solution lies some element that was clearly seen in the mind's eye.

Fatima's brilliant stratagem to save Ali Baba stemmed from her manipulation of visual images. Her master, after his escape with the treasure of the forty thieves, had been followed home by one of them, who painted an identifying mark on the door, planning to return later with his comrades. Fatima tried to erase the mark without success.

Now follow her thought processes: She visualizes the door without the mark; its absence will save her master. She defines her problem: "How can I erase the identifying mark?" She visualizes soap and water. To no avail: no matter how hard she scrubs, it will not come off. She tries other cleansers; again, without result. Now she finds it necessary to abandon her formulation of the problem, for within the boundaries of the present formulation there is no possible answer that can be visualized.

But then she asks: "How can I leave this mark, yet render it ineffective as a sign of identification?" This frame of reference permits a new set of visualizations. She visualizes the door, the mark, the whole setting—and has her solution. In her mind's eye, she sees all the doors of the neighborhood with the same mark—which makes Ali Baba's house immune from identification. In the process she has moved from the generalization "Houses marked differently can be distinguished" to "Houses with the same marks cannot be distinguished." Visualization contributed to the solution.

Visual Language

That visualization has played a part in the development of scientific solutions is clear from the very names we give to intricate concepts. In 1904 the Englishman, Ambrose Fleming patented the "thermionic valve"—an adaptation of the hitherto unexplained "Edison effect" that the American inventor had observed in 1884 but had never understood. Fleming had seen the point that Edison missed: that negative electricity was moving in one direction—from the filament to the tube—*as if it were* a stream flowing through a one-way valve. As a result, radio was on the way.

"The sea of air" was a visualization that led to Torricelli's correction of Galileo's error and to Boyle's Law which advanced man's understanding of gases. The falling apple gave Newton the visualization with which he could see the relationship between the vast bodies in the universe.

William Harvey, author of the crucial medical concept of the circulatory system, found his thinking advanced by his ability to visualize the operations of the heart. "The working of pumps and water supply was becoming a familiar matter," writes W. P. D. Wightman in his history of scientific discoveries. "Harvey was thus able to regard the heart and arteries as a pump subject to the limitations of any other kind of pump." In Harvey's words, "the arteries dilate because they are filled like bladders or leather bottles; they are not filled because they expand like bellows." He is able to continue surefootedly on his logical path because he is not content with vague abstractions; he must "see" what he is talking about and he describes the arteries being filled with blood "like the fingers of a glove."

Harvey's analogy has been so fruitful that it has produced the modern miracle of heart surgery. Pushing forward the concept of the heart as a pump, cardiac surgeons now use an artifical heart, which is really a pump, to keep the blood circulating while an operation is being performed.

Another illustration of such visualization is the corpuscular theory of light: light is like "a stream of bullets." When this theory is inadequate, the scientist thinks of light as a phenomenon of waves.

To launch the revolution of automation and "electronic brains" (the term itself is a visualization), the scientists at Massachusetts Institute of Technology talked about "feedback" and saw before their eyes the "self-correcting rudder of a ship on course"; they called their science "cybernetics" after the Greek word for "steersman."

Lord Rutherford and Geiger (whose name is linked with radioactivity through the "Geiger counter") penetrated into the structure of the atom when Rutherford exclaimed at the deflection of alpha rays as they passed through a thin film of aluminum: "It's as though a fifteen-inch shell were being bounced off a sheet of tissue paper." Then, observing that the alpha rays were passing through matter, they reasoned: The rays are passing through atoms, which means that they penetrate into a loose structure. "So," said Rutherford, "they must be like solar systems—not solid spheres." And the now familiar models that show the structure of atomic elements began to emerge.

In political affairs, too, the visualization of solutions is demonstrated by the terms used. "The open door policy" becomes the answer to international trade conflict in China. "The good neighbor policy," with its image of friends cooperating across their fences, evolves to guide relationships in the Western Hemisphere. Concepts of static military defense are answered now by references to "Maginot Line policies."

In the business world some of the key generalizations that have shaped our civilization are reducible to visualizations. "The principle of interchangeable parts" was picked up by Henry Ford and viewed in the setting of the automobile factory; it was followed by the concept of the "assembly line" that accompanied "mass production."

"A Flow of Suggestions"

Again, a word of warning. There are visualizations and visualizations. An old joke distinguishes between describing a woman as a "vision" and as a "sight." Our visualization may present us with a genuine vision or expose us to a gruesome sight. Visualization may be the poetry of imagination which pays off in the prose of reality, but it cannot be treated as proof of a proposition. It makes its contribution by *merely suggesting possibilities that still require examination.*

When you are halted by a problem, as John Dewey suggests, the important thing is to "promote the flow of suggestions" into your mind. The visualization is useful to thought because it gives you additional associations of ideas, possibilities, potential solutions. In visualizing, you make your generalizations jump through hoops. You are forced to abandon vagueness in favor of concrete images, even though you are dealing with abstractions and relationships. Made definite, your visualizations point up distinctions between objects; and the elements involved in your generalization emerge with greater clarity in your mind.

This is the process, as Dewey describes it:

> As soon as any quality is definitely discriminated and given a special meaning of its own, the mind at once looks around for other cases to which that meaning may be applied. As it is applied, cases that were previously separated in meaning become assimilated, identified, in their significance. They now belong to the same *kind* of thing. [We now have an abstraction.] Even a young child, as soon as he masters the meaning of a word, tries to find occasion to use it; if he gets the idea of a cylinder, he sees cylinders in stove pipes, logs, etc. In principle, this is not different from Newton's procedure in the story about the origin in his mind of the concept of gravitation. Having the idea suggested by the falling of an apple, he at once extended it in imagination to the moon as something also tending to fall towards the earth, and then to the movements of the planets in relation to the sun, to the movement of the ocean in the tides, etc. [Visualization has taken place.] In consequence of this application of an idea that was discriminated, made definite in some one case, to other events, a large number of phenomena that previously were believed to be disconnected from one another were integrated into a consistent system.

The Use of Visual Analogy

Some writers warn that visualization is no more than a figure of speech and has no greater value in problem-solving than analogies have in logic. It is true that analogies do not prove, but they do explain. To say that the earth's pull on the moon is analogous to the falling of an apple is not proof of the existence of gravitation, but it does help us to understand the relationship between bodies and find the proof.

What happens when we use analogy? John Stuart Mill, in

his book *A System of Logic* says that our minds operate along these paths when we reason by analogy: "Two things resemble each other in one or more respects; a certain proposition is true of the one; therefore it is true of the other."

Thus, by analogy, oil men were able to conceive of the modern pipeline. Water is a liquid; oil is a liquid. Water can be transported through a pipe; therefore oil can be transported through a pipe.

As a method of demonstrating truth, however, analogy is a weak instrument of logic. That is so because no perfect analogies exist. There are always some differences between the items being compared. But the analogy is helpful if we discipline ourselves to keep the differences clearly in mind. Mill puts it this way:

> If we discover, for example, an unknown animal or plant, resembling closely some known one in the greater number of the properties we observe in it, but differing in some few, we may reasonably expect to find in the unobserved remainder of its properties, a general agreement with those of the former; but also a difference, corresponding proportionally to the amount of observed diversity.

Faulty analogy can cause many difficulties in problem-solving. I remember when I was a law student in the early 1930's, our professor of insurance law told us that unemployment insurance was not feasible. Unlike life insurance, he said, there was no actuarial basis for figuring the frequency of unemployment, whereas in life insurance we have statistical probabilities as to the number of people who will die in a given period. But unemployment insurance, despite his dire predictions, has worked because it is not really analogous to life insurance.

Scientists are specialists in using analogy as an instrument of thought. They know the importance of discovering new relationships by detecting *how certain things are like other things*. J. Robert Oppenheimer, the atomic physicist, elaborated this point. In an address to the American Psychological Association on "The Analogy of Science," he said:

"Whether or not we talk of discovery or invention, analogy is inevitable in human thought . . . We come to new things with what equipment we have, which is how we have learned to think about the relatedness of things."

An analogy, according to the dictionary, is "an agreement or likeness, or correspondence, a matching up between the relations of things to one another." The analogy does not have to be a complete likeness. The comparison can be based on "a partial similarity."

To develop an analogy, we must be able to keep many objects in mind simultaneously so that we can make the comparison. Memory or free association must help us bring to the surface material that can be stacked up against our present problem.

The effectiveness of analogical thinking is not just a matter of *what* is seen, but *how* it is seen. Things must be seen in a relationship.

Today we solve many problems in industry with the help of analogies. Certain data-processing hardware, called "analog computers," are based on the assumption that "analogy exists between the operation of the computing device and the type of problem it is intended to solve." Information is stored up in the machine to correspond, for example, to the movement of freight cars in railroad yards and on tracks across the country; by letting the machine operate, the programmer is able to make decisions on routing the traffic.

It is interesting to note that the same authors I have just quoted, George H. and Paul S. Amber, say that "analog computers are not ordinarily as accurate" as other types of computers. For example, predictions of election results made by such computers must be allowed their margin of error because the analogies from past elections do not always hold true.

I have discussed the subject of analogies here because visualization of our problems often leads us to make comparisons. We shall observe, when we discuss symbolization in the next chapter, that symbols also help us to handle analogies.

The point I want to emphasize now is that an analogy can be trusted only to suggest possibilities, which may then have to be confirmed by other evidence. Fortunately, in the process of problem-solving, we are not engaged in *proving* a proposition, as the word is understood today: presenting evidence to establish the truth of a statement or assertion. We are engaged, however, in *proving* as that word was originally understood: probing, testing. (The exception proves—that is, tests—the rule.)

Problem-solving is not a courtroom proceeding in which the parties systematically present testimony for one side and then for the other; instead, it is a laboratory procedure in which there are no sides but tentative surmises being examined experimentally. The lawyer, a partisan, dominates the courtroom; the researcher, an objective observer, commands the laboratory. The tentativeness of scientists makes them notoriously poor witnesses, and they are easily victimized by cross-examiners.

The problem-solver, like the pure scientist, is looking for a generalization that will bind together the facts of his situation in a manner that will point to solution. To tie the knot, he may use visualization and analogy, but he is not certain that it will hold until he has tugged at it with all his might. Ideally, what he does is to use visualization to give him a grip on his hypothesis. He cannot be sure of himself, however, until he has proved—that is, tested—his hypothesis.

Again let us take an illustration from pure science. For years physicists found it necessary to visualize a particle in the atom without which, they thought, certain things could not happen. Into their atomic designs, they placed a something they called a neutrino. In 1953 Dr. Conant wrote: "To date, as far as I am aware, there is no experimental evidence for the existence of this particle, nor does it seem likely, I am told, that experimental tests can be devised to establish or disprove its existence." But one year later, atomic physicists hailed Frederick Reines and Clyde Cowan, Jr., for demonstrating its reality.

The path stretches clearly from visualization to experimentation to confirmation.

A Debated Analogy

I recall the vivid impression made on me by a faulty illustration presented by Dr. L. Susan Stebbing in her otherwise excellent book *Thinking to Some Purpose*. Writing in 1939, she quoted and derided the following statement by the great physicist, Sir Arthur Eddington:

> The inside of your head must be rather like a newspaper office. It is connected with the outside world by nerves which play the part of telegraph wires. Messages from the outside world arrive in code along these wires; the whole substratum of fact is contained in these code messages. Within the office they are made up into a presentable story, partly by legitimate use of accumulated experience but also with an admixture of journalistic imagination; and it is this free translation of original messages that our consciousness becomes aware of.

Dr. Stebbing condemned this statement because

> Eddington does not use his analogy purely for the sake of illustration; he uses it in order to draw conclusions with regard to the nature of the external world and the nature of our knowledge about the external world.

Quite so. And from her vantage point in 1936, Dr. Stebbing rejected Eddington's view, based on his visualization of the human brain as a central office of journalistic communications.

But time has given Eddington the last word. A whole new science—cybernetics—has developed from this very concept of the human nervous system as an intricate network of communication wires coming into the editorial office. The practical application of this visualized structure is to be found in the electronic computers that, in almost a terrifying sense, attempt to duplicate the nervous system of the human being.

By 1951, Eddington's intuitive picture of the way the brain

functions was a commonplace accepted by the experts. Professor J. Z. Young, the British biologist, wrote a book called *Doubt and Certainty in Science*, subtitled *A Biologist's Reflections on the Brain*, in which he summarized his own experiments on the nervous system of the octopus. He developed certain conclusions about our own human processes: "In order to have some picture of how the brain works it is useful to think of it as a gigantic government office—an enormous ministry, whose one aim and object is to preserve intact the country for which it is responsible. Ten million telegraph wires bring information to the office. . . ." And so on to an elaboration of the Eddington concept of the brain.

The ability to visualize relationships and abstractions—thus visualizing generalizations—leads to extraordinary and unexpected results, depending on the kind of visual images you are able to handle. The development of automation is itself an example of how a fresh mind from a different background can bring his visualizations to a problem that has baffled others, and can help to provide solutions.

Dr. Norbert Wiener, pioneer in this field, recounts the process by which the young science was launched during the war years. At Massachusetts Institute of Technology, a group of mathematicians, engineers, physicists, and others were working on the problem of achieving "fire control." The armed services had asked them to develop a means of bringing down enemy planes attempting to attack our ships.

The complexity of this problem, viewed just from the mathematical standpoint, is enormous. Think of all the computations involved: the speed of the ship on which the gun is mounted, the speed of the enemy plane, wind drift, the speed of the projectile, etc. By the time you have made all your calculations and aimed the A-A gun, the bomber will have dropped its bombs and be back at its base.

In the course of studying the problem, the development of the electronic computer became a reality—a reality that will shape the future of peacetime civilization as the atom bomb has shaped the course of war.

Dr. Wiener describes the turning point in the research. He tells of the arrival of Walter Pitts at M.I.T. as a member of the scientific team. Pitts "was already thoroughly acquainted with mathematical logic and neurophysiology. . . ." With that background, he saw the problem in a completely new frame of reference and made his unique contribution. "From that time," says Wiener, "it became clear to us that the ultra-rapid computing machine, depending as it does on consecutive switching devices, must represent almost an ideal model of the problems arising in the nervous system."

Once more, the ability to see the problem visually—*in terms of something already known*—made progress toward solution possible. For all of us who tackle problems on a smaller scale, the technique of the scientist points the way. The use of visualization makes our generalizations more real to us and consequently more helpful in solving our problems.

[9]

MANIPULATING SYMBOLS

WHEN YOU can't visualize, symbolize.

Some of the generalizations that take us on our path toward solution are too broad to be susceptible to visualization. In such cases, we can use another tool invented by the ingenuity of man—symbolization.

The first organized system of symbols was language itself. In recent years, the semanticists have been somewhat successful in getting people to realize that words are merely symbols for reality and not reality itself. Words are useful but potentially deceptive if we forget that we are engaged in the process of symbolizing.

Symbolic Language

Man invented language for very practical purposes. If you want to handle the concept of a marauding beast in the foliage, you can symbolize it with the word "Lion." Without the word, the only way you can communicate about it is to point your finger—after it has made its appearance. In effect, once the word-symbol has been established you only have to say it and your hearer can visualize the reality at once.

Periodically man finds new languages less prone to confusion than words. Mathematical formulas, and chemical equations, written in a variety of symbols unknown to the layman, speak more accurately about the realities of the physical world than the languages of the nations. In astronomy, chemistry, and physics the symbols of the mathematician are better tools for manipulating the abstractions and relationships that make up the proudest discoveries of science. Indeed, the scientist is not content with his knowledge until he has symbolized it in mathematical terms.

Mathematical Symbols

Many sciences remained unborn until certain symbols were developed that made it possible to manipulate the intricate generalizations involved. Algebra was just such a set of symbols that spelled out relationships—often between abstractions that are unknown quantities in themselves. The ancient Babylonians, now recognized as the founders of astronomy, were able to map the recurrent sweep of the planets in their orbits only because they had developed a rudimentary algebra. Later the Hindus, who invented modern algebra, were able, by reason of their mathematical progress, to outdistance the Babylonians and their successors the Greeks. Ironically, the most valuable legacy we received from the Indian culture is called "Arabic numerals" because of the Arabs who carried them westward in the camel caravans. Without this system of symbols the West could not have achieved the scientific and technological progress that still distinguishes the Occident from the Orient.

Mathematics is symbolism in its purest form. In algebra we can manipulate unknown quantities and come out with known data. In logic we can manipulate unknown x's and y's and z's and arrive at conclusions. "If all x are y, and all y are z, then all x are z," we say with perfect validity—even though we don't know what each of the letters stands for. But the power of these symbols is such that they can give us guidance in thinking through intricate problems. They are abstractions, and these mathematical principles pave the way to an understanding of relationships.

Symbolic Knowledge

The symbol is an unknown, standing in temporarily for information that will take its place in the final calculation. Our x's and y's and z's, symbols that we can manipulate, are like sealed containers that will not spill and lose their contents while we are carrying them back and forth in the journey toward new understanding.

"If all x are y, and all y are z, then all x are z" is pure generalization, but we can fill these vessels with content: "If malaria (x) is a disease carried by the anopheles mosquito (y), and all diseases carried by mosquitoes can be defeated by killing the mosquitoes (z), then malaria (x) can be defeated by killing the mosquitoes (z)." With such reasoning, keyed consciously or unconsciously to the symbols of our logic, we can handle the relationships involved in solving the medical problem created by the insect.

The more complicated our problems, the more necessary it is to rely on symbols. Some philosophers, like Ernst Cassirer, insist that "human knowledge is by its very nature symbolic knowledge." Galileo, who lived before mathematics experienced its greatest development, said: "The book of Nature is written in mathematical language." A glance at the blackboards in Princeton's Institute of Advanced Study is enough to prove the point.

The writer of scientific history might well say: "In the beginning was the symbol." In 1905 Einstein published the symbol $E = mc^2$. This atomic equation became reality 40 years later when the blast went off at Alamogordo. But before the atom could split, the physicist needed the symbol that made it possible to handle complex ideas.

The symbol is necessary when there is no other way to visualize the generalization. We can visualize *three men, three kings, three mountains,* but we cannot visualize pure *three-ness.* As a substitute for the visualization, we use the symbol 3, which by itself means three-of-anything. The numeral is a symbol for the abstraction.

Such symbols save us a great deal of time and mental effort. If I tell you that apples cost 3 cents a piece and you want 10, you need not go through the process of visualizing 10 applies with 3-cent signs behind each, and then add 3 plus 3 until you have moved visually along a line of 10 apples. Because you can use symbols to manipulate your generalizations, you multiply the symbol 3 times 10, knowing that it always makes 30. You then translate the conclusion of your generalization into the specific circumstances you are dealing with and pay the 30 cents.

Einstein's successful effort to describe the complicated relationship between the amount of energy that would be released and the mass of the element involved led to the famous atomic equation. But in other relationships of life the effort to summarize what we cannot visualize may take on nonmathematical but nevertheless symbolic forms. The outstanding example of course is the symbol "God"—the representation we give to the most enigmatic concept yet evolved by the mind of man. And since the term itself is not enough, man contrives other symbols for it: the tablets of Sinai, the cross of Calvary, the Black Stone of Mecca.

The Essence of a Symbol

It is now a commonplace that words are symbols used in the process of thinking. "Brains think with words," says Charlton Laird. "For practical purposes most people think only about things for which they have words and can think only in the directions for which they have words." The original thinker goes further because he can invent and define new words that correspond to new realities.

Since symbols, then, play so important a role in thinking, we had better understand exactly what they are and what they do for us. The essence of their character and their function is that *one simple thing is made to represent a more complicated thing for purposes of solving problems.*

Let us look at some of the ways in which we arrive at happy solutions by allowing a very simple object to represent a complicated concept. Glance up at the calendar on your wall. Each little box stands for one day in the month. By following the boxes one by one—in short, by using them as symbols for a 24-hour period of light and dark—you know when the rent has to be paid to the landlord.

We think ourselves quite clever because we can keep track of the days, but let us remember that for a long time the human race dwelt in a confusion of dates that historians have not yet been able to unravel. Learned scholars still debate whether Jesus Christ was born on December 25th or some time in January, the changes in the reckoning of time have been so many.

Some unknown genius had to invent the idea of a calendar —a system of symbols—or we should not have succeeded in making our computations of time. Consider the predicament of the Persian King Darius, father of the Xerxes who beat the ocean with lashes. Darius, preparing to invade Scythia, found it necessary to leave guards to protect a bridge over the Danube; they were to remain there for 60 days. But how were they to tell that the 60 days had passed, since the soldiers had no calendars? Darius solved the problem for his men by giving them a symbol to manipulate: a leather thong with 60 knots. Each day they were to untie one knot; when the last knot was untied, they could leave the bridge.

A similar use of symbols—that is, simple objects standing for more complicated objects—led to the development of the abacus. This is a system of wires with beads that symbolize numerical values and can be moved about to solve arithmetical problems. Its use is not confined to the kindergarten, where children find it a valuable and pleasant learning tool, nor to China where, as the famed Swan-pan, it is still used by merchants; you can find it keeping score quite accurately for the contemporary pool player. To add another symbolic note: *Calculation* comes from *calculus*, meaning little stone or small pebble originally used in the Roman abacus.

In many other respects we are also influenced to this day by the kind of symbols our ancestors used to tame and manage the abstractions of arithmetic. Our decimal system is an outgrowth of the fact that *homo sapiens* learned to count on his fingers, of which nature had provided only 10. Had we been gifted with an extra digit on each hand, the round dozen might well have been the basis of our system of calculation.

Many of our daily problems are solved by a translation of the unseen into some kind of visible symbol. Our watches and clocks are just such devices: the revolution of the hands *corresponds* to the passing of a day. Once we depended on the falling sands in the hourglass to symbolize the flight of time. Now we can keep appointments because each of us looks at a symbol on his wrist.

Our use of these familiar symbols makes us confuse them with the object they are supposed to represent. We are apt to forget that the dial on a watch is only a symbol of time—not time itself. Only when we try to teach our children how to "tell time"—that is, to find word symbols for the symbolic values on the watch face—do we realize how intricate is our time conception.

It is striking how often the mere creation of a symbol is itself the solution to the problem. The terribly complicated problem of controlling traffic—which is far from final solution —has at least been rendered manageable because we have been able to create symbols for abstractions like *Danger!* or *Curve Ahead*. Colors have been made to symbolize such ideas as *Stop* and *Go*, and for even more complicated combinations of ideas such as *Proceed with Caution* (a yellow blinker light) and *Stop, then Proceed with Caution* (a red blinker). Lines in the center of the road can be given various meanings: a solid white line paralleled by a broken white line tells the driver from one direction that it is unsafe to enter the other lane, while the driver from the opposite direction is told that he may.

We have even extended our use of color symbols by teaching them to animals. Through reward and punishment, a chimp can be made to recognize colors and give them symbolic values. He can be shown a colored patch, which he will treat as a signal to press a red button; a green patch means pressing a green button. Thus the chimpanzee Enos paved the way for our astronauts with a two-orbit flight because he could receive radioed instructions that turned on differently colored lights, directing him to push levers and press buttons as required.

Relation to Reality

In all phases of thinking our tools can enlarge our vision or narrow it. So too with symbols. If we use them improperly, we defeat solution. This happens when we forget that we are dealing with symbols and think we are actually dealing with the realities to which they refer.

Take, for example, the common, ordinary photograph. You look at a picture and say, "Yes, that's John, of course." To be sure, you don't really mean that it is John; you know it is merely a collection of dots and shadings and outlines that symbolize or correspond to John's features.

But the idea of a photograph is readily understood by us. That's why a policeman can use it to identify a criminal whom he has never seen before.

Yet there are people—outside our culture—who do not comprehend the fact that the two-dimensional photograph stands for a real three-dimensional person. Native tribesmen shown photographs, simply cannot correlate them with specific people because the symbol does not contain the third dimension.

Many people who must deal with the inhabitants of underdeveloped areas are constantly frustrated because there are too few shared symbols through which communication can take place. Dr. Biesheuvel in Johannesburg told me, for example, of the difficulty he encountered in trying to use safety posters with African gold miners recruited fresh from the jungles of Nyasaland. A picture of a worker holding a sledge hammer against the background of a building was interpreted by them as a giant about to smash the structure. They could not understand the symbolism of perspective, which indicates distance to us.

Each culture has its own symbols, and we can communicate across cultural lines only as we come to understand each other's symbols. A few years ago, an American ambassador to a Far Eastern country—not a career diplomat—had to be recalled because he had offended the local community. His first error had been to walk about with a swagger stick in his hand, an object still viewed as the hated symbol of the British imperialists.

The emotionalism surrounding symbols does not decrease with an increase in Westernization. In fact, our culture creates an ever-expanding number of such symbols. The very photograph which a primitive tribesman cannot understand can arouse intense feelings in us.

Verbal Symbols

An important practice, then, is to make a conscious effort to translate your ideas into one of the symbolic forms—the most familiar of which is to *put them into words.* This seems elementary, but many people refuse to take the trouble to find the words that describe their problem.

Writing in the *Harvard Business Review,* Richard L. Larson says: "Executives can improve their skills at decision-making if they make it a habit to set down in writing their perceptions of the major problems before them. They can profit from *verbalizing explicitly* the problems they think they are, or should be, attacking *before* they proceed far in seeking solutions."

Few of us do that, because the value of the written form is not properly understood. We tend to believe that a written communication is something we compose for somebody else. The truth is that a document we write is very often more illuminating to us than it is to the recipient.

A brilliant lawyer, whose courtroom arguments are noted for their clarity and persuasiveness, once told me that he always writes out what he intends to say. His purpose is not to memorize it; he finds he can think more clearly about the issues if he sees them black on white. He can do a better analytical job on his own case if he has it laid out on paper before him. In court he speaks extemporaneously; the sole value of the written argument is that it has equipped him to handle the legal problem in whatever form his adversary might raise it.

Some people who "block against writing" use another method by which they can achieve somewhat similar results. They "talk it over" with others. Almost all of us have had the experience of seeking counsel from a friend who knows less about the problem than we do. Even when he offers no advice or when we deliberately reject his advice, we go away with a feeling that we have been enlightened. We have been —simply because we found ourselves translating the problem into verbal symbols.

Avoiding Confusion

We are helped with a problem if we can find the appropriate symbols to represent it. But in doing so, we must avoid the error of assuming an identity between the symbol and the reality it is supposed to mirror.

I have mentioned the African tribesmen who cannot make any sense out of a photograph. Once they have learned from repeated exposure to photographs and have seen the persons photographed, they are able to establish the symbolic relationship. Then they may find themselves at the opposite pole: they begin to consider the picture and the person as one. Some British colonial officers in the nineteenth century used this confusion to the advantage of the Empire. They hung photographs of Queen Victoria in native huts, and the people believed that the Queen was physically present to observe their behavior and overhear any rebellious conversation.

The fact is that many sophisticated Westerners slip easily into similar notions. Somehow we feel that we are face to face with reality when we are merely seeing the product of light's chemical reaction on silver nitrate. We burst into tears, or are deeply moved in any event, by the misfortunes enacted before us on the movie screen. Here, assuming Hollywood has done a good job, the symbol is performing its valued function for us: it is indeed giving us a grip on an emotional reality we would otherwise never have known.

But take the case that Wendell Johnson describes. A group of students, in a psychological test, were asked to pierce a series of photographs with a pair of scissors. They did so—until suddenly each came upon a picture of his own mother and could not carry out the instructions. The symbolic nature of the act was too much for them.

Actually, of course, there is no *identity* between the symbol (the photograph) and the reality (the mother). But because the symbol does serve so often to bring the reality nearer, it has great use. Hung on the wall of a soldier's barracks, it can give him the emotional reality of being closer to home and love.

One necessary step in using symbols is to ask yourself: "Which of the elements in my problem are symbols for reality and not the reality itself?"

This question is important because many of our problems are created by a confusion of the two. A case in point is that of the business executive who complained that he could not get his people to understand his instructions. He cited as the most recent illustration a memo in which he had included every possible relevant fact so that he would not be misunderstood. Yet his subordinates had failed to carry out his orders. "My communication could not have been more detailed," he said.

It took him quite a while to understand that his long document was not "communication" but only a symbol for communication; in fact, the abundance of his "communication" had actually blocked real communication, which is the transmission not of a piece of paper from hand to hand or even of words from mind to mind. It is the transmission of an idea from mind to mind.

Religious Symbols

But the power of symbols to solve problems—by making abstractions and concepts more intelligible even to the humble mind—is demonstrated by the use to which religion has put them. Nowhere is this more strikingly revealed than in a passage by George Bernard Shaw which proves the exact opposite of what he had intended.

In his preface to *Androcles and the Lion,* the brilliant dramatist and social commentator argues against the truth of the Biblical miracles, not on the ground that they never occurred but that they are completely irrelevant to the religious message being propagated by the wonder workers.

> But the deepest annoyance arising from the miracles [Shaw says] would be the irrelevance of the issue raised by them. Jesus's teaching has nothing to do with miracles. If his mission had been simply to demonstrate a new method of restoring lost eyesight, the miracle of curing the blind would have been entirely relevant. But to say "You should love your enemies; and to convince you of this I will now proceed to cure this gentleman of cataract" would have been, to a man of Jesus's intelligence, the proposition of an idiot.

Which only goes to show how completely Shaw misses the point. He fails to realize that the intent of the miracle is to serve as the symbol for the great abstraction of love. To make concrete the idea of "love thy neighbor as thyself," Jesus offered a specific symbol—cure thy neighbor of his infirmity. Great minds, no doubt, can grasp the intangible concept, but for most people a symbol has to be given. Thus, throughout the ages, the cry has been, "Give me a sign, O Lord."

Curiously, modern theology has been revolutionized by a new appreciation of the role played by symbols in religious thinking. In a commentary on the work of Albert Schweitzer, Charles R. Joy clarifies how symbols are used to solve religious problems. By contrast, Shaw looks as naïve as the native who cannot read the symbolism of a safety poster or a photograph. Joy writes:

> Schweitzer points out that it is conceivable that religious truth might be preached independently of any age, truth

that is universally and everlastingly so, truth that is valid for every succeeding generation and century. The simple fact, however, is that the truth that Jesus taught is not of that kind. He had a gospel of love to teach and then he wrapped it up in the ideas of his contemporaries. [That is, he used their system of symbols.] We cannot appropriate to ourselves this gospel of love by refusing to recognize the wrapping. Each age must unwrap the gospel and then apply it afresh to itself, which means, in all probability, enveloping it again in temporary covers. After all Jesus is profoundly concerned with love itself without which no man will enter into his Messianic Kingdom. There is, then, this enduring kernel in his teaching which we must learn to make our own in our own way.

Similarly, Maimonides, the great Jewish philosopher, explains the symbolic language of Genesis, which describes God as going down to the Garden of Eden. "The Torah speaks the language of men," he declares.

Getting Behind the Symbol

Ultimately you have to get behind the symbol, without abandoning it, if you are to reach the reality which is essential to your solution. The executive with his problem of communicating must tear himself away from the pieces of paper that symbolize communication and must ultimately face up to the reality, which is not the transmission of paper but the exchange of thought.

Let us take a more elaborate problem in communications than the executive faced. When Samuel Morse was wrestling with the challenge of sending thought across vast reaches of space, he found it necessary to convert his messages into symbols—the dots and dashes. These symbols can be sent along a wire as electrical impulses; once received, the symbols can then be reconverted into the original message. The manipulation of simple symbols, representing a meaningful reality, produced the solution of Morse's communication problem.

The illustrations can be multiplied. Radio uses electrical

symbols to represent sounds: the transmitter converts sound into impulses, and the receiver reconverts them into sound. In the case of television, images are broken down into dots which are converted into electrical impulses, then carried through the air, then reconverted into dots again to give us a final symbol which we translate mentally into the original image.

Your first step, then, is to be aware of the fact that you are engaged in a process of symbolization. Once that is clear, you are in a position to take the second step. You ask yourself: "Does my symbol abstract and highlight the reality with which I am dealing in its major characteristics?"

This question is easy to ask, but beware. The answer may come too easily, and you will pay the price of self-deception. For the fact is that in our kind of world philosophers can explain why man can be likened at once to the beasts in the forests and to the angels of heaven; why the structure of the infinitely small atom can be symbolized with the same balls and wires as the infinitely grand design of the universe with its planets and orbits; why the awe-inspiring family of nations meetings in the General Assembly of the UN bears a resemblance to a family of Australian aborigines huddled in their jungle shelter and why it represents a hopeful aspect of modern institutional life. It is because there is a likeness that the symbol can be made to stand in place of the reality —*for certain purposes but not for all.*

Note very carefully the qualification that I have emphasized in the preceding sentence. At most a symbol can correspond to the reality only to a limited extent. We can see this most clearly when we examine the symbolic character of words. Unfortunately, as symbols, they carry different connotations to different minds. Thus two men speak of the same object—the human eye. One is the poet Christopher Fry who describes man as

> ". . . a perambulating
> Vegetable, patched with inconsequential
> Hair, looking out of two small jellies."

The other is Leonardo da Vinci, proud of the human eye and exclaiming: "Who would believe that so small a space could contain the images of all the universe?"

Symbols are metaphorical, intended by the poet and artist to stimulate us to certain thoughts and feelings. They can be bent to our purposes and help us to achieve our goals by encouraging imagination. They have a value in themselves, as things of beauty; but they serve also a utilitarian function.

So when Burns symbolizes his love as "a red, red rose" he intends to represent the lady by the flower for only limited comparison. He does not mean that she lives for only one season, though many a love is indeed short-lived; he means that she is like the rose in beauty. In other words, his symbol is useful only for some purposes and not for others.

"Extending the Metaphor"

Anatol Rapoport, the mathematical biologist and semanticist, has emphasized this point in his book *Operational Philosophy*:

> Long before the perception of similarities between seemingly unrelated things was molded into the scientific outlook, such similarities were pointed out for the sheer pleasure of perceiving them. In literature and poetry, this matching of widely dissimilar things according to some perceived similarity is called "metaphor". . . . Theoretical science is essentially disciplined exploitation of metaphor.

What the scientist does is to use the symbolic quality of words to help him extend meanings already in his possession. Frequently the result seems to be accidental. In fact, though, it is the product of a logic that symbols themselves possess. They, too, fall into a pattern of cause and effect.

This has been made clear by the psychoanalyst's use of the symbolism in dreams. It was Freud who first saw clearly that in sleep we continue to wrestle with our problems, using visual images conjured up in dreams. The psychoanalyst

views the dream as a continuation of the individual's effort
to handle a problem that arose during the waking hours. He
looks for two elements: (1) the wish-fulfillment that the
dreamer is seeking, and (2) the particular event during the
preceding day that is the subject of the dream.

A typical example is the case cited by Dr. Erich Fromm,
in *The Forgotten Language*, which discusses symbolism from
the psychoanalytic point of view. The patient recounts an
anxiety dream in these words: "I have taken an apple from
a tree while I am passing an orchard. A big dog comes and
jumps at me. I am terribly frightened, and I wake up yelling
for help."

As Dr. Fromm explains:

> All that is necessary for the understanding of the dream
> is the knowledge that the dreamer had met, the evening
> before the dream, a married woman to whom he felt
> greatly attracted. She seemed to be rather encouraging, and
> he had fallen asleep with fantasies of having an affair with
> her. We need not be concerned here whether the anxiety
> he felt in the dream was prompted by his conscience or
> by the fear of public opinion—the essential fact remains
> that the anxiety is the result of the gratification of his wish
> —to eat the stolen apple.

By ignoring our dreams, we often discard a whole night's
work that our minds have devoted to a current problem of our
waking lives. Dr. Fromm quotes the Talmud: "A dream which
is not understood is like a letter which is not opened."

Sometimes we wake up having forgotten the dream, but
fortunately the answer it has generated continues to unfold
in our unconscious. Then we are startled that the answer
suddenly bursts into our conscious minds, as if from nowhere.
The sleep process has produced the solution because in the
dream we manipulated special symbols of relationships and
drew closer to the realities of our problem.

That is why there is truth in the folk wisdom which leads
us to say, "Let me sleep on it." In doing so we are not
postponing action on the problem; we are merely referring

it to another court in which the issues can be tried by other procedures which are also valid. When reviewed by the court of logic which has jurisdiction over our daytime problems, the verdict is often sustained.

There is good reason for this. The nighttime decision is not based on whim but on the wisdom of the unconscious. As Dr. Fromm says, "In our sleeping life, we seem to tap the vast store of experience and memory which in the daytime we do not know exists."

These unconscious solutions point up the value of symbols on which conscious attention has been focused. The symbol, consciously held, has its chain of unconscious associations which are activated just by virtue of our contemplating them. And when the solution comes as if from nowhere, it is really the product of a seemingly undisciplined "extension of the metaphor," as Rapoport has called it.

Actually, there are two ways to extend the metaphor:

1. *Analytic extension.* This is a consciously systematic approach, breaking down the problem into its components and exploring each.

2. *Contemplative extension.* Here the unconscious mind roams freely over the subject, jumping back and forth among ideas in uncontrolled fashion.

Let us look at each method.

Analytic Extension

The scientist relies primarily on the analytic technique to help him extend the metaphor. Because the spirit of science permeates our age, we usually tend to favor the analytic method. We attack a problem by dissecting its components into symbolic values, asking ourselves: "What does this element in my problem represent and what does it resemble? And if A is like B in these respects, in what other respects will it be like B?"

This was the case when Einstein discovered relativity. Because he was interested in the relationship between time and space, he conceived a symbolic presentation of the situation flowing from his need to understand the meaning of *simultaneity*, a very difficult abstraction. He reduced his problem to a metaphor: simultaneity was like lightning striking at two different points and seen from a moving train. He visualized himself on board the train with double mirrors that allowed him to see both points. He visualized another man standing beside the tracks similarly equipped.

Now see how he extends the metaphor in a major paper first published in 1916:

> If we say that the bolts of lightning are simultaneous with regard to the tracks, *this now means*: the rays of light coming from two equidistant points meet simultaneously at the mirrors of the man on the track. But if the place of my moving mirrors coincides with his mirrors at the moment the lightning strikes, the rays will not meet exactly simultaneously in my mirrors because of my movement. [Remember that Einstein is on a moving train.]
>
> Events which are simultaneous in relation to the track are not simultaneous in relation to the train, and vice versa. Each frame of reference, each system of coordinates therefore has *its special time*; a statement about a time has real meaning only when the frame of reference is stated, to which the assertion of time refers.

To arrive at this, Einstein used metaphors within metaphors. He said to himself, My proposition requires a set-up which allows for demonstration. Suppose I use the word "hunchback." Such a term can have real meaning only if there is some standard by which it can be determined that a man is a hunchback. He writes:

> Similarly with the concept of simultaneity. The concept really exists for the physicist only when in a concrete case there is some possibility of deciding whether the concept is or is not applicable. Such a definition of simultaneity is required, therefore, as would provide a method of deciding. As long as this requirement is not fulfilled, I am deluding myself as a physicist (to be sure, as a non-physicist, too!) if I believe that the assertion of simul-

taneity has a real meaning. (Until you have truly agreed to this, dear reader, do not read any further.)

After some deliberation you may make the following proposal to prove whether the two shafts of lightning struck simultaneously. Put a set of two mirrors, at an angle of 90° to each other ($<$), at the exact halfway mark betwen the two light effects, station yourself in front of them, and observe whether or not the light effects strike the mirrors simultaneously.

With such analytic reasoning, based on the metaphor of the lightning striking in two places on a moving train, Einstein was able to upset the long-established view that time and space are absolute. He could learn that time and space are interrelated and that one is relative to the other.

Contemplative Extension

I have used Einstein's great achievement to illustrate the analytic method of extending the metaphor. A second method I have called the contemplative, which scientists are commonly thought to use less frequently. Actually, the well-known absentmindedness of the scientist is often due to a meditative mood. In such a state, he is not thinking in systematic fashion about his problem but is letting his mind ramble haphazardly over the elements of his problem. He has put aside his blackboard, his diagrams, his equations; he is not mapping out sequences of items to be considered in their proper order; he may not even be dealing with demonstrable facts. Instead, he is doing a great deal of "supposing"; he is letting intuition operate; he is groping for hunches.

This process of contemplation is different from what some writers have called "incubation"—which involves putting the problem aside altogether on the assumption that the unconscious mind will take over and continue to rework the problem material. Contemplation is a relaxed procedure in which the mind responds as if to a psychoanalyst's instruction to associate freely. His question is, "What do you think of when you think of apples?" He does not ask, "What *should* one logically think of when he thinks about apples?"

Before the age of science, the major instrument of thought was contemplation. Scholars would deliberate over a single sentence from an ancient text to "extend the metaphor." Thinkers would thus muse over problems and gain new insights which proved correct and useful. If this were not so, the human race would not have survived. Many of the social institutions which still help to preserve mankind were the product of contemplative, not analytic, thinking. Sometimes it took centuries to translate the results into logical systems of cause and effect.

But because scientific method has proved so effective in modern times, there has been a tendency to discard the contemplative method which produces the intuitive or instinctual solution. The psychologist Jung has warned us: "The forlornness of consciousness in our world is due primarily to the loss of instinct, and the reason for this lies in the development of the human mind over the past eon."

The abandonment of the contemplative method for the more glittering, systematic method of science is comparable to the abandonment of walking because the automobile is now available. Yet walking has many virtues—for both body and spirit—that riding does not have. It is interesting that Aristotle, an advocate of the disciplined mind, "walked, talking, and talked, walking, . . . with the students . . . who were called the *Peripatetics*. The thoughts were really and actively 'walked,' 'stood' and 'under-stood' with limbs, heart and head."

Some psychiatrists are even afraid that the preoccupation with structured problem-solving is blocking the use of the less systematic contemplative and intuitive method which can contribute to our needs. Dr. Franz E. Winkler goes so far as to say: "Intuitive perception and creativeness waned in the course of time, while analytical intellect increased in strength. In no other creature has intellect become as formidable an adversary of intuition as in man."

But there is no need to pit one method against the other. Both can be used, and where each produces a contradictory result, we are forewarned that further checking is necessary.

How is the contemplative method used? The ancient sages, relying on meditation, could sit for hours, thinking about a single object. The Zen Buddhist monks have apparently been capable of producing ideas and experiences even by pondering statements that are meaningless to the Western mind—for example: "A monk asked Chao-chou, 'What is the meaning of the First Patriarch's visit to China?' 'The cypress tree in the front courtyard.'" According to Zen Buddhists, the purpose of contemplating such questions and answers is to force logical thought out of the mind and make room for intuitive action.

Hubert Benoit, the French psychiatrist and former surgeon who has been profoundly influenced by Zen Buddhism, has made an effort to describe his process of meditation. He seeks relaxation and does not follow the peripatetic method of Aristotle. "Alone, in a quiet place, muscularly relaxed (lying down or comfortably seated), I watch the emergence within myself of mental images, permitting my imagination to produce *whatever it likes*. It is as though I were to say to my image-making mind, 'Do what you please, but I am going to watch you doing it.'"

In other words, the countemplative method of "extending the metaphor," as Rapoport called it, is simply to invite a free play of images on the movie screen of the mind. That this method produces results is evidenced by the distinguished French mathematician Henri Poincaré who describes how he arrived at one of his most original mathematical conceptions. In the process, he found himself, like Benoit, a spectator of his own spontaneous images. He writes:

> For fifteen days I strove to prove that there could not be any functions like those I have since called Fuchsian functions. I was then very ignorant; every day I seated myself at my work table, stayed an hour or two, tried a great number of combinations and reached no results. One

evening, contrary to my custom, I drank black coffee and could not sleep. Ideas rose in crowds; I felt them collide until pairs interlocked, so to speak, making a stable combination. By the next morning I had established the existence of a class of Fuchsian functions, those which come from the hypergeometric series: I had only to write out the results, which took but a few hours.

Our culture offers us little training in thus letting the imagination run rampant. We are given many lessons in "thinking to some purpose" but very little in "imagining to some purpose." We are even taught to disapprove of daydreaming. And yet the same executive who rebukes an employee for "letting his mind wander" will swing his feet up on his desk, stare off into the distance and let his mind do what it pleases, often producing practical business solutions.

Sometimes it takes a situation of boredom to create for us a genuinely contemplative mood. When the preacher is droning on, in sheer self-defense we take off from a chance word that he has uttered, and we are startled by the destination at which we arrive. Lying awake at night, we ponder a business problem with none of the paraphernalia of analytic thought at our disposal—no pencil, no paper, no secretary to dictate to, no memoranda drawn from the file cabinet, no colleague to consult over the telephone for a piece of information. Yet we come up with answers that we could not discover in the formal arena of systematic thought, the office.

All too frequently the solutions we have found in the middle of the night are forgotten the next morning. The rituals of analytic thinking have created in us a suspicion of the free-wheeling method of contemplation and force us to discard the conclusions.

But while the scientific spirit of the times has led even laymen to think that the only legitimate avenue to solutions is the rigorous, disciplined analytic method, scientists themselves know the value of undisciplined contemplation. A physicist who now works exclusively on defense problems told me that he uses what he calls "a preanalytic phase of research,"

another name for the contemplative approach. Many businessmen have used a technique they call "brain-storming,"
a group method of developing solutions: participants are
encouraged to place on the table the wildest possible ideas,
and nobody is permitted to criticize.

Eventually, of course, the physicist must return to disciplined analysis of the ideas suggested by his musings. And
the businessman must bring critical judgment to bear on
the products of the brain-storming.

Einstein undoubtedly used both the analytic and the contemplative methods in developing his theory of relativity.
His work really began when he was a boy of 16, puzzled by
the behavior of light beams. As James R. Newman has
written:

> At the heart of the theory of relativity are questions
> connected with the velocity of light. The young Einstein
> began to brood about these while still a high-school student.
> Suppose, he asked himself, a person could run as fast as a
> beam of light, how would things look to him? Imagine that
> he could ride astride the beam, holding a mirror just in
> front of him. Then, like a fictional vampire, he would cause
> no image; for since the light and the mirror are traveling
> in the same direction at the same velocity, and the mirror
> is a little ahead, the light can never catch up to the mirror
> and there can be no reflection.

These images danced before his mind's eye again and
again. As his collaborator Leon Infeld pointed out in later
years, Einstein had an enormous capacity for "wonder." He
could ponder over the same problem again and again on long
walks—Einstein also belonged to the peripatetic school—
"until darkness is transformed into the light of understanding." Because of his capacity for wonder, he could think up
imaginary experiments—"experiments that could never be
performed in practice, but which, when properly analyzed,
strangely clarify our understanding of the world around us."

In a study of problem-solving, few things are more profitable than an examination of Einstein's thought processes.

He knew the value of thinking in symbols and did most of his work by using mathematical symbols instead of laboratory experiments. The latter were done by others, following up on his theories. If he proved so right in his speculations about what experiments would show, it was because he had already performed the experiments visually and symbolically in his own mind.

A psychologist once asked him to describe the internal or mental images he used in his thinking. His answer reveals the power of symbols or signs, as distinguished from words on which so many of us rely exclusively. Einstein said:

> The words or the language, as they are written or spoken, do not seem to play any role in my mechanism of thought. The psychical entities which seem to serve as elements in thoughts are *certain signs and more or less clear images which can be "voluntarily" reproduced and combined.*
>
> There is, of course, a certain connection between those elements and relevant logical concepts. It is also clear that the desire to arrive finally at logically connected concepts is the emotional basis of this rather vague play with the above mentioned elements. But taken from a psychological viewpoint, this combinatory play seems to be the essential feature in productive thought—before there is any connection with logical construction in words or other kinds of signs which can be communicated to others.

This, of course, is the method of the genius who can use abstract symbols in his thinking without the need to translate them into words.

How to Set Up Nonverbal Symbols

Against this background of theory, we are now ready to look at some of the typical instruments with which we can symbolize the elements in our problems to achieve solution. We shall be discussing diagrams, maps, indexes, control charts, models, and similar devices of thought. They are useful both in creating and explaining ideas because they are symbolic representations of relationships.

Such devices are valuable because they lead not only to the discovery of solutions but, equally important, to the discovery of problems that might otherwise be overlooked. Businessmen keep graphs that spell out relationships between prices and costs, betwen inventories and sales, revealing problems that might remain undetected until too late for action.

Graphic presentations of problems are effective because their preparation involves asking and answering these questions:

1. *What are the key relationships relevant to my problem?* In drawing a visual representation, the irrelevant and accidental elements have to be eliminated. The mind is forced to think in terms of relationships.

2. *How can these relationships best be represented visually?* This forces the mind to think in terms of analogy. Lines, arrows, circles, arcs, rectangles, all kinds of geometrical forms, are used as "stand-ins" for forces, relationships, parallel developments, conflicting pressures.

3. *What is the logical sequence in which the elements of my problem must be arranged?* This question, more specifically, involves asking: What follows what in point of time? What follows what in spatial arrangement? What causes what? What accompanies what?

4. *What scale can I use to represent degrees in the various elements of my problem?* Such degrees may be quantitative, as in an atomic model, or qualitative, as in a company organization chart showing levels of authority.

In answering these questions, an effort must be made to keep the visual representation as simple as possible. The effect of such simplicity is to bring out more graphically the relevant elements, the basic relationships, the pattern of sequence and the degree to which the different elements affect your problem.

All of these four characteristics of a good symbolic representation will be illustrated below as we discuss diagrams, maps, indexes, control charts, and models.

Diagrams and Maps

The dictionary defines a diagram as "a figure, or set of lines, marks, etc., to accompany a geometrical demonstration, give the outlines or general features of an object, show the course or results of a process, etc."

The most familiar kind of diagram is a map, used constantly for solving the problem of getting from a physical place (A) to a desired destination (Z).

Note how Question 1 is applied by cartographers in constructing a roadmap. The most relevant relationships are *distance* and *direction*. For the designer of a roadmap, terrain is irrelevant: he ignores mountains, forests, lakes, because these have no bearing on his purpose, which is to indicate primarily distance and direction. A designer of air maps, however, is concerned also with altitude and must therefore include mountains that might endanger planes flying at night or in fog.

Motoring maps are satisfactory if they merely indicate distance and direction. But a third element is necessary if the user of the map is to be helped; he must also know his *present location*. The cartographer can afford to omit this element because he knows that towns proudly display their names. The designer of air maps, on the other hand, must provide a method of identifying present location from the air. Consequently, air maps have to include railroads, golf courses, water towers, race tracks—easily identifiable landmarks.

This difference between a roadmap and an air map illustrates how we can determine what is relevant. The test is purpose. A map whose purpose is air travel must include many more elements than a map intended to guide us on an auto trip.

In working out his diagram, the mapmaker must also tackle Question 2: "How can I best represent the relationships of distance and direction?" Here he thinks in terms of analogies. A road is like a geometric line, going from one point to another. As Wendell Johnson says, "For a map to be useful to a traveler it must be coordinated with the territory, its structure must be similar in certain respects to that of the territory it represents. The arrangement of the symbols, the dots, lines, etc., of the map must accord with the arrangement of the actual cities, roads, rivers, etc., of the territory." A right angle on the map must coincide with a comparable turn on the road. A vertical line on the map must coincide with a north-south direction, if the map follows the usual plan for representing the points of the compass.

Such maps are useful not only in physical travel but in

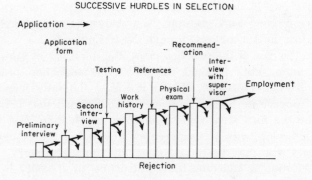

SUCCESSIVE HURDLES IN SELECTION

the effort to move toward a solution in nonphysical problems. For example, in hiring employees—or "selection," as personnel experts call it—companies want to be sure to get qualified people. "Make the selection process a series of hurdles that the applicant must overcome if he is to be hired," say the textbooks on personnel administration. From such a frame of reference, a whole program can then be developed, in the course of which it is desirable to diagram the proposed procedure. A typical result is the accompanying illustration, which I have borrowed from Dale Yoder's *Personnel Principles and Policies.*

Such a chart is valuable because it makes it easier for

us to grasp all the key elements of a proposed solution to the problem of hiring. The diagram suggests questions that we should ask. Looking at this graphic representation, we can spot duplications and determine if any can be eliminated. We can ask: Why not, on the basis of Dr. Yoder's diagram, eliminate the preliminary interview and start with the filling out of an application form? We can also discover omissions. After the physical exam, should we not also have an interview with a psychologist, as many companies now do in hiring executives?

Roadmaps and such devices as the selection chart also illustrate the value of Question 3, dealing with logical sequence. In the case of the map, sequence is obviously all important. If the dots representing the cities indicate the order is New York, Boston, New Haven, we are likely to get lost in our travels through New England.

In the case of the selection chart, the questions of sequence are more subtle. Should the physical examination precede the second interview? Should it follow the interview with the supervisor? Some companies have decided that it ought to be the final step, since it involves much more cost than an interview with the supervisor: why spend the money on a man who may be turned down by the supervisor?

Question 4 concerns the construction of a scale. In the literal sense, a scale represents measurement of degrees. In mapwork it is the ratio of distances on the map to distances on the territory—for example, every inch representing 20 miles.

Where precise quantities are not really relevant, the scale need not be exact. To guide a friend to your house, you may draw a crude map with rough approximations of distance. In the personnel selection chart, if amount of cost is considered relevant—as it might be in a cost-conscious company—the vertical bars representing the hurdles might be drawn higher or lower to correspond with the expense. If the amount of time consumed in each step of the hiring process is important, the horizontal axis could represent degrees of time in the form of wider or narrower spacing between the hurdles.

We have all become attuned to certain diagrammatic symbols which help us solve problems. Direction is almost invariably indicated by arrows. Boy Scouts have developed their own method of diagramming direction when arrows are lacking: they lay out stones in a special pattern.

Since arrows suggest sequence, they are also used to indicate cause and effect. For an illustration, see how diagramming with arrows helped us, on page 119, to think our way through such concepts as facts, abstractions, and relationships.·

Such diagrams have a further advantage. They help us see the process as a whole. Because the details have been eliminated, the true pattern is visible. Modern mapmakers have a great advantage over their predecessors precisely because they can get away from details. From planes, and with the aid of aerial photographs, they can discern contours more clearly. An astronaut, looking at the earth from space, needs no intricate logical argument to tell him that our planet is round.

But, while a diagram shows us the whole all at once, it also facilitates study of each component in the problem one at a time. The mere act of drawing a diagram forces us to make preliminary decisions as to what is relevant and important. And at the same time, it sets in motion a train of associations, clearing the path to new ideas by showing us resemblances between the unknown relationships (our problem) and relationships which are already familiar to us.

Einstein's Diagram

Remember Einstein's problem of simultaneity, which led him to the concept of relativity. He has visualized himself on a moving train as lightning strikes at two points; he is contrasting his perception with that of a man standing on an embankment as the train goes by. Einstein knows that the problem can be better understood if he diagrams the situation. So he draws this picture:

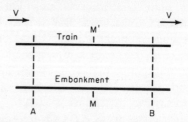

Einstein's own example of the relativity of time

He uses V to represent the velocity of the train. The arrows show the direction in which it is moving. One black line symbolizes the train, the other the embankment. A and B are the two points where the lightning strikes. Seen in the mirrors at M on the embankment, the lightning flashes appear to hit simultaneously. But viewed from M', the point of observation on the train, the flash at B seems to come first because M' is moving toward the beam of light at B and away from the beam of light at A.

Einstein concludes that both observers would be right. It all depends literally on the point of view. The observer on the train is right, relative to a system involving a moving train; the observer on the ground is right, relative to a stationary system. As James R. Newman sums it up:

> There is nothing to choose between these views, and they can be logically reconciled only by accepting the principle that simultaneity of events is meaningful only with respect to a particular reference system; moreover, that every such system has its own particular time, and unless, as Einstein says, we are told the reference system to which the statement of time refers, a bare statement of the time of an event is meaningless.

The form of a particular diagram, of course, must vary with the nature of the problem. Einstein's problem dealt with relationships between space, velocity, direction, and time. He reduced these elements to their bare bones, thus simplifying the relationships. At the heart of his diagram is an analogy in which a moving train represents an astronomical body and lightning flashes are substituted for the traveling of light through space. In effect, his diagram is an analogy carried one step further toward simplification because it illustrates his figure of speech.

Automation—The Story in a Diagram

Einstein's thinking, as we have seen, began with an analogy. Whenever you attempt to diagram a problem, it pays to ask yourself quite consciously: "What situation with which I am already familiar does my present problem resemble?"

I have already described (in Chapter 5) some of the thinking that preceded the development of automation. You will recall that the answer came to the scientists of Massachusetts Institute of Technology at the suggestion of a neurologist member of the team. He said that the basic frame of reference for the problem was how to duplicate the human nervous system in mechanical devices.

It's your frame of reference that may suggest the analogy or be suggested by it. You decide to look at the problem from a given point of view, hoping that it will prod you to make comparisons with other situations. In the case of automation, the frame of reference was the establishment of a communications system comparable to the nervous system.

The thoughts of the scientists are then able to move along these lines, as if in the courtroom examination of an expert witness:

Q: What are the basic elements in the nervous system?
A: Input and output.
Q: What is input?
A: The feeding in of information.
Q: What is output?

A: The production of useful activity.

Q: Can you illustrate input and output in the nervous system?

A: Yes. A good example would be the case of an airline pilot approaching the airport. The input is information— some of it stored up in his mind as a result of previous training, either in memory or habit; some of it in the form of instructions sent to him from the radio tower; some of it, information received through his eyes as he looks at the dials on his control panel; some of it through the sense of hearing as he listens to the sounds made by the lowering of his flaps; some of it through touch, as he feels the plane moving into the angle of descent. All this information is being fed into his nervous system.

Q: Can you illustrate output?

A: Well, something has to happen before he can produce the output, which is the actual work of landing the plane.

Q: What do you mean, something has to happen?

A: He has to process the information that has come to him, and he must make certain decisions—for example, on speed, angle of descent, lowering a wing of the plane in order to bring him in line with the runway, and so forth. Then, after making these decisions, another step must be taken: he has to actuate his equipment, set certain things in motion to implement his decisions. In this process of actuation, he must also be prepared to make certain corrections—speed up and slow down lest he overshoot the runway. So his nervous system must be equipped to give him feedback on what is happening during the control action. This feedback has to be based on his observation of the kind of output he is getting, and the feedback has to become a new input.

Q: In other words, the whole business is like a continuing circle, if I understand you correctly.

A: Yes, you might call it a closed loop.

This, then, is a picture of the human nervous system producing an output from a given input. And the problem of the scientists working on automation was to duplicate this system. To think it through, a useful method would be to diagram the operation of the nervous system, thus reducing the challenge to certain key elements. The diagram could tell what kinds of solutions are necessary.

Out of such thinking comes a diagram of this kind:

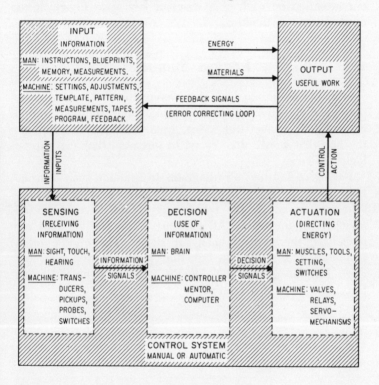

As we saw when we discussed the subject of purpose in Chapter 2, it is important in problem-solving to have some idea of what the solution will look like. The diagram is a symbolic representation of the form an answer might take. Now the diagram suggests to us what we must do to solve the problem. We will need *sensing equipment,* capable of receiving information—transducers, pickups, probes; a *decision-maker*, capable of processing the data and making choices—controllers, mentors, computers; *actuators*—valve openers and closers, electrical relays, servomechanisms; and as we obtain our output, we will need feedback devices to report what is happening to the output.

In short, the diagram is like a teacher's pointer, focusing our attention on each of a series of key areas to which we must apply our thinking.

Logical Symbols

Students of formal logic are among the first to recognize the value of nonverbal presentations. They translate verbal content into geometrical forms, usually circles, to eliminate the bias that words often carry. In this way, they can expose logical fallacies.

For example, they use diagrams to examine such abstractions as "The Fallacy of the Undistributed Middle"—a faulty syllogism in which the middle term fails to refer to all members of the class. "All men are *mammals*; all dogs are *mammals*; therefore all men are dogs." The middle term, *mammals*, is supposed to link the two subclasses, *men* and *dogs*. But the reasoning is clearly seen to be invalid when translated into these symbols:

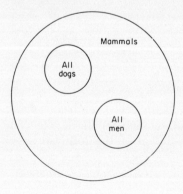

All men fall into the class of mammals; all dogs come within the same circle, but, as the diagram reveals, they do not necessarily fall into the same inner circle as men. The flaw lies in the fact that *mammals*, the middle term intended to show the relationship between *men* and *dogs*, is undistributed—that is, it never really refers to *all mammals*.

"Socrates is a man; all men are mortal; therefore Socrates is a mortal" does have a distributed middle term—*all men* and is therefore logically valid. Here, again the diagram helps to tell the story:

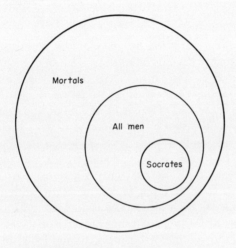

Socrates does fall within the category *all men*; the category *all men* does fall within the category *mortals*. Consequently, we have a valid spelling out of relationships.

A small amount of ingenuity, but a great amount of clarity, is necessary to prepare an adequate diagram of an abstract problem. First of all, you must know what relationships constitute your problem and the nature of the terms you are using; you must then be able to strip away the nonessentials so that you can set up the bone structure; then you must be able to contrive the simplest possible visualization. Simplicity is the key, because simplification is clarification. It is an axiom among scientists that the simplest statement of the problem produces the best and truest understanding of the forces at work in nature.

"The Symbol of Science"

Wendell Johnson has said: "The essential structure of the language of science can be represented by a very simple diagram, one that is familiar to all of us. We may regard it as a universal symbol of science and of the scientific way of life. It may one day supersede the many other symbols by which men have tried for so long to focus their energies and fashion their wills."

Such is the description he gives of the typical graph used to show quantitative relationships. As one factor rises, it is represented on the vertical axis, called the "ordinate"; as the other factor rises, it is represented on the horizontal axis, or the "abscissa." The resulting line on the graph is what Johnson calls "the sign of the curve."

We are all familiar with it as a device for recording, in most simplified form, how economic trends rise and fall with the passage of time. Several curves put on the same chart can show us how different factors compare with each other or may influence each other. The economist, with one glance, can see how a rise in purchasing power is associated with an increase in the volume of business. If, suddenly, he discovers that there is a decline in purchasing power, he can project a decline in business.

This "symbol of science" is now in wide use among executives. They wrinkle their brows over curves which show a rise in sales expenditures as compared with a small rise in profits. Then they are able to arrive at decisions based on the realization that they are heading toward a less favorable ratio between the sales dollar and the profit dollar. The result is to focus attention on the need to reduce sales costs.

The head of a purchasing department, who is responsible

for keeping the right amount of raw materials on hand, tackles his problem by preparing a chart which shows him the relationship between inventory and new orders from customers. If he finds that new orders are falling below the level of sales that has prevailed so far, he examines whether he ought to be reducing inventory.

The value of the symbolic representation in the graphs and charts is that they clarify existing relationships and suggest measures of control. Here is an example.

A Case History

The head of a group of salesmen has a problem: he must increase sales. He calls a meeting of his salesmen and delivers a "pep talk." He expatiates on the virtues of the company's product. He holds out the picture of bigger commissions, special bonuses. He reminds his men that "the little woman back home wants to be proud of you; now go on out, and bring back the bacon." He tells the salesmen customers are hungry for the product. His eloquence moves his men. In fact, one of them is so inspired that he rushes out of the meeting, hails a taxi-cab and tells the driver: "Take me anywhere; I have customers waiting for me everywhere."

But the net result is an insignificant increase in sales. Our sales manager reads the reports filed by his salesmen on every call they make. Then he decides to apply "the symbol of science." He prepares a chart, showing the relationship between *the number of calls* and *the number of sales*. He discovers that for every six calls, his salesmen average one sale.

Now he has a handle on his problem and asks himself the question: "How can I increase the number of calls my salesmen make each day?" He draws a simple visual diagram of a salesman's day, based on his observation that the average man makes five calls. It looks like this:

9 A.M.   5 P.M.

☐ Productive time

▨ Unproductive time

The horizontal line represents time—the hours of the day. Each white rectangle stands for a call, time actually spent with a customer. The shaded rectangles represent unproductive time—that is, time not spent with a customer, including everything from sheer dawdling to unavoidable time spent traveling from customer to customer.

With this symbolic presentation of his problem, he can now see clearly the direction in which he must move. The number of white spaces must be increased. Since the working day, when customers are available, is a fixed amount, he must effect a reallocation of the salesmen's time by reducing the shaded areas and allowing more room for the white.

He examines the facts about unproductive time, and learns that

1. time is wasted in just covering the physical distance,

2. time is lost in zigzagging back and forth to keep appointments in different places to suit the convenience of the customer's schedule,

3. time is frittered away on arrival in a new city because the salesman can't resist seeing the sights,

4. time is lost in finding parking space,

5. etc., etc.

Having located the specific causes, he now proceeds to do something about them:

1. He reduces the size of each salesman's territory to avoid excessive travel time.

2. He instructs his salesmen to resist accepting appointments that will make them zigzag through their territory.

("Better to set a later date for your presentation," he urges them.)

3. He meets the sight-seeing problem by telling his men, "On hitting a new town, take a few hours to see the sights, but after that, it's strictly business on all subsequent visits."

4. He advises his men to avoid the parking problem by telling them, "Once you get into town, park your car and use cabs."

Now he turns to the problem of increasing the value of the *productive time*—the time actually taken in trying to sell the prospect. He comes up with these specific questions and answers:

1. "How can I shorten the presentation?" His answer: "I will equip my salesmen with visual displays so that the nature of our product can be communicated more quickly. Also, the visual presentation will keep the salesmen from rambling on at length and getting off on tangents, which only prolongs the call and hampers the sale."

2. "What can I do about 'waiting time' in the customer's office?" He puts such time to use by instructing the salesmen that call reports on visits to customers should be prepared while sitting in the next customer's anteroom.

He continues to think about the problem of productive time—time actually spent with prospects—and comes up with these additional questions:

3. "What can we do about the time wasted on customers who are not likely to buy?" This leads him to another question: "Can we identify the customers who are least likely?" Looking over his records, he finds that "well-established firms are likely to have strong ties with one of our competitors; new firms are more likely to switch over to us." So he instructs his salesmen to put the emphasis on the latter.

4. This line of reasoning suggests another question: "Can we reduce the amount of time spent on customers who are likely to buy—for example, those who habitually reorder from us, month after month? Is a call to pick up the reorder really

necessary? Why not make it a practice to conduct these transactions by alternating telephoning and visiting?"

After going through this process, he keeps careful records of the results. Not all of his "solutions" work. Some of the men don't "buy" all of his ideas. But in outlining his program to them he has accomplished several results: he has made them aware of the need for increasing the number of productive calls, and he has given them methods by which they can do it.

The returns come in. Once more he relies on the symbols of problem-solving. He discovers that the increased number of calls is producing a higher level of sales. But "the symbol of science" shows him that something else is now happening. Some of his men have actually reached a level of eight calls a day, but they are not selling more. His graph looks like this:

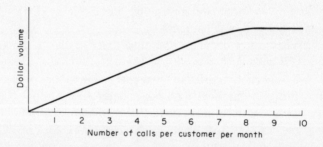

Number of calls per customer per month

Now he realizes that he has reached the point of diminishing returns. Perhaps his salesmen are tired by the time they make the eighth call.

Or perhaps the market simply cannot absorb additional purchasing, as the Lamp Division of General Electric discovered from such a chart. The answer was to reduce the frequency of calls to find the point at which sales volume would drop off. As one of the company's consultants put it, "The current frequency of salesmen's calls was well over the threshold of saturation so that increasing or decreasing the number of calls made little change on volume of sales." With this knowledge, the company was then in a position to make important new decisions. It knew now what was the desirable number of salesmen, and was able to reassign some of the men to other products whose market was far from saturated.

Charting Production Problems

Business organizations place great reliance on diagramming and charting as an aid to problem-solving. The engineers in the design department solve most of their engineering problems on the drawing board. In fact, technical education in many fields—from architecture to zoology—is to a large extent a study of how to make diagrammatic presentations.

Manufacturing firms would be lost if they did not have flow process charts to help in analyzing the problems of production. Floor layout plans, drawn on graph paper with the use of templates and sometimes prepared only after the use of three-dimensional models, are customary tools in setting up a factory or an office.

When the mass production system got started, it became absolutely essential to set up methods of "control." For instance, thousands of different components go into one automobile. To get the product manufactured on time requires that each component be ready when it is needed for assembly into larger units, which in turn have to be assembled into others, and so on until the auto is completed.

The man who came up with the first basic answer to the problem of control was H. L. Gantt, one of the pioneers in what has come to be called "scientific management." The Gantt Production Planning and Control Chart now hangs on the walls of many manufacturing executives. It is the height of simplicity, but at a glance the production planner knows whether he is on schedule, or must go into overtime, or assign more machines to the work or increase the number of workers on the job.

In recent years production has become fantastically complicated. The delicate assemblies of modern rocketry have forced engineers to think about even more efficient ways to diagram the multitudinous phases of production. Charts are prepared in networks, allowing for alternative plans, particularly as new developments are being researched. Then data about the charted alternatives—figures on the time and costs involved—are fed into computers, and the most economical methods are used to achieve the earliest or most desirable delivery date.

Such charts are tools in a system developed by the U.S. Navy in building the famous Polaris submarine missile. The method is called PERT, a very attractive abbreviation of the more mouth-filling title, Program Evaluation and Review Technique. The Polaris project required the manufacture of more than 70,000 separate parts, some of them never produced before. By dovetailing the steps in a PERT pattern and by processing detailed data in electronic computers, the Navy was able to produce the Polaris *two years ahead of schedule.*

This provided a neat, pert method that many private businesses now use in solving production problems by diagramming. The General Electric Company has worked out a similar approach which it calls the Critical Path Method.

On page 189, I reproduce a typical network chart, showing the interrelationship of different phases in the production process. Each of the circled numbers represents an "event"— a major milestone in the unfolding of the program. The events are interdependent, since some of them cannot proceed until others have been completed. A whole series of "activities," represented by interconnecting lines, links the "events." The "critical path" through which the "activities" must move toward completion is represented by heavy black lines.

Models

The most elaborate method of diagramming is to build a model. Use of the word immediately brings to mind the toy models we played with as children—trains, automobiles,

TYPICAL NETWORK CHART OF PARTIAL PROGRAM

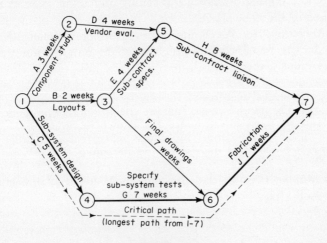

EVENTS

1 Start preliminary design
2 Complete component study
3 Complete layouts
4 Complete sub-system design
5 Start sub-contractor liaison
6 Start fabrication
7 Start sub-integration

miniature dishes, etc. One result of this association is that we tend to think of models as small-scale reproductions. But a model may be of any dimension. It may come life-size. For example, early in the design of a new automobile, a clay model is prepared—a full-size reproduction with the actual dimensions the car will assume. Or a model may be bigger than life-size, as in the case of a physicist's reproduction of an atom's structure.

A model is more useful than a diagram because it adds a major third dimension, to length and width. A floor layout in a factory may be prepared on graph paper, but the problem-solver may overlook height; when he installs the equipment he may discover that one of his machines is too high for the ceiling. He may then have to turn to a makeshift solution, cutting a hole in the ceiling and using some of the space in the floor above.

According to W. Walter Grey, the brain specialist, a model can be effective in problem-solving only if these three conditions are present:

1. Several features of the mystery must be known.
2. The model must contain the absolute minimum of working parts to reproduce the known features.
3. The model must reproduce other features, either as predictions, or as unexpected combinations.

He emphasizes also that the simpler a model is, the more helpful it's likely to be.

Simplicity

Simplicity is important in a model precisely because we solve our problems only if we can simplify them. The most fruitful way to find solution is to reduce complex matters to their bone structure. In fact, the path of progress in human history has always been from the more complex to the simple, as Toynbee has demonstrated:

> The ponderous and bulky steam engine with its elaborate "permanent way" is replaced by the neat and handy internal-combustion engine which can take to the roads with the speed of a railway train and almost all the freedom of action of a pedestrian. Telegraphy with wires is replaced by telegraphy without wires. The incredibly complicated scripts of the Sinic and Egyptiac societies are replaced by the neat and handy Latin alphabet.

In part, this progress through simplification is the result of our ability to simplify our problems symbolically. Language itself, as we have seen, is the first of our symbolic tools; it too has been undergoing simplification through the generations. The older languages—Latin, for example—are more involved and have many more inflexions than contemporary speech.

In the interest of simplicity, we use models. Usually they do not relate to the whole project but concentrate on only one aspect of it. Airplane designers will produce models of a new craft that emphasize primarily the *shape*. They can then create model conditions by exposing the design to currents of air in a wind tunnel.

In the effort to simplify the model down to its most basic elements, problem-solvers in recent years have developed a new technique for transforming physical models into mathematical models. The appropriate equations or the mathematical formulas of the computer programmers are now referred to as "models." This is no mere figure of speech. One of the key objectives in building a model is to reproduce the minimum number of essential relationships that affect the problem. When these can be expressed mathematically you have the simplest possible model.

Irwin D. J. Bross, in *Design for Decision*, explains why this is so:

> It might be puzzling to understand why the astronomers should go from a nice simple physical model with little spheres on wire arms to a symbolic model with all sorts of queer mathematical signs when, if sufficient care were taken in the construction of the physical model, it would be possible to use it directly in order to predict eclipses. . . . From the astronomer's point of view it is the mathematical model which is the *simple* one and the physical model with balls and wire which is complex. Since the physical model is made out of metal it not only has attributes which are intended to simulate the solar system, but it also has a lot of attributes which depend on the materials used in its construction and the way in which it is made.

The substitute materials can be misleading or can cause oversights because they have qualities that differ substantially from the reality they are supposed to represent. These irrelevant qualities may involve friction, vibration, stress, etc., that are not characteristic of the real situation being studied. As a result, the purpose of the model, which is predictability, may not be met.

Automobile engineers learned this fact quite painfully. The clay model produced in the early stages of design has the properties of clay, not of metal. Consequently, when the curved windshield was first introduced by a leading auto manufacturer, a serious error was made. Only after the car was on the market was it discovered that jacking it up to change a flat tire caused the windshield to crack. Shifting the weight of the car produced stresses that could not be anticipated from the clay model.

It must always be remembered that the conclusions drawn from a model must be subjected to further testing. This can be done either by eliminating irrelevant characteristics inherent in the model or by creating additional models that will concentrate on characteristics omitted from the original model. One advantage of a mathematical model is that the equations avoid the deceptive qualities inherent in the materials of a physical model. In the case of the cracked windshields, mathematical models based on the engineer's equations of stresses and strains might have avoided the error.

Again, it is the simplicity of the mathematical model that makes for greater accuracy in prediction. As Bross points out, it is curious but true that "Einstein is working with an extremely simple model in his theory of relativity, while a schoolboy is working with an extremely complex model when he builds an airplane."

Like the diagram, the model suggests the direction in which action should be taken. But it does more. It reveals the gaps in information which must still be filled. Space scientists found it profitable to build life-size models of capsules long before they knew the detailed nature of the contents. The models themselves then suggested further resarch.

For example, shape is an important element in motion through space; therefore the model must abstract form from the mass of problems involved, and the model is built accordingly. Similarly, the abstraction *heat* is crucial; the model must therefore provide for this characteristic, and the scientist models some kind of heat-shield.

"Wrong" Models

Even if it turns out that your model does not work, it can help you along the road to solution. Each faulty model can guide you toward devising a better one. Philosophical and scientific formulations about the nature of the world are models of reality; they are never complete, nor are they always right. But error carefully examined and exposed is a finger pointing in new directions.

Inventors, who are specialists in model-making, do not consider time lost because they have produced a model that failed. They would have lost much more time, energy, and money if they had worked only with the final product itself. Just consider what the cost would be if the aircraft industry were to produce a real plane, and actually try to fly it, without having worked up models of the various elements. It is cheaper and faster to build miniatures to scale and study them in wind tunnels that are models of the air conditions in which the plane must ultimately fly.

The reason a model saves time and heartache is that it helps to narrow the area in which thinking is to be done. It allows for depth in the thinking because the mind does not have to ramble over a wide variety of data, both relevant and irrelevant.

There is a limit to the number of ideas the human brain can juggle simultaneously. Dr. William Shockley of Bell Laboratories claims that some rare individuals can balance as many as five ideas at a time but that most of us can keep only two or three intellectual balls in the air simultaneously.

A model, however, reduces the number of items to the bare essentials. By presenting them in one composite form, it steps up the number of ideas you can handle and eliminates the distraction of extraneous elements. The secret of the juggler is not only his coordination but his concentration.

Building a Model

To construct a suitable model, you have to take the following steps:

1. List all the factors you consider relevant to your problem.

2. Isolate the key ones—those that you believe are most crucial to solution.

3. Choose the physical forms that will best suit your problem—that is, most nearly conform to your purpose.

4. Put the parts together.

5. Test—by seeing how it works, exploring the new questions that it suggests and collecting more facts to answer those questions.

6. Repeat the process.

Note that the model itself—or any diagram, for that matter —is not itself the solution. It is a tool that helps you along the way. It shows you essential relationships, which may have to be readjusted. It helps you fill the gaps in your information. In short, it brings you closer to the point where you can actually formulate the type of solution that is most appropriate for your problem.

[10]

TYPICAL SOLUTIONS—PATHS AND PITFALLS

SOLUTIONS do not spring from the brain fullblown like Athene from the head of Zeus. They are born in the personality as well as the mind and are responses to the needs of "the whole man."

Two able men will tackle similar problems and will come up with dissimilar yet equally effective solutions. Why? Because their inner nature leads them to choose different answers. But each could learn from the other's method and could adapt it to his use by putting on it the imprint of his own personality.

In this chapter I discuss different kinds of solutions. Though I categorize them into seemingly neat compartments, real life is too rich with variety to permit any such list to be either exhaustive or so sharply defined. Besides, these categories can be combined in practice, making available to men an even richer cornucopia of thought.

Beyond Formulas

My list of different types of solutions is abstracted from the cases of problem-solving discussed in previous chapters. But do not assume that they add up to a formula in which you can mechanically substitute your quantities for the X's and Y's and automatically come out with a Q.E.D. Thinking, under the best circumstances and with the best of aids, still requires thought.

Also by way of qualifying the recommendations in this chapter, I would like to stress a truth that seems important to me. Problem-solving is not a game played on the football field of any one man's mind. Individual cerebration is an important part of the process, for which there can be no substitute. But there are other players on the team: the knowledge gained from the experience of others; the thought patterns created by our times and our culture; even the element of the accidental—the good fortune of being in the right society at the right time. Da Vinci designed a workable parachute, but he could not make it because his age had not yet produced the necessary materials.

Sometimes a man transcends his age, bursts the bonds of his culture, perceives a truth and fashions a concept that may be alien to the spirit of his times. This is true creativity, going far beyond the limits of ordinary problem-solving.

Jacques Barzun, in his provocative book *The House of Intellect*, laments the Hollywoodian hyperbole of our time which permits us to call even the writing of advertising copy "creative work." That term must be properly reserved for the mysterious process by which a man lays hold on a truly great insight. It is genuinely creative just because it is inexplicable—because its author has reached some height of innovation that all the preceding steps cannot explain. The rest of us, who take his findings and adapt them, may deserve the proud title of problem-solvers, but we are not Einsteins. We are *explorers* following in the footsteps of the *discoverers*.

It is useful to know in what general categories solutions are available. The most typical are the following:

1. *The Panoramic Method.* This method involves laying out the whole spectrum of alternatives and studying the consequences of each.

2. *The Classification Method.* In effect, we find the answer to our problems by asking, "Into what classification of problems does my problem fall?"

3. *The Critical-Factor Method.* We locate the critical factor that creates the problem and take action with reference to it.

4. *The Method of Innovation.* Here we find a novel answer by making a basic change in our frame of reference. We are able to introduce fresh, experimental changes into the situation because our openmindedness brings us new vision.

5. *The Adaptation Method.* We borrow an existing solution that has been applied to another problem and alter it to fit the aspects of our new problem that diverge from the original problem.

These types of solutions are different ways of looking at the same problem. Sometimes we begin by using one method, but a turn of thought suddenly leads us into another—which is exactly as it should be. The function of such categories of solutions is to provide as many avenues to Z as possible. If, as we move down the main road, a short-cut becomes apparent, it would be folly to reject it.

1. *The Panoramic Method*

In the rolling hills of Westchester County, New York, in a complex of attractive buildings looking out on green fields, a team of physicists, psychologists, engineers, sociologists and military strategists, are working on cold war problems for the U.S. government. With an extraordinary, even frightening, objectivity, they dig into such questions as the economic consequences of atomic attack, civil defense measures, and strategies of negotiation with the Russians.

I sat in one of the briefing rooms of the Hudson Institute and watched these experts using one of their favorite techniques—a method I call "panoramic problem-solving" because it consists of spreading out a panorama of alternatives. The question they were exploring was, How might World War III start? On the walls were charts setting up every (to them) conceivable alternative relating to the problem under discussion. The charts read:

Tense Situation: Soviet Union Strikes First
Tense Situation: U.S. Strikes First
Tense Situation: Accidental War
Non-Tense Situation: Soviet Union Strikes First
Non-Tense Situation: Accidental War

In effect, the mental process used in the panoramic method consists of these steps:

1. List the basic alternatives.

2. Break each of them down into a set of alternatives within the alternatives.

3. Assemble every possible bit of data relevant to each.

4. Examine the possible consequences of each to give you predictability.

5. Since "predictability gives control"—the basis of applied science, as John Dewey says—you can now take steps to minimize or maximize the consequences, whichever is appropriate.

The panoramic method of solution appears to be the one most commonly used in private life. For example, we are earning a certain amount of money beyond our immediate needs. The problem: How can we put it to the best use?

We have two basic alternatives—to spend the money as we earn it or to save it for future use. Each of these alternatives includes networks of alternatives. The spending alternative opens up a wide variety of choices: buy new furniture, buy a home, buy a car, take a trip to Europe, and so on. The savings alternative opens up another set of choices: let the money earn interest in a bank account, invest in common stocks, buy government bonds, take out a life insurance policy, buy educational annuities for the youngsters' college education, etc.

The panoramic method involves following a chain of reasoning through alternatives and subalternatives. A charming satire on this method is found in Nathan Ausubel's *Treasury of Jewish Folklore*:

The old rabbi had left the room for a moment, then returned to his studies, only to find his eye-glasses missing. Perhaps they were between the leaves of his book? No. . . . Maybe they were somewhere on the desk? No. . . . Surely they were in the room? No. . . .

So, in the ancient sing-song, with many a gesture appropriate to Talmudic disputation, he began:

"Where are my glasses? . . .

"Let us assume they were taken by someone. They were taken either by someone who needs glasses, or by someone who doesn't need glasses. If it was someone who needs glasses, he has glasses; and if it was someone who doesn't need glasses, then why should he take them?

"Very well. Suppose we assume they were taken by someone who planned to sell them for gain. Either he sells them to one who needs glasses or to one who doesn't need glasses. But one who needs glasses has glasses, and one who doesn't need them surely doesn't want to buy them.

"So much for that.

"Therefore . . . this is a problem involving one who needs glasses and has glasses, or who either took someone else's because he lost his own, or who absentmindedly pushed his own up from his nose to his forehead, and promptly forgot all about them!

"For instance . . . me!" And with a triumphant sweep of thumb to forehead, signalizing the end of his analysis, the rabbi recovered his property.

"Praised be the Lord, I am trained in our ancient manner of reasoning," he murmured. "Otherwise I would never have found them!"

The panoramic method is likely to be the most time-consuming because it requires exploration of every possible alternative.

Evaluating Consequences

The most difficult step in the panoramic method is evaluation of the consequences of each alternative. Three factors will determine how successfully we do this:

1. The completeness of our list of alternatives.

2. The accuracy of the predictions we make about the consequences of each alternative.

3. The personal values we hold dear, which constitute the standard by which we judge the consequences.

One of the major perils in using this method is a faulty enumeration of the alternatives. Intellectual laziness—or weariness—may lead us to close the list of possibilities prematurely. All too often our projects wind up as failures and are buried under the epitaph, "I never thought of that."

Similarly, we run into trouble because wishful thinking sends our prediction of consequences wide of the mark. Or the fault may be lack of data, due again to laziness—an unwillingness to do the spadework and dig up the necessary facts.

Or it may be due to an unavoidable condition of human existence: all the facts about the future simply cannot be known to us. Chance intervenes with greater frequency in human affairs than we are willing to admit. A businessman decides to purchase a large supply of a given commodity because the price is right; a week later a new, secretly developed, better and cheaper product comes on the market and his inventory is obsolete. How could he have known?

Perhaps the only safeguard against such perils is *consciousness of risk* and the preparation of a substitute Plan B. This is the essence of mental flexibility: the ability to switch one's course in mid-flight as circumstances change.

Personal Values

In the evaluation of choices, we cannot help but bring to bear on the problem the set of standards we have developed in response to the needs of our own personality. In the spending-versus-saving problem, we must decide what is most important to us. Unfortunately, our failure to make conscious judgments as to which value we are satisfying results in poor solutions of our problems. All too often we allow Freud's pleasure principle to operate and we ignore the reality principle which requires longer-range thinking. Tomorrow has less worth to us than today.

But more frequently the difficulty is that we are under pressure from a set of values that may be inherently consistent but in a given situation creates internal conflict. I encountered just such a problem in a seminar conducted with a group of supervisors in a large metropolitan hospital. Though their basic approach was professional, it seemed to me that they were paralyzing their own problem-solving capacities because of poor evaluation of alternatives. It was essential, therefore, to examine their set of values.

I put the question directly to them: "What are the standards you use in your department when judging among the alternatives open to you?" The answers offered by different individuals, but assented to by all, were these:

1. Will my solution meet the needs of the patients?
2. Will it keep my department running smoothly?
3. Will it help my fellow-supervisors?
4. Will it satisfy my boss?
5. Will it keep my staff happy?

I insisted that the list was by no means complete, that they had other values which must also be enumerated. Finally, these items were added to those already on the blackboard:

6. Will it serve the institutional interests of the hospital —its financial needs, its public image, etc.?
7. Will it serve my personal needs—self-approval, social approval, economic interest in the form of promotion opportunities, etc.?

"Now," I asked, "are there any situations in which you have found that these values clashed?"

A flood of illustrations came pouring out. "Yes, I had to fire an employee for incompetence, even though she was very popular. Meeting the needs of the patients brought me into conflict with the need to keep my staff happy," said one participant.

"Yes," said a nursing supervisor, "I had to upset the smooth running of my department and assign some of my nurses to Pediatrics because they were shorthanded, and we got bitter complaints from our own patients and a pretty nasty note from the Superintendent because some of the complaints got to him."

In such situations the individual obviously is being forced to give priority to one set of values over another. But all too often no conscious analysis of the values precedes the decision; there is no systematic weighing of priorities in the light of the circumstances. Obviously the supervisor who spends a sleepless night in anticipation of a firing interview would suffer much less if his decision were geared to a clear understanding of the values he hopes to serve by the action.

This panoramic method is usually effective in areas where we are fortunate enough to possess a large body of information.

It works well in cases where the alternatives can be clearly discerned. But if we find that all the known alternatives have to be rejected as inadequate and we are compelled to look for an unknown alternative, then a more complex type of solution is required.

2. *The Classification Method*

This type of solution depends on your ability to determine into what class of problems your particular problem happens to fall. Once you know that, you're in a position to apply known solutions that have worked with other problems in that class.

This is the method used by most professionals. Their education and training are geared to a knowledge of useful categories. When a client presents a case to a lawyer, he tackles it by asking himself: "Is this a problem in contracts? in torts? in criminal law?" The more experienced he is, the more quickly he can assign the case to its proper category.

Failure to find the right category prevents solution. We saw how the men who developed automation were frustrated until a newcomer to their team was able to say, "Gentlemen, this is a problem in neurology." The reason such an analysis provides solution is that the mere determination of a classification puts order into what would otherwise be a jumble of facts.

The Greeks, according to some historians, were the first to recognize the intellectual power inherent in classification. Aristotle says, "We must make up our minds about the method of our investigation and decide whether we will consider, first, what the whole group has in common, and afterwards the individual peculiarities; or begin straightway with the particular instance." Aristotle favored the first, and in science it proved to be the beginning of wisdom, though in later years it became necessary to redress the balance and call for greater attention to the particular instance through careful observation.

The function of science and the fruit of its labors is the creation of classified knowledge. Once data have been systematized, we have facts put into orderly relationships. So, in the study of animals, the zoologist classifies his data into genus, species, and so on. The anthropologist sets up types of societies: food-gatherers, hunters and fishermen, pastoralists, agriculturists, and artisans. A knowledge that the Masai tribesmen are pastoralists automatically gives us information about the type of housing they dwell in—short-lived mud huts.

When I was in the Congo just before independence, I visited a tribe of pygmies and was told, with great amusement, about the futile efforts that the Belgian authorities had made to encourage them to grow their food and raise their standard of living. Government officials gave them seed, which they dutifully planted under the eyes of the white men from Leopoldville. But no sooner had the agricultural experts left than the pygmies dug up the seeds and ate them. What stumped the experts was their failure to appreciate the anthropological classification in which the pygmies fall. They are hunters and therefore must follow the game. They do not remain in one place long enough to work on a crop; good sense told them that the only use for seed was to eat it. The white man was a fool for thinking they would do something as irrational as leaving it buried.

The function of classification is to arrange knowledge in an orderly fashion. Then, when we are confronted by a problem, we can retrieve the stored information that is relevant to solution.

History, like science, is also concerned with classification. Its purpose is to classify human experience. Alfred Korzybski, the pioneer in general semantics, says that the distinction of man in the universe is his time-binding quality: "The human class of life differs from animals in the fact that, in the rough, each generation of humans, at least potentially, can start where the former generation left off." But that is true only because, by classifying knowledge, we are able to make it usable for problem-solving purposes.

It is important, then, to understand the nature of a classification. To begin with, it is a generalization about all members of the class. The classification *vertebrates* is a way of linking together all fishes, amphibians, reptiles, birds, and mammals as belonging to a group all of whose members have jointed backbones. The classification establishes a relationship among the members by emphasizing the characteristics they have in common.

"Togetherness"

Alfred North Whitehead offers what seems to me the best explanation of the term "classes." Though he is thinking in mathematical terms primarily, we can readily apply his definition to the solution of other types of problems.

A class [he says] is a composite entity arising from the togetherness of many things in symmetrical connection with each other. There are three requisites that any concept of "class" must satisfy: (1) The members of the class are "together"; (2) The class is the totality arising from that composition; (3) In respect to membership of the class, one member is as good as another.

What constitutes the *togetherness* of the things? It may be that they are all the products of the same causes, or have qualities that may produce the same results. Consequently, a knowledge of one member of the class tends to enlighten us about other members of the class. The effect is to make our limited knowledge an instrument for relieving our unlimited ignorance.

Let us examine a relatively simple case reported in the Sunday magazine section of *The New York Times*:

> A clerk at Chicago's Drake Hotel found that a good part of his time was taken up figuring the astronomical cost of broken dishes. He suggested that sample pieces of glassware and china be tagged with their actual cost to the hotel and displayed in a cabinet where they could be seen by all employees. As a result, breakage was reduced by $7,328 in the next year, and the clerk got a $730 award.

What was the process at work in the mind of the ingenious clerk? His purpose was to reduce the breakage of dishes by the employees, and therefore he had to reach them with some message that would change their behavior. In effect, his key question has to be, "What kind of problem do I have?" Like the man at M.I.T. who responded to the challenge of automation with the realization, "We have a problem in neurology," the clerk had to realize that "I have a problem in communication."

Since his problem belongs "together" with other problems of communications, he can now expect his remedy to be like the remedies others have applied. Almost automatically, the process of association can now bring to his mind a basic communications precept: "Make it visual; make it dramatic." Applied to his circumstances, this means: "Create a visual, dramatic presentation of the high cost of breakage." All that remains is to implement this concept with available materials. Result: an exhibit of the broken dishes with the price tags.

The method of classification has its pitfalls. Improper classification may result in failure. Many an employer, frustrated by poor employee performance, classifies his difficulty as a problem in motivation, when it may well be a problem in employee selection—he has simply hired the wrong people for his kind of work.

Even when a problem has been correctly classified, other dangers may beset the unwary. A classification must be used as a type, not a stereotype. That is to say, a classification does not mean that all the members are identical, but only that they are similar in some respects. However important the similarities may be, there are always some differences that distinguish the members.

Monkeys and men belong in the same classification, mammals, but they are obviously not identical. Because of the similarities, monkeys are useful in testing new drugs, but the findings are not conclusive until they have been tested on human beings.

The method of classification is useful because it spells out relationships among facts, or "togetherness" as Whitehead uses the word. An understanding of any given subject means that you have a grasp of logical groupings, which can be instruments for advancing your thought. Emerson has said: "Nature is an endless combination and repetition of a very few laws. She hums the old well-known air through innumerable variations." Your problem may be one of the variations, but you are on the way to solution if you know the basic melody.

The Key Classification Questions

A successful use of the method of classification requires the asking of these basic questions:

1. Into what class of problems does my problem fall?

2. What are the solutions usually applied to this class of problem?

3. In what respects does my problem conform to the other problems in this class?

4. In what respects does my problem differ from the other problems in this class?

It is the first question among the four that presents the greatest difficulty. Finding the right classification is difficult if you do not already have a broad knowledge of the subject matter. The reason experienced people in a given field come up with quick, sound answers is that they are thoroughly familiar with the existing categories.

When a problem has us baffled, it may be due to either of two difficulties: (1) we may be undecided into which of several classifications our problem falls, or (2) there may seem to be no conceivable classification at all that can contain the problem.

In the former case, we can respond to the situation by testing the several classifications. This means seeking out additional information about each.

The possible classifications themselves tell us what we ought to be looking for. Suppose we suddenly encounter additional expenses—say, because of an increase in our family or because a son is now entering college. The problem, as we define it, may be to earn more money. But such a problem can fall into many classifications:

Is it simply a problem of persuading the boss that we deserve more?

Is it a problem of finding a better-paying job?

Is it a matter of taking on an additional job?

Just by looking at the possible classifications, we have discovered a series of alternatives among which we may choose. Now we are in a position to use the panoramic method, seeking out the characteristics of each classification and projecting the consequences.

Reclassifying the Problem

The most troublesome situation, however, is one in which we simply do not know of a classification into which the problem might fall. It resembles no other problem that we can think of and consequently it has no "togetherness' vis-à-vis other problems. At this point we have to invent or assume a classification—that is, we have to make a hypothesis.

Suppose you are faced with the problem of protecting ships at sea. You consider that this is a problem in observation—you must develop methods of seeing the enemy as he approaches. Your solution, then, is to post men in the crow's nest, equipping them with telescopes and powerful binoculars.

This proves to be fairly effective against approaching battleships. But then the situation changes, and the enemy begins to use submarines. The reach of sight is now too limited, and the submarines can come within range undetected. You are forced to the conclusion that you cannot cope with the situation so long as you consider it *a problem of sighting the enemy visually.*

Now you set up a hypothesis: "If I could hear the enemy submarine while it is still out of sight, I can take timely action." In doing so, you have assigned your problem to a new classification: *problems in hearing.* You explore listening devices which can pick up the sound of a motor or a propeller under water—which is exactly what the U.S. Navy did.

But then as time passes, submarines begin to carry improved, longer-range torpedoes. They become more adept in tactical evasion of depth charges that you fire at them. Now the existing classifications—problems of sighting and problems of hearing—are less productive of answers to your difficulty. So you start out once more to find a new classification, which turns out to be *problems of automatic communications and control.* The result is the development of a torpedo that can be dropped from a plane; it moves slowly in the water until a receiver picks up electronic impulses from the submarine's motor; then it changes its course in the direction of the source; once on target, it picks up speed and races in for the kill.

One reason for the fantastic proliferation of new devices is the increase in technological classifications—our growing mastery over light, sound, magnetic impulses, electronics. New solutions are possible because our classifications, which establish the relatedness of their individual members, also have a relation to each other. Oil constitutes one classification and water another, but both are members of a common classification *fluids.* When Alexander the Great first heard of oil as a "water that burns," he was incredulous. In Mesopotamia he tested it by pouring it over a boy and setting fire to it. In doing so, he proved that he was Alexander the Small; if he were truly great he would have used a model to give him the answer, and would have poured the oil over wood.

The ability to think of your problem as falling into several classifications is the hallmark of a flexible mind. We are constantly confronted with the need to reassign our problems to new categories because the environment in which our problems exist is constantly changing. This is a lesson which Toynbee draws from the history of 5,000 years of human experience. In our own times, we have seen the need for reclassifying our problems, as Toynbee indicates in the simple illustration of what has happened to the highway traffic problem:

> On this road the problems of speed and haulage have been solved, as is testified by the motor-lorry with its train of trucks that comes lumbering along with more than the momentum of a charging elephant and by the sports-car that goes whizzing past with the swiftness of a bee or a bullet. But, by the same token, the problem of collisions has become the traffic problem *par excellence.* Hence on this latter-day road the problem is no longer technological but psychological. The old challenge of physical distance has been transmuted into a new challenge of human relations between drivers who, having learned how to annihilate space, have thereby put themselves in constant danger of annihilating one another.

Such changes in the nature of our problem—that is, in the classification to which they belong—need not take years or decades, as in Toynbee's illustration. It can happen in a matter of moments.

For example, during World War II a young naval officer was brought to the alert by a cry, "Floating mine to starboard." Standard operating procedure offered a solution. Under such circumstances, the practice was to stand off at a sufficient distance and explode the mine by a well-placed shot fired from the deck. To the officer's horror, he saw immediately that the mine was too close to be discharged, and at any moment it would hit his hull. The problem was no longer in the category of withdrawal-and-discharge; fortunately, he realized immediately the nature of the new classification. He ordered his men to turn one of the ship's hoses on the mine, pushing it away from the ship until a shot could be fired. His decision was based on the split-second conclusion that instead of a withdrawal problem he was confronted with a pushing-away problem.

Classifications are vital in problem-solving because they give us a frame of reference within which to operate. They marshal facts into efficient units of thought. The classification method is a valuable instrument where all the essential facts are at hand but need interpretation. In such a case, we must ask ourselves deliberately: "What binds these facts together? What makes a consistent whole of them? What is the significance of this whole?"

This was what the ancient Greeks introduced into the Western world. As Edith Hamilton has said: "Homer's hero who cried for more light even if it were but light to die in, was a true Greek. They could never leave anything obscure. Neither could they leave anything unrelated. System, order, connection, they were impelled to seek for. An unanalyzed whole was an impossible conception for them."

Justice Oliver Wendell Holmes commented on the same thought in words more directly addressed to our own times. To a group of Boston students in 1900, he said, "Your business as thinkers is to see the relation between your particular fact and the framework of the universe." Such a relationship is established through the use of classifications.

3. The Critical-Factor Method

If you can locate the critical factor or factors in your problem, you are within reach of your solution. Such a factor, as Peter F. Drucker has pointed out in *The Practice of Management*, is the element or elements in the situation that have "to be changed before anything else can be changed, moved, or acted upon." Or it may turn out to be an element that has to be newly introduced into the situation to make the change.

In some cases, the critical factors can more properly be called limiting factors—that is, elements in the problem that set the boundaries on potential solutions. Without knowing the limiting factors, we can wander all over the lot, coming up with impossible answers that don't apply at all to the situation confronting us.

Often the critical factor is not a single element but a combination of elements. A given result is not always the product of a single cause but may be due to a series of causes acting simultaneously. In a dice game, the critical factor may be the appearance of the number 7. But that can happen only if two cubes come up in the right combination: a 6 and a 1; a 5 and a 2; a 4 and a 3. If a player could control only one of the cubes, he would still be in danger of losing. Both dice have to be loaded.

In most cases, a problem has not been adequately defined if the statement does not in some way point to the critical factor—the key elements in the problem. As long as the critical factor remains elusive, you must continue to redefine the problem.

Karl Duncker, the psychologist who has specialized in problem-solving, provides an illuminating example in the form of a problem that confronted doctors treating inoperable stomach cancers with X rays. Radioactivity destroys malignant tissue, but unfortunately it also destroys healthy tissue. In treating the tumor, the X rays may do so much damage to normally functioning cells that the patient may die from the treatment before he can benefit from the cure.

The doctors therefore defined the problem in these words: "Given a human being with inoperable stomach tumor, and rays which destroy organic tissue at sufficient intensity, by what procedure can one free him of the tumor by these rays and at the same time avoid destroying the healthy tissue which surrounds it?"

The nub of the situation was the fact that the X rays entering the body had to be strong enough to kill the cancer and would therefore be strong enough to kill whatever they encountered on the way to the cancer. This was the critical factor that had to be changed or acted upon.

The critical factor may take either of two forms: (1) an obstacle to be eliminated from the situation or (2) a condition to be newly created in the situation. The cancer problem falls under the first heading, since the objective was to eliminate or reduce the destructive effect of the X rays on the healthy tissue. (A simple example of a critical factor requiring the introduction of a new condition would be the case of an employer who adds an employee to his staff to correct a falling behind in work schedules.)

Let us continue with the cancer problem. Suppose we need nine units of radiation to destroy the tumor. We can diagram the problem as follows:

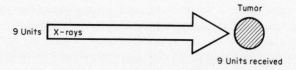

The critical factor, unfortunately, is that the nine units will destroy the healthy tissue all along the path as well as the tumor which is their destination.

Dr. Duncker reconstructs the kind of thinking that led to a solution. The experimenters had quite successfully isolated the critical factor—the factor that had to be changed—and their thoughts could then run along a series of possibilities:

1. Can we send the rays to the stomach through the esophagus, so that they will encounter less tissue on the way?

2. Can we desensitize the healthy tissues by means of a chemical injection?

3. Can we reach the tumor directly by operating?

4. Can we decrease the effect of the rays on the way and increase their effect at the target point, as is done with injections of fluids by a long hypodermic needle?

5. Can we protect the healthy stomach walls by having the patient swallow some inorganic coating material?

6. Can we alter the location of the tumor, bring it nearer to the surface, perhaps by applying pressure?

7. Can we use a cannula—a tubular instrument that doctors introduce into tumors to allow fluids to escape?

8. Can we condition the healthy tissues in some way so as to make them more resistant than the tumor to the radiation?

9. Can we divert, diffuse, or disperse the rays to weaken them at certain points and have them cross at the site of the tumor, thus concentrating the intensity? This was the "jackpot" question that produced the following answer:

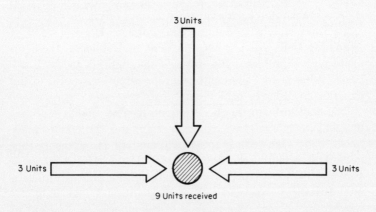

In this way the tissue along the three paths is exposed to only three units, but the tumor receives the full impact of nine.

All of the proposed measures, the successful one and those that proved impractical for various medical reasons, could also have been derived from a persistent application of the classification method. The problem could have been assigned to these three classifications:

1. A problem in the avoidance of contact between the rays and the healthy tissue. Questions 1, 3, 5, 6, and 7 fall under this heading. But these questions proved unanswerable.

2. A problem in desensitizing or immunizing the healthy tissue. Questions 2 and 8 are in this category, but they also were unproductive.

3. A problem in reducing the intensity of the radiation on the way. Question 4 is in this classification, but it was unfruitful because no mechanical method could be found to alter the intensity of the ray once it left the X-ray machine. Question 9, however, did produce a method of varying the radiation—increasing the number of paths through which it moved.

This line of thought reveals a close relationship between the critical-factor method and the classification method. By locating the critical factor you can spot the category that is appropriate to your problem. But the critical-factor method deserves separate consideration because it offers an additional angle from which to examine the problem. Here, instead of beginning with existing classifications and stacking them up against your problem, you direct your attention to the question: "What must I eliminate from the situation or add to the situation in order to achieve my goal?"

The critical-factor method frequently uses models and diagrams. The symbolic presentation eliminates the nonessential, as we have seen—which means eliminating all elements that have no bearing on the critical factor. If the critical factor in your problem is shape, as in aircraft design, you can make a model that is concerned only with shape and take it to the wind tunnel. This is the method of the laboratory. You set up an experiment that will permit you to exclude all elements except the critical factor so that you can manipulate it and determine how it will behave under various circumstances.

Locating the Critical Factor

It is not easy to identify the critical factor precisely because it is surrounded by a great many other noncritical factors. Unless you have an unerring instinct for the critical, you are not likely to approach it in a straight line. The mental pattern is more likely to be in the shape of a whorl, like the lines in a fingerprint. Your mind moves around the problem in a series of uneven circles with ever-narrowing diameters.

You start out with broad questions, which tend to grow more specific as you proceed.

A wartime shipping problem provides an excellent example. For centuries sailors took it for granted that vessels must collect barnacles, periodically be laid up in drydock, and be scraped clean. Someone concentrated on barnacles as the critical factor—the element that had to be eliminated. His solution: Mix poison into the ship paint and kill off the marine life before it can cling to the bottom. As a result, the United States was able to keep thousands of tons of transport in action during World War II. Today the shipping industry saves millions of dollars a year.

In solving this problem the reasoning moved from broad to narrow questions, funnelling down to the critical factor. Here is the process:

Q. How can we increase our shipping?
A. By increasing our use of the available ships.
Q. How can we increase our use of the available ships?
A. By reducing drydock time.
Q. How can we reduce drydock time?
A. By avoiding bottom-scraping.
Q. How can we avoid bottom-scraping?
A. By keeping barnacles from forming.

Now we have discovered the critical factor—the prevention of barnacle formation. Having reached the ultimate point in being specific, we are ready for the payoff questions:

Q. How can we prevent the barnacles from forming?
A. Kill the crustaceans that cause them.
Q. How can we kill the crustaceans?
A. Mix poison with the paint.

The first rule in spotting the critical factor, then, is to force your questions to move from the general to the specific.

A Historical Approach

Another method of approach to the critical factor is to study the history of the problem. Here are some suggestive questions that may help you unearth the answer:

How long has the problem existed? When did it arise and under what circumstances?

Did it generate any other problems? Was it the result of a solution to some other problem?

How much of a problem is it? Has it been more of a problem at some time and less of a problem at other times?

Whom does the problem affect? Who has been affected before and is no longer?

What has been the record of efforts to correct the problem?

Sometimes you have to go a long way back in history to find your critical factor. During the war with Egypt that followed the establishment of the Jewish state, Yigael Yadin, the Israeli general, had to position his men for a military operation. The critical factor involved moving his troops as quickly as possible. This had been a problem for generals through thousands of years, even long before Joshua sounded his trumpets at the gates of Jericho. Yadin, an archeologist in civilian life, knew that Solomon had once confronted the same question and had built roads for his armies and caravans of commerce. Those roads no longer existed, but the archeologist-general reasoned that what had been suitable terrain for a highway then would probably be the best route now. As a student of Biblical archeology, he knew their approximate location. Across the millennia, Solomon's wisdom still shed light on a contemporary critical factor.

Relation to Purpose

The strategy is to select from among the relevant factors in the situation *the ones that are most closely related to your purpose.* In the case of X-ray therapy, all of the nine questions were certainly relevant, but the one that was most relevant to the purpose—preventing damage to the healthy tissue —was the dispersal technique.

Conscious awareness of your purpose itself helps you to recognize the most relevant factor. If you know what you are looking for, you have a better chance to see it. "It's a big, red book," we say, when someone asks us where to find a given volume on the shelves.

It is the purpose itself that makes the factor critical, and the most critical factor is the one most closely related to the purpose. All too many people go searching for the critical factor but fail to keep purpose in mind.

G. K. Chesterton was once asked the trite question about what book he would like to have with him if he were shipwrecked on a desert isle. He did not say the Bible, though he was devoutly religious; nor did he mention Shakespeare, though he was a lover of literature. He answered promptly: "Why, I think above all else I should want a copy of Johnston's Manual of Practical Shipbuilding." He knew that in such a situation, the critical factor would be shipbuilding skill because his purpose would be escape, not edification.

Military Examples

If we fail to find, or if we ignore, the critical factor, we seriously limit our ability to solve the problem. Hitler, for all his mad genius, marched down the road to destruction because he ignored a critical factor in warfare—mobility. Churchill points this out in his monumental history of World War II:

> On June 17, at Margival, near Soissons, Hitler held a conference with Rundstedt and Rommel. His two generals pressed on him strongly the folly of bleeding the German Army to death in Normandy. They urged that before it was destroyed the Seventh Army should make an orderly withdrawal towards the Seine, where, together with the

Fifteenth Army, it could fight a defensive but mobile battle
with at least some hope of success. But Hitler would not
agree. Here, as in Russia and Italy, he demanded that no
ground should be given up and all should fight where they
stood. Hitler's method of fighting to the death on all fronts
at once lacked the important element of selection.

Churchill uses the word selection. What must be selected
out of all the elements is, of course, the critical factor. Julius
Caesar, faced with a situation in which he was surrounded
and besieged, knew he must restore his mobility if he was to
win. He did so by the only means available to him: he had
his troops divert the course of a river to encircle the enemy,
reduce their mobility, and enhance his own.

A similar solution was used by the Russian Cossacks when
they found themselves being beaten by invading nomads,
whose mobility derived from their horsemanship. The Cossacks matched the nomads at their own game by learning to
ride as well, and thereafter won fame as outstanding cavalry-
men. But they went further: they outdid the enemy in mobility by also acquiring skill in navigating rivers.

During the American Civil War the South wreaked havoc
with the Union forces because of greater mobility—until
Grant showed that he could maneuver with startling speed,
sometimes moving so fast that higher echelons had no time
to countermand his plans. On one occasion, knowing that his
superiors favored a static war, he telegraphed General Hal-
leck that he was attacking and cut the wires to forestall the
order forbidding it.

The reluctance to act is often a cover-up for an inability to
see or acknowledge the presence of a critical factor. Even
General Robert E. Lee, who knew the importance of mobile
warfare, sometimes fled from it. At the end of a day of fighting in which he had taken a heavy toll of the northern troops,
he was urged by Stonewall Jackson to administer the coup de
grace with an assault after dark. "They are demoralized!"
said Jackson. "A night attack on them and we have them all."
Lee demurred, on the ground that his men would not be able

to distinguish comrade from foe. Since the critical factor was identification, Jackson offered this answer: "Let us all strip ourselves perfectly naked for identification and then charge them." Lee refused. He was too much the gentleman to undress in the presence even of a critical factor.

In another civil war, thousand of years before, identification also had been a critical factor. It was solved this way: "As an Ephraimite came up, . . . then said they unto him, Say now, Shibboleth; and he said Sibboleth: for he could not frame to pronounce it right. Then they took him, and slew him." In World War II, American GI's in the Pacific used the same technique by asking persons out in the darkness to identify themselves by saying, "Lallapalooza."

People who can spot the critical factor with no delay quite properly win for themselves the title "quick witted." They perceive the important element and address themselves directly to it. Here is an example taken from a United Press dispatch:

> Robert Moore, a repairman, shouted and beat his fists in vain on the six-inch walls of a tavern refrigerator in which he had accidentally locked himself. After 30 minutes of futile effort, Moore got a brilliant idea. He shut off the supply of beer to the bar upstairs. Seconds later the bartender came down to investigate and the shivering Moore was released.

Before he could effect his release, however, he had to know that the critical factor was getting attention. Then he could ask himself, "How can I make my presence known?"

A friend of mine, a salesman, told me of a situation which involved the same critical factor. He had tried to see a company president and had placed as many as 40 telephone calls. "I finally got an appointment and went to keep it. He kept me waiting an hour and a half and then phoned out to say he couldn't make it. I tried again and again but he wouldn't give me another appointment."

Then the salesman read a Western Union advertisement which said that a telegram always gets attention. He knew, however, that a telegram wouldn't be enough unless it included content that merited attention. So he wired the president:

> My product is sponsored by your national association. Whenever I present it to members of your local chapter I am first asked the question, "Has Fred bought it yet?" Apparently your influence is considerable. You could do the association, yourself and me a great favor if we could meet.

He got his appointment—and the order.

Acting on the Critical Factor

Implicit in Peter Drucker's definition of the critical factor are two phases: (1) locating the factor and (2) doing something in relation to it. The first step obviously must come first. "Before you can scratch, you have to know where it itches." By identifying the factor you already have a leg up on the steps that might help.

Fortunately, knowledge itself has consequences. A true understanding of the factor automatically suggests the direction in which the action should be taken because you already know the answer to the question, "What has to be changed if I am to accomplish my purpose?"

Sometimes the only change needed is to nullify the factor. That's what the bellhop in the London hotel did when he made the mistake of entering the bathroom while her ladyship was in the tub. He promptly turned on his heels and said, "Excuse me, your lordship."

A friend once made the usual parental complaint to Winston Churchill: his son, away at school, wasn't writing to him. "That's easy," said Churchill. "Tell him you're enclosing a five-pound note and forget to put it in." Perfectly obvious: to get a person to write, give him a reason.

On a more serious level was the revolutionary action taken by "the father of Turkish democracy." Kemal Ataturk knew that the critical factor in modernizing his country was to break the grip of the past. He simply passed a law requiring that all books be printed in the Latin alphabet. This shut off the younger generation almost completely from the old culture without necessitating a burning of the books.

Great men often have an intuitive skill in locating the critical factor and perceiving immediately how it can be changed. But for most of us it is a laborious process. As affairs become more complex, consisting of enormous quantities of data, we may have to call in specialists who can ferret out the critical factors.

Today this function is carried out on scientific, governmental, and business levels by men who have been trained in a method called "operations research." They have at their disposal mathematical and statistical techniques which bring the critical factors into so clear a focus that they point directly to a solution. Here, for example, is a typical problem that such specialists have worked on:

A department store does considerable business in C.O.D. orders. As a result of ads, customers will phone in orders. While the C.O.D. business on the whole is profitable, thousands of dollars are lost because some of the customers refuse to accept the goods on arrival and the packages are returned unopened. The company, meanwhile, is out of pocket because of the handling costs, the record-keeping, the two-way delivery charges, breakage en route, the loss of the order itself. What can it do?

I have presented this problem to hundreds of people in management classes and executive development seminars. The discussion usually runs along these lines:

"Cut out the C.O.D. orders." But that means eliminating the profitable C.O.D. orders because of the unprofitable ones.

"Require the customer to put down a deposit." But that would eliminate telephone orders, since no deposit can be paid over the phone.

"Raise the price on C.O.D. items to offset the losses." But higher prices might reduce the total volume of business.

...ach false starts, someone may say: "Wait a
...rying to solve the problem before we've found

...unt begins for the critical factor—the element in
...on that has to be changed if the losses are to be
. The group turns its attention to the data-producing
...ns that might reveal the critical factor. After a while
...ave the following items listed on the blackboard:

...In what price range are the rejected items?" (Maybe
...ice is the critical factor.)

"In what categories are the rejected items?" (Hardware,
clothing, etc.)

"Is there any particular combination of items that is more
often rejected than others?"

"Do the rejected items tend to be ordered from certain
areas of the city?" (The inference is that certain economic
classes might be responsible for the rejects.)

"Does the way we deliver the items—by parcel post or by
our own trucks—make a difference in the acceptance or rejection of the order?"

"Do the rejected orders tend to be items ordered in response to advertising?"

"Does the lapse of time taken in delivering the item make
a difference in the frequency of rejection?"

In actual fact, the last question proved to be the critical
one. The operations research men who had been retained by
the company spent many weeks collecting statistics on all of
the above possibilities. The figures showed clearly that the
longer the interval between the placing of the order and its
delivery to the customer, the greater the likelihood that it
would be refused. It was demonstrated mathematically that
the critical period was five days. If delivery could not be
made before then, it simply did not pay to send out the item.

Now the necessary action was clear: If you can't fill the
order in five days, don't fill it at all. The company thereupon
adopted practices to implement the policy. The shipping department was instructed to give priority to C.O.D. orders. If

the order could not go out on time, no matter what the reason—shortage of help, misplacement of the order, failure of the supplier to deliver—a postcard would be sent to the customer reading: "Due to the great demand for the item you ordered, we have run out of stock. We regret that you have been inconvenienced. If you still wish to purchase it, please reorder." The company then had another five-day period in which to meet the request.

Again, the significant element is that the critical factor, once it has been identified, points to the remedial action.

But notice one very important point about all of the cases I have described. When the critical factor has been identified, the action taken has to be commensurate with its magnitude. In air travel, for example, weight is a critical factor. An airline, inviting opinions from its passengers, once received this suggestion: "Remove the pits from the dinner olives before each take-off."

Always remember that the action you decide on must make an appreciable difference in altering or eliminating the critical factor.

4. *The Method of Innovation*

In the history of the human race, the most dramatic solutions have been those that emerged from a flat rejection of existing premises. The pre-requisite is intellectual daring. Old frames of reference must be shattered, and new ones built.

The process is painful because you must be willing to strike out into completely unexplored territory, with no knowledge of the dangers that lie ahead. But the most painful part of the process is that you must challenge your own knowledge. You must be prepared to answer the sometimes frustrating question that Morris Raphael Cohen, the great philosophy teacher at the City College of New York, used to put to his students: "I know that everybody knows it, but how do *you* know it?" When you begin to ask yourself that question, you discover that the world is a haven of wrong answers but also a port of embarkation for new and better ones.

The Mind of Henry Ford

Father H. L. Bruckberger, the French scholar and priest, in his book, *Image of America,* singles out Henry Ford as the great innovator who contributed much to the "second American revolution"—the development of a society in which new premises went to work for the first time in world history. Despite his obscurantism in many fields of culture, Ford was able to shatter old premises and install new ones.

All about him, in existing factories, Ford saw men moving about from place to place in order to produce goods. Do you want to step up output? Instead of bringing the man to the work, said Ford, bring the work to the man—and he created the automobile assembly line.

In the matter of price and profit, Ford found most businessmen solving their pricing problems by calculating their costs and then adding a margin of profit. No, he said, cost is not the starting point in pricing.

> Our policy is to reduce the price, extend the operations, and improve the article. You will notice that the reduction of price comes first. We have never considered any costs as fixed. Therefore we first reduce the price to the point where we believe more sales will result. Then we go ahead and try to make the prices. The new price forces the costs down. The more usual way is to take the costs and then determine the price. . . . What earthly use is it to know the cost if it tells you that you cannot manufacture at a price at which the article can be sold? But more to the point is the fact that, although one may calculate what a cost is, and of course all of our costs are carefully calculated, no one knows what a cost ought to be. One of the ways of discovering . . . is to name a price so low as to force everybody in the place to the highest point of efficiency. The low price makes everybody dig for profits. We make more discoveries concerning manufacturing and selling under this forced method than by any method of leisurely investigation.

Ford's systematic practice of standing things on their head and coming up with better answers made it necessary for him to fight the prevailing premises of his time. Even in the matter of making money he was unorthodox, and some of his stockholders—including the Dodge brothers, who founded a competitive company because of their differences with Ford —brought suits against him.

Ford decided to buy out the stockholders and as a result found himself faced with the possibility of extinction. His working capital was down to a minimum, in part because he was also caught in the post-World War I depression. But again he solved his problem by reversing the traditional premises.

At the beginning of 1921 his back was against the wall. His bank account was $20 million, but in less than four months he would have to meet obligations amounting to $58 million. He adopted a series of dazzling steps, the most daring of which was to reduce his working capital further by investing in fixed capital. He bought a railroad for $5 million!

His plan was to use it "in such a way as to reduce the time required in processing and transporting his materials, so that he could henceforth reduce his inventory by one third, thus freeing 28 million dollars of capital." Less than three months later, as a result of this and equally decisive actions, he had $87 million in the bank. All because he had the resilience to challenge the convential assumption that you don't spend money on more fixed capital when you don't have enough working capital.

Principle of "Tamar Verkehrt"

Obviously, the secret of Ford's successful thinking lay in his ability to reverse gears and change his direction completely. Dr. Abraham Myerson, the neurologist and psychiatrist, discussing this principle in his brilliant and charming book, *Speaking of Man,* says: "The ancient Jewish scholars had a name for it; they called it *'Tamar verkehrt,'* which means that turning things upside down may bring as satisfactory results in the seeking of truth as logic itself." In effect, the Talmudists would develop a line of reasoning, and would then say, "But suppose we deny our premises, what conclusions will result?"

Take the case of the railroad that was stuck in its own tracks. In the freight yards, traffic was becoming congested because switch engines had to start up, move up, and back up to get from one set of rails to another. On the basis of the accepted railroad premises, everything in a railroad yard just has to move on rails.

But one of the engineers on the Pennsylvania Railroad had the wit to ask himself: "*Tamar verkehrt?* Suppose we turn things around and assume that it doesn't have to be done on tracks. Suppose we think about removing the switch engine from the tracks altogether." With the help of the Le Tourneau-Westinghouse Company, he put the switch engine on huge, rubber-tired wheels that could cross the tracks as well as ride them.

This approach can be called "the principle of reverse gear."

From examining a whole series of cases in which it has been used, I come to the conclusion that there are at least four different ways of accomplishing reverse thinking. They involve asking these questions of your problem:

1. *Can I turn my premises upside down?* This requires some formal restatement of the problem, which may at first glance seem ridiculous. What is needed is a tolerance for the absurd.

For instance, immediately after the attack on Pearl Harbor, where the Japanese bombers destroyed U.S. planes on the ground, American Air Force engineers were ordered to concentrate on the problem "What's the quickest way to get airplanes out of the hangars?" They introduced some improvements until it seemed that no further progress could be made. Then someone refused to accept the basic premise of the problem as stated. He turned the question upside down, and asked, "How can we get the hangar away from the planes?"

The result was a 172-foot diamond-shaped hangar that can be separated at the widest part of the diamond. Each section is mounted on wheels that are powered to move the sections of the hangar away from each other at a speed of 35 miles an hour. When the call comes to the pilots for a "scramble," instead of the planes being pulled out of the hangar one by one, every plane is in a position to move simultaneously to the runways.

Some of the questions and statements that can help you turn your problem upside down are:

"What if this were reversed?"

"If it's horizontal, suppose it were vertical (and vice versa)."

"If it's long, suppose it were short; if high, low; if narrow, wide (and vice versa)."

"If it's inside, suppose it were outside."

"If it's on top, suppose it were on the bottom."

"Does it have to be this way?"

"Suppose it didn't have to be this; could it be that?"

"Does it really have to be done here; why not there?"

"Could somebody else do it, instead of the people who have always done it?"

"It's always been this way, but suppose nobody had done it before; how would I start?"

At the U.S. Army's Watertown, Massachusetts, Arsenal, the engineers decided to do things backwards and see what results were produced. They found a way to produce better guns by firing armor plate at projectiles, instead of the other way round. Reversing the normal procedure gave them a better way to measure the strain and impact of a shell.

2. *Can I tear it apart and rearrange it?* People who deal with manufacturing problems or with questions of design use this approach effectively. General Electric Company developed a program called Value Analysis, which many other companies are also using to solve the cost-reduction problem.

They take a product, break it down into its components, arrange it item by item on a "bread-board" or a peg-board for critical examination, and explore its value to determine whether its cost is justified. The same approach can be adapted to solving abstract problems as well as physical ones.

Here are examples of the type of question asked by the problem-solver engaged in "tearing it apart":

"What are the different parts of the problem?"

"Is any one of them the key to another part?"

"Do I have to change any of the parts?"

"What if I changed the size, making it larger, wider, thicker, smaller, thinner?"

"What if I changed timing, making it faster or slower?"

"What if I changed the sequence?"

"What if I changed the form—to liquid, powder, solid, paste; to rod, tube, triangle, cube?"

"Suppose I transpose cause and effect?"

Professor Robert Crawford of the University of Nebraska illustrates the rearrangement approach by showing what can be done with a common picture frame:

> Shape: usually rectangular, but could it be round, elliptical, continuous like a mural, three-dimensional like a shadow box?
> Material: often wood, but can't we use aluminum, glass built into the wall, plastic, plaster, or even no frame at all?
> Covering: normally glass, but how about lucite, or any clear plastic, or a shade, or nothing at all?
> Support: in most cases wire and hooks, but why not have a brace hinged or fixed on the back, or have the frame simply rest on a narrow shelf?

Herbert Kondo, writing in the *Scientific American*, tells how Michael Faraday discovered the principle of the electric generator by deliberately transposing cause and effect:

> But an irrepressible idea remained on his mind. If an electric current could yield magnetism, could not a magnet produce electricity? In 1824 and again in 1825 he tried to induce current in a wire by placing a magnet near it, but

these attempts failed. He did not yet appreciate the central importance of motion in the phenomena that Oersted had demonstrated. It was the motion of the electric current in the wire that produced magnetism. To obtain the reverse effect the magnet had to be moved in relation to the conductor.

On August 29, 1831, he began to see light. "I am busy just now again on electro-magnetism," he wrote, "and I think I have got hold of a good thing, but can't say. It may be a weed instead of a fish that, after all my labor, I may at last have pulled up." On October 17, 1831, he had the answer and produced the generator. He had pulled up a treasure from the ocean of nature.

3. *What would happen if I abandoned my basic beliefs about the problem?* John Arnold, professor of creative engineering at Massachusetts Institute of Technology, says: "We're afraid to 'fantasy.' We don't look often enough for the weird solution." To open up new horizons for his students, Professor Arnold set up what he called the "Arcturus laboratory." His students had to assume that they live on a mythical planet, Arcturus. There no normal frame of reference is permitted. The pull of gravity is eleven times that of earth, the atmosphere consists only of marsh gas, temperature ranges from 122° to 230°F., and so on. Under these conditions, the students are forced to solve various engineering problems.

Thinking in this new, and unreal, frame of reference often produces madcap and unworkable suggestions. But the ultimate result is a habit of producing ideas that are practical right here on earth—for example, a powerful tractor with two engines, one for each track; a typewriter that can manipulate 4,000 symbols; surgical instruments that fit over the fingertips, instead of being held in the hand, and that can probe into the heart valve itself.

Similarly, by transporting yourself to your own personal Arcturus, you can get useful answers out of questions like these:

"If I could forget all specifications, how could the basic function be performed?"

"What led people to accept the conventional premises, and how have conditions changed since then?"

"What if I carry my thinking to extremes at either end of the spectrum of available possibilities?"

"Suppose I ignore some of the elements in my problem and exaggerate the weight I give to others?"

"Suppose I didn't have this limiting factor in my situation, what would I do? And what can I do to alter the limiting factor?"

George Santayana, the philosopher, was able to develop many original thoughts because he too had his own personal Arcturus:

> All my life I have dreamt of travels, possible and impossible; travels in space and travels in time, travels into other bodies and alien minds. Not having been suffered by fate to be more than an occasional tripper and tourist, I have taken my revenge in what might be called travels of the intellect, by admitting the opposite of all facts and of all beliefs to be equally possible and no more arbitrary.

Many of the things we now take for granted were the result of the fact that at some point in history somebody was not content with the usual assumptions. The ancient Babylonian conqueror and law-giver won for himself the name of Hammurabi-nukhush-nishi, Hammurabi the Abundance of the People, because he knew how to reverse the usual premises. Instead of having the people go and fetch their water, he brought the water to the people by building canals.

The most world-shaking solutions to human problems are those achieved by thinkers who are willing to test the wisdom of the Psalmist: "The stone which the builders rejected, the same is become the head of the corner."

5. *The Adaptation Method*

This method is based on the simple fact that you can use the experience of others to solve your problems. It is frequently applied in business. The coal industry in the United States, for example, has been suffering as a result of the competition of oil as a fuel. Because the movement of oil through pipelines is cheaper than transportation by railroad, coal is at a disadvantage. To solve their problem, coal operators are now thinking along these lines: "If we could ship coal like oil through a pipeline, our costs will come down and we'll be able to compete." As a result, the industry has developed a method of converting coal into a liquid called "slurry," which can be pumped through a pipeline and, on arrival at its destination, can be reconverted into a solid.

In a competitive society it is standard operating procedure for men to borrow from their competitors' experience. But since their circumstances are never really identical, they must usually make some adaptations of their own. Whoever borrows lock, stock, and barrel, without regard to his own conditions, may find himself firing a weapon that explodes in his hands.

Some people, however, congenitally resist the ideas of others and will not even attempt to make adaptations. They say, "My problem is different" and insist on letting the differences obscure the similarities. The practitioners of adaptation are those who can (1) discern the similarities and (2) make adjustments to compensate for the differences.

Man stands at a higher level than the animals because he has been able to observe their experience and apply it to his own problems. The sheep, for example, was equipped with wool as a solution to the problem of cold. To keep warm, man borrowed the solution and the sheep's wool with it. He adapted the idea of a wool covering, wrapping the sheep's skin, wool and all, around his own body. Then he made a further adaptation by just taking the wool: he sheared the sheep and wove the fleece into cloth.

In the process of adaptation, we take the experience of others but manipulate it in our own way for our own purposes. Samson used the jawbone of an ass to articulate his point of view to the Philistines; he did not use the jawbone to express an ass's ideas. Whenever you borrow somebody else's techniques, make sure you focus your attention on your purpose, not his.

Likenesses and Differences

Adaptation requires that you see relationships—how your problem is like and unlike the situation from which you are borrowing. In so doing, you must

1. compare,
2. contrast,
3. look for causes and effects,
4. associate items that may be the product of the same or similar causes,
5. juxtapose (simply put items alongside each other, whether or not they seem related),
6. combine,
7. add,
8. subtract,
9. rate (that is, assign relative values),
10. check consequences, and
11. trace back the history of comparable experiences.

All eleven processes play a part in bringing critical judgment to bear on your own and others' experience. Experience alone is not enough. Industry often goes wrong because of the way it looks at experience. We ask a job applicant how many years he has worked in previous jobs rather than what he has learned from them. There is a vast difference between *exposure* to experience and *learning* from it. Unevaluated experience is itself a hazard to problem-solving. It leads us to say, "I've been doing it this way for 17 years, so there's no reason to change now."

As a matter of fact, we do not really understand an experience unless we are capable of adapting it, just as we do not really understand a passage in a book unless we are able to express it in our own words. Duncker says:

> To the same degree to which a solution is understood, it can be transposed, which means that under altered conditions it may be changed correspondingly in such a way as to preserve its functional value. For one can transpose a

solution only when one has grasped its functional value, its general principle, i.e., the invariants from which, by introduction of changed conditions, the corresponding variations of the solution follow each other.

In other words, we must first *recognize the general principle represented by the solution* if we are to apply it effectively to our set of circumstances. An example of this kind of transplanting of experience is the automobile mechanic who took his son to the dentist. Watching the dentist explore the youngster's mouth with the aid of a small light attached to the dental probe, the mechanic suddenly saw the possibility of solving his own problem in getting at dark areas under the auto hood. Borrowing the *general* idea, he made his *particular* adaptation by combining a small flashlight with a screwdriver.

Every professional—whether a doctor, a lawyer, a teacher, a minister—makes systematic use of accumulated experience. But nobody has such a keen interest in the organized use of past experience as the student of history. The historian Will Durant was once asked how he could write so massive a work as his *Story of Civilization*. He answered:

> I accumulate around 30,000 notes for each volume. It's what I call "Operation Theft." You can't write history out of your imagination. You have to find out what happened. . . . When the research is done, "Operation Theft" ends and "Operation Sweat" begins.

This is almost a formula for solving problems by adaptation:

Operation Theft involves developing careful habits of collecting experiences and storing them away for future use. Or it may mean deliberately going out to learn how other people who had problems similar to your own handled their difficulties.

Operation Sweat involves summoning up the relevant experience, identifying how it relates to your situation, and modifying it to meet your own specific needs.

Sometimes the process of combining elements out of past

experience requires that we proceed in several phases. Even a chimpanzee is capable of a two-step adaptation. Suppose he wants to get a banana that is beyond his reach. Within range of his arm is a short stick, not long enough to reach the banana. But within reach of the short stick is a longer stick that could make contact with the banana. He solves his problem with a double adaptation. He lengthens his arm with the short stick and draws to himself the longer one. Then he makes the completely satisfactory adaptation of his arm by using the long stick to reach the banana.

The successful use of the method of adaptation depends on a willingness to explore these two basic questions with equal thoroughness:

1. In what is our problem *like* the other case?
2. In what way is it different?

Just as some people can see only the differences and therefore discard the available solution, so others see only the resemblances and misapply the potential answer.

For example, a company that had long prospered by manufacturing laboratory glassware started to turn out cheap, ornamental glass parts. The executives were astonished when they found they were losing money due to excessive production costs. They had assumed their experience in producing expensive glass could simply be transferred to the cheaper line with the same efficiency. On investigating, they learned that their veteran craftsmen, accustomed to quality control procedures, had carried them over to the new, less demanding products, and that the purchasing department was still buying the same high-quality materials that were once essential. Failure to adapt their practices to the new circumstances —that is, the failure to recognize the differences—had produced substantial loss.

Approach as Well as System

In this chapter, I have discussed different types of solutions. In reality, they are simply different methods of arriving at the same result—namely, the achievement of the purpose inherent in your definition of the problem.

While I have necessarily discussed them as if they were sharply differentiated, the problem-solving mind in search of solutions cruises in and out among them. A line of thought that begins by examining the panorama of alternatives may find itself moving into the realm of innovation; what has been a search among classifications may settle down to an analysis of a critical factor; in the course of innovating or in exploring a novel adaptation the problem-solver may find himself reviewing possible classifications from which he may draw the answer he needs.

[11]

THE PROBLEM-SOLVING ATTITUDE

IN THE EARLY DAYS of the automobile, two inventors developed a car that operated on steam. It was efficient and economical. Old-car enthusiasts still remember the Stanley Steamer with more than nostalgic regret.

The Stanleys, twin brothers, worked long hours, at top speed, with the aid of expert helpers. But they never turned out more than 650 cars a year and never caught up with their competitors. Why did they fail?

They couldn't delegate; they couldn't use other people's ideas or experience; they couldn't accept the new principle of mass production. Until each car had been checked by one of the brothers personally, it would not be sold. It any technical problem developed in one of their products and a customer complained about a defective part, the twin who handled the situation promptly returned the man's money, refusing to listen to the details. "Give back the car," he would say, "we don't want your kind riding in it."

The Stanley Steamer, as the Broadway columnists would say, went ph-t-t-t! The business died.

A State of Mind

Nothing was wrong with their engineering skill. What was wrong was their problem-solving attitude. Finding solutions to problems is more than logic and scientific method. You must be able to put aside old ideas and habits without paying too high an emotional cost. As psychologists put it, you must be *open to experience*.

All of us have a tendency to shut out some facts encountered in our experience. Even our modern-day belief in scientific method has led us to refuse scientific examination to some possibly relevant data. If we mistrust the source, we refuse to look at the idea. If we do not like the package, we throw away the content. We jeer at "old wives' tales" and refuse to investigate them. But Dr. William Withering did not allow the "unscientific source" to deter him from looking sympathetically at an old Shropshire grandmother brewing foxglove tea. The result was his discovery of digitalis for the treatment of heart disease. As a true scientist, he could remain open to experience.

In these pages, we have met men of all kinds and in all fields who succeeded in solving problems—scientists, businessmen, inventors, statesmen, generals, writers and artists, philosophers, humble workmen engaged in the daily tasks of earning a living, housewives dealing with their children. If we ask ourselves, "What personal qualities did they bring to bear on their problems?" we find these common characteristics:

1. Flexibility—a tolerance for living with the unknown and with gaps in their own knowledge

2. Realism—an ability to compromise, to accept small gains, to utilize the slight edge that makes the big difference

3. A sense of time—a factor all too often ignored in the formulae advocated by "experts" on thinking

Let us look at each in some detail.

1. *Flexibility*

We feel safer with the old; therefore we spurn the new. And cold logic is our justification. After all, what is old and has survived has proved its workability. The probabilities are on its side. Why run the risk of the unproved? Consequently, we cling to the familiar.

At the age of 32, Edison became a nationally known figure because he alone had solved the problem of the electric light. Everybody else had tried to get light out of a current by *reducing* the resistance of the electrical conductors. But Edison refused to follow in their tracks. He wanted to know what would happen if you *increased* the resistance. The others insisted on studying the effects of leading the current through a filament surrounded by air; he tried it in a vacuum.

"I start where the last man left off," he said in later years. Because he was willing to try the untried, as one biographer wrote, he "had the penetration to seize the relationship of facts and principles, and the art to reduce them to novel and concrete combinations."

Edison had the two basic qualities of flexibility: (1) the ability to tolerate, even have an affection for, the unknown; and (2) the ability to recognize that the unknown is all around us, even in the most familiar things.

In a study of the lives of outstanding problem-solvers, Dr. A. H. Maslow concludes that they have a special "relationship with the unknown." They are "uniformly unthreatened and unfrightened by the unknown. . . . They accept it, are comfortable with it, and often are even *more* attracted by the unknown. They not only tolerate the ambiguous and unstructured: they like it."

Einstein is the foremost example of such individuals. He felt that "the most beautiful thing we can experience is the mysterious. It is the source of all true art and science. He to whom this emotion is a stranger, who can no longer pause to wonder and stand rapt in awe, is as good as dead; his mind and eyes are closed."

The ability to live with the mysterious is essential if we are to develop the sense of tentativeness that marks the flexible mind. Men who possess this quality can take their generalizations—precious as they are and should be—and treat them as merely "the most convenient way of ordering these facts," to use Conant's words. They can use hypotheses for what they are, arrows on the signposts that tell them not where to go but where to look. Those who cannot tolerate uncertainty remain at the signposts.

Tolerance of the unknown is a powerful quality because it helps us postpone solution and thus avoid the unsound solutions that come to mind first. The record of failure is long because of the impatience of would-be problem-solvers who had to rush to a destination, any destination, even if it was not theirs.

Two elements seem to characterize the flexible mind: first, it is quick to recognize changes in the environment; second, it responds to the new picture with changed responses. But the ultimate in flexibility is the capacity to keep reviewing your present premises even in the absence of changes in your environment; otherwise, you remain in the old grooves. Most of us, however, do need stimulation from our environment to get us to change. Hence the value of exposing ourselves to new situations, new places, new people, new books.

Problem-Centered or Solution-Centered?

A cardinal attitude in problem-solving is to *remain problem-centered rather than solution-centered.* "Here is where ordinary thinking and thinking that is scrupulous diverge from each other," says John Dewey in his book *The Quest for Certainty.* "The natural man is impatient with doubt and suspense: he impatiently hurries to be shut of it. A disciplined mind takes delight in the problematic, and cherishes it until a way is found that approves itself upon examination."

Because we chafe under the touch of the unknown, we leap to the first answers that occur to us. Every teacher knows that if he puts a problem to the class, most of his students will immediately offer answers; the thoughtful minority put off answering until they have first had a chance to analyze the difficulties. "*Describe* before you *prescribe*," says Irving J. Lee. Therapy should not come before diagnosis.

We are all aware that a given culture will produce a certain type of common-denominator solutions. That is because we take the first materials that come to hand as the stuff with which to build. If we live in forested lands, our temples will be made of wood. But if, as the Greeks did, we dwell on a hard, stony soil, we are more likely to build of marble.

In short, we allow our immediate environment to dictate

our solutions, instead of letting a concentration on the problem lead us to the best answer. Why did the British forge ahead of the United States in ocean travel? Not only because they lived on an island. Americans also lived on the shores of the Atlantic, and they too developed vessels. But they focused on the paddle steamer, which was ideally suited for the great rivers and inland waterways, ignoring the screw propeller, which was more efficient for ocean travel.

Frustration and Hostility

Not only do we rush to accept the immediate, but our unwillingness to suspend decision and stay with the problem leads us to look for devils to blame. Preoccupation with the search for the demon blinds us to the real cause of the difficulty. Problem-solving then becomes problem-evasion. We find a villain to shoot at, and by sighting on him we avoid the harder task of aiming at the problem.

Some of us have so low a tolerance for problems *per se* that we respond immediately to their existence by becoming hostile. Instead of looking for the solution, we devote ourselves instead to a search for what Dr. Fritz Roethlisberger at Harvard calls the double s.o.b.—the "spherical son-of-a-bitch—the son of a bitch from every angle."

Tolerance for the unknown is important because deferred solution may otherwise create frustration which ultimately turns to hostility. In experiments conducted in Harvard's psychological laboratories, a group of students were given problems to solve. Their work was timed, but they weren't told that the problems actually couldn't be solved at all. Trying hard, and failing continually, the unfortunate subjects became highly frustrated, and then very aggressive. Some of them, being naturally bolder, expressed their hostility directly to the psychologists. But many others, unable to make an open display, turned on their fellow workers, and some even on themselves.

Many people suffer from an inability to tolerate the presence of "contradictory facts." Their minds must immediately reject one or the other, instead of exploring ways to make them compatible. Saadi, the Persian poet, said: "Ten dervishes can sleep on one rug, but two kings cannot be accomodated in the same kingdom." The flexible mind, however, can keep two rival ideas in mind without suffering emotional stress. In fact, the awareness of contradiction is itself a revelation that fruitful discoveries and potential solutions are just under the surface.

To the effective problem-solver the realization that facts don't fit is a welcome discovery. It serves notice that a frame of reference may have to be changed. Or it may be a portent that other facts are buried nearby and should be unearthed. Or it may be like the clicking of a Geiger counter, warning that dangerous material is in the vicinity.

Mental Rigidity Test

The flexible mind is energetic, and does not fear the long way round. Yet it is likely to be more direct and get to the point much faster than the rigid mind. Psychologists who devise tests for mental rigidity rely on a fairly simple principle: expose an individual to a series of problems that require a complicated method of solution; then subject him to the same type of problem that requires only a simple solution. The mentally rigid will almost invariably insist on staying with the complicated method. Here, for example, is a simple version of such a test:

"What does M-A-C-T-A-V-I-S-H spell?" The answer usually given is, "MacTavish."

"What does M-A-C-D-O-N-A-L-D spell?" the answer: "MacDonald."

"What does M-A-C-H-I-N-E-R-Y spell?" The rigid, preconditioned mind replies, "MacHinery," particularly if the questioner has been careful to pause after the C in each case. The more flexible mind, of course, is alert to spot the word promptly.

In these cases, the rigid mind is trapped by its own laziness. A pattern has been created, and, rather than engage in fresh thinking, it moves along the familiar route of assuming that Scotch names are being spelled out.

The rigid mind, eager to escape the work of thought, is glad to rely solely on precedent or past practice. But its dependence on authority is worse than laziness. A man may be lazy and yet not steal, but the slave of authority does no intellectual work of his own and merely lives by seizing on the product of others. It is no sin to use the work of another, provided one pays for it with some coin that he himself has earned. The slavish plagiarism that takes another's thought without thinking is an offense punished by a heavy sentence: imprisonment in the past and banishment from the present.

There are some people who think that an idea is to be rated like wine: the older, the better. The resort to antiquity's cellar may yield vinegar as often as it produces wine. Vinegar has its uses—and the citation of authorities too can add flavor to one's intellectual cooking. Authority may be symbolized by that literary device, the footnote, which is all too often dedicated to the proposition that nothing is true without the say-so of another scholar. If nothing can be learned except from our predecessors, from whom did they learn?

The Essence of Flexibility

Affirmatively, what are the characteristics of the man with the flexible mind?

He is open to experience, receptive to what is new.

In the seemingly unrelated, he looks for possible relationships.

He finds similarities in the dissimilar, and differences in the similar.

He uses generalizations but is aware of exceptions; he knows also that obsession with exceptions can paralyze action.

He can turn his back on the familiar and risk association with the strange.

Because he is truly decisive, he can decide to postpone solution until he has completed analysis.

He does not ignore the probable because of the possible; yet he does not overlook the long shot because everybody is betting on the favorite.

He welcomes the unknown, knowing it conceals opportunities.

2. *Realism*

The desire for dramatic solutions is one of the greatest enemies of solution. People who are continually looking for the nonexistent "one big chance" overlook the hundred little chances that do come their way. In the real world, the crash program is rarely the answer.

> A successful individual typically sets his next goal *somewhat, but not too much,* above his last achievement, [wrote Dr. Kurt Lewin, who founded the Research Center of Group Dynamics at Massachusetts Institute of Technology]. In this way he steadily raises his level of aspiration. Although in the long run he is guided by his ideal goal, which may be rather high, nevertheless his real goal for *the next step is kept realistically close to his present position.*

Problem-solving I have said at the outset, begins with purpose. But to define your purpose in illusory terms is to reduce yourself to purposelessness. In handling our problems, we are more likely to find the available answer if we are content to play for the slight edge.

In every competitive field, it is incontrovertible that the successful individual is really only somewhat better than his rival. Research has demonstrated that the margin of difference between making the grade and falling behind is statistically very small. And this is true both in physical and intellectual accomplishment. Where large gaps seemingly exist between the best and the worst, they are due primarily to an accumulation of small advantages.

To be sure, while the differences that produce success or

failure are small, the consequences are big. The small amount of heat from a lighted match won't raise the temperature much by itself, but it can set fire to a whole house.

One of the most impressive facts about problem-solving that I have ever encountered is to be found in a rather technical book called *The Range of Human Capacities* by Dr. David Wechsler, chief psychologist in the Psychiatric Division of New York City's Bellevue Hospital, and inventor of the famous Wechsler-Bellevue Intelligence Test which has been administered by the U.S. Army to millions of draftees. In strictly scientific and statistical terms, he reports that

the differences which separate the mass of mankind from one another, with respect to any or all of their abilities, are small. . . . As compared with other ratios or orders of differences met with in nature, they are pitifully insignificant.

In a world where forces, velocities and distances exist, which are thousands, nay millions of times as great as those of any others with which they may be compared, one cannot, except by sheer arbitrariness, fail to accede that the differences met with in human beings are anything but insignificant. One need not turn to astronomy for contrasting examples; the realm of living things teems with illustrations. How small are the variations in human stature compared with those to be found in the heights of trees, the differences in the physical strength amongst men when compared with that of the elephant, or of his speed of locomotion when matched with the flight of birds. . . .

But, as Dr. Wechsler points out, the small differences that do exist within the range of human capacities produce big effects:

The difference between 5 feet 11 inches and 6 feet 0 inches is admittedly small, but the ability to jump this extra inch may save a man's life.

A cosmic example of the big difference that results from the slight edge can be found in space science. Arthur C. Clarke gives this explanation of why the United States failed in its first moon probes while the Russians succeeded:

To escape completely from the earth's gravitational field, a rocket must attain a speed which, in round figures, is 25,000 miles an hour. At a fraction less than this speed it must fall back to earth. At a fraction more, it has attained the freedom of space. The first Army and Air Force shots missed the crucial figure by only about 2 percent—but that was enough. Then came the Russian moon probe, which beat it by about the same slim margin—and that was enough to take it not merely to the moon but, at the extreme end of its orbit around the sun, more than 200,000,000 miles from earth, or almost 1,000 times as far away as the moon.

So, too, in solving day-to-day problems, we must be able to recognize that the line between successful solution and failure may be a hairsbreadth. It may take only a slight change in the critical factor to produce the answer we want. For a pugilist, the critical factor is speed, but all he needs is split-second superiority over his opponent.

Small Gains vs. the Jackpot

The genuine problem-solving attitude makes it possible for us to concentrate on the small things that ultimately make the big difference. Successful businessmen know this. A Swiss executive visiting the United States told me proudly that he and his fellow countrymen apply the slight-edge principle in their foreign trade policy. Swiss watchmakers don't rely on cheaper price to gain a big trading advantage over their competitors in world markets. Nor do they rely on lower labor costs, as the Japanese have done. Instead, they turn out a *somewhat* better product so that they can charge a *much* better price. A small margin of superior quality brings back a proportionately much larger reward.

The problem-solving perceptiveness of the man who plays for the small gain is illustrated by the case of the foreman who was trying to improve his department's output. While others might have attempted to raise the production of the poor producers, he focused on the better men. Employee A turned out 10 units a day; Employee B, 50 units. He knew that a 5 per cent increase in B's output would give him more than a 10 per cent increase in A's production.

But our natural tendency is to go for the jackpot. There's a cultural reason for this, at least in the United States. In pioneer communities, with open frontiers, the big killing was a real possibility. If things were going badly on the little farm, a man could hitch up a covered wagon and go West, where cheap and extensive land awaited him. This psychology lingers on today, even though the geographical frontiers have disappeared.

To be sure, there are cases when you have to "go for broke," as the gamblers express it. In a sudden crisis, when time is lacking, you cannot solve your problem with small improvements. But usually, even when the critical factor looms large, you can make more headway by trying for small but possible gains.

What you do is to establish a series of realistic subgoals that will ultimately bring you to the accomplishment of the long-range purpose. For example, to keep abreast of the industry's growth, a company needed a 10 per cent increase in its annual output. It asked each supervisor to play for the slight edge, to increase his production each month by just 1 per cent over the figure for the preceding month. At the end of the year, the total was up more than 15 per cent— not only because the one per cent increase compounded itself but because the small improvement seemed realistic and easily attainable.

3. *The Sense of Time*

In addition to flexibility and realism, the problem-solving attitude characteristically includes a special sense of time. Problem-solving takes place in a time dimension.

Animals rate low as problem-solvers because they live primarily in the dimension of the present. But even a dog has some sense of the future: it will bury a bone to cope with tomorrow's hunger.

Time is among the assets of the problem-solver. It is indeed one of man's most important possessions. As the "time-binder," to use Korzybski's word, he can put to work three facets of time—the past, the present, and the future.

Time is one of those abstractions that have troubled philosophers and scientists. Little wonder. After writing at length on the mystery of time, St. Augustine concluded: "My soul yearns to know this most entangled enigma. . . . I confess to thee, O Lord, that I am as yet ignorant what Time is." Yet the problem-solver must make the effort to understand his own relation to time.

The most novel ideas about this subject have come from the new school of "phenomenological psychiatrists." Such therapists believe that emotional illness involves a special attitude towards time. Many schizophrenics, for example, have lost all sense of the future. They live only in the narrowest span of the present.

Psychiatrists used to think that this loss of the future was a result of mental illness, that after health is restored the patient can then recover his awareness of the future. But the phenomenologists take the opposite view. They say the illness is not the cause but the result of losing one's sense of the future. To restore health, the doctor must work on the patient's perception of time.

Dr. Eugene Minkowski, describing one of his cases, says the cause of "the more basic disorder is the distorted attitude toward the future." This was the state of mind of the patient: "There was no action or desire which, emanating from the present, reached out to the future, spanning the dull similar days. As a result, each day life began anew, like a solitary island in a gray sea of passing time."

The implications are important for all of us. Our success as problem-solvers depends on our attitude toward the future. If we are to go from A to Z, from our present position to the goal we seek, we must see ourselves in a definite relationship with the future, appreciating its link to the past and the present.

Intellectually, a child may be fully equipped to handle a

particular problem, but he will come up with no solution because he lacks the right attitude toward time. Many routine jobs in business, like filing correspondence, would not tax the mental capacities of a 10-year old; yet he cannot do it successfully because he does not see the relationship between his task and a future that has reality.

Psychological research has revealed these facts about the individual's sense of time at various ages:

Age	*Sense of Time*
1 year	no future—only the present
3 years	awareness of regular hours in the day
4 years	understands meaning of "today"
5 years	understands "yesterday" and "tomorrow"
8 years	can understand "weeks," each of which seems endless
15 years	basic time unit is the "month"
20 years	a "year" is tangible
40 years	spans of "years" and even "decades"

These are approximations, of course, and some 15-year-olds may have the point of view of the average 20-year-old.

For the problem-solver time itself presents many hazards in each of its facets—past, present, and future. William James has emphasized the difficulty of understanding time and in so doing has described one of its characteristics:

> Let anyone try, I will not say to arrest, but to notice or attend to, the *present* moment of time. One of the most baffling experiences occurs. Where is it, this present? It has melted away in our grasp, fled ere we could touch it, gone in the instant of becoming.

He suggests that we treat time as *duration*. We measure the duration as a continuing series of "now," "now," "now," and so on. Each "now" is a bit of time, and the pieces when put together make up a *continuing present* that stretches for us into a future. The important point is the relationship of the present to the future. If we did not sense that relationship, we could not even speak. We can only begin a sentence in the present; we will need a part of the future to finish it.

Unfortunately, most of us tend to overvalue the present and the near future, finding the long-range future more elusive to our grasp. Often we know that a half-hour of thorough preparation will get the job done three hours sooner. Nevertheless, we neglect the preparation. Why? Because the preparation would take a half-hour out of the here and now, whereas no preparation will mean that we pay the price of three hours out of the future. When we fail to do adequate planning, we are mortgaging the hours and forcing ourselves ultimately to pay a heavy rate of interest. We can avoid the usury of time only by strengthening our awareness of the future and making it more real.

The Three Dimensions of Time

Our faulty sense of time, leading us to gloss over preparation, often cripples our problem-solving. We press on to examining solutions before we have defined the problem, before we have looked at the facts, before we have analyzed our frame of reference, before we have really explored the critical factors—all because of our reluctance to sacrifice the present to the future.

Man is truly the "time-binder" when he fulfills his unique human relationship to time. In solving our problems, we must give proper attention to each of time's three dimensions: we must tie together long stretches of the past and the future, knotting them at the point of the present.

We frequently strike the wrong balance between past, present, and future because of our tendency to visualize time as if it were a continuum stretched out in space. We think of the past as something "behind" us; the present we see as something "here," at this point of space where we now stand; the future is "ahead" of us, a direction in space toward which we are moving.

The result of these spatial ideas is that we develop certain unsound attitudes toward time. Because the past is behind us, we feel it is gone. But in truth the past is always with us.

It is a body of experience right at hand which can be used over and over again. Because the present is "here," we may tend to give it dominating value on the theory that it's a "bird in the hand." Often the present is important only because it makes possible a bigger and richer future.

Whatever its handicaps, our spatial feeling about the future has one important advantage for us. The fact that it is "ahead" gives us hope. It helps to compensate for the sufferings of the past and the discomforts of the present. Without it, aspiration and effort would become impossible. The world of problem-solving is necessarily oriented toward a better tomorrow.

Problem-Solving and the Future

The problem-solving attitude is essentially optimistic. It is based on the idea that intelligence, coupled with the human will, can find ways of implementing our values. Problem-solving is a function that derives from our compulsion to serve the values we hold, whether they be noble or selfish or both.

We who believe in the democratic way of life want freedom because it enlarges the area in which we may undertake to solve our problems for ourselves. We do not delegate to others the right to impose on us their prefabricated solutions.

If we fail as problem-solvers, we may find ourselves stripped of the right to tackle problems altogether. As the problems have grown greater, the need to think soundly has increased. A society in which the individual proves ineffective in dealing with his own small-scale problems cannot hope to be strong enough to cope with the world-shattering issues of our times. The critical factor in democracy is whether the people, who have ultimate authority, are capable of thinking.

The advocates of totalitarianism say we are not. They believe that in an industrialized world, where specialization is the keynote, only a handful are equipped to perform the specialized function of problem-solving. History will judge.

Jacques Barzun has said that the problem of our age is that we don't know quite what to believe and don't quite believe what we know. We do not know all we need to know about coping with our difficulties, but we do have more knowledge than we have yet been willing to apply. Even if we know less than we ought to, we must have the conviction to put it to work. An ancient sage has said: "He whose works exceed his wisdom, his wisdom shall endure; but he whose wisdom exceeds his works, his wisdom will not endure."

We must use the skills of problem-solving to translate our wisdom into works. Only so can the race of man survive and prosper.

Appendix

[Appendix]

PROBLEM-SOLVING QUESTIONS

I. Defining Your Purpose
A. "Where am I?"
B. "What results do I want to accomplish?"
C. "Can I be specific in defining my purpose?"
D. "Can I at the same time achieve a breadth of scope?"
E. "What subgoals must I pursue to accomplish my purpose?"
F. "Am I distinguishing between means and goals?"
G. "Does my definition of purpose give me some idea of what a solution would look like?"
H. "Can I organize my problem into a series of manageable units?"

II. Asking the Right Questions
A. "What questions will yield data relevant to my purpose?"
B. "How can I restate these questions in other forms?"
C. "What new questions are suggested by the restatement of my original questions?"
D. "Are my questions meaningful—that is, do they foreshadow what a possible answer would look like?"

III. Dealing with Facts
A. "What facts have my questions yielded?"
B. "How would these facts look in a different setting?"
C. "How would these facts look through the eyes of other people involved in the situation?"
D. "How would they look to people not involved in the situation?"
E. "Have I delayed judgment as long as possible in evaluating the facts?"
F. "If this fact is true, what other facts are likely to be true?"

G. "What is the pattern of which the fact is merely a part?"

H. "How does the fact relate to my purpose?"

I. "Concerning each fact—who, what, when, where, why, how, how much?"

J. "What facts in my problem still remain unknown or incompletely understood?"

K. "Have I added *Etc.* to my list of facts to remind me that some of the facts are still unknown?"

L. "Are there alternative explanations for the facts in my possession?"

IV. The Frame of Reference

A. "What frame of reference am I using?"

B. "Does my frame of reference suggest that there are gaps in my knowledge?"

C. "What additional facts are suggested by my frame of reference?"

D. "What new meanings will my facts take on if I change my frame of reference?"

E. "Does any new fact, which fails to fit the rest of my facts, constitute a challenge to my present frame of reference?"

F. "How can I reword my frame of reference so that I may see it in a new light?"

G. "How do new facts fit into my frame of reference?"

H. "Against what facts have I been prejudiced by my frame of reference?"

I. "Do seemingly irrelevant facts have some hidden relationship to my frame of reference?"

J. "Would another frame of reference make more sense out of the facts at my disposal?"

K. "Would a rewording of my frame of reference help me fill the gaps in my information?"

V. Using Generalizations

A. "What generalizations lie at the heart of my frame of reference?"

B. "What new details of fact are added to my knowledge by the generalizations I am using?"

C. "Do my generalizations tie all the facts together in a reasonable pattern?"

D. "Do any of the facts conflict with my generalizations?"

E. "Since I must use abstract terms in my generalizations, what detailed facts do those terms represent?"

F. "What important details are omitted in my statement of abstractions?"

G. "Are the dominant details represented in my statement of abstractions really the most important and the most relevant to my purpose?"

H. "Are the qualities alleged to be characteristic of each item in my generalization really present?"

I. "Exactly what is identified by my generalizations and abstractions, and how is it classified by my generalizations and abstractions?"

VI. Spelling Out Relations

A. "What facts go together—either as a result of cause and effect or as a result of the same causes?"

B. "Which facts are more important than others?"

C. "What arrangement of the facts will suggest courses of action that lead to my goal?"

D. "In the absence of knowledge, can I set up a tentative theory or hypothesis that will establish relationships among the available facts?"

E. "Does my tentative theory suggest other facts for which I ought to look or any experiment that will test my theory?"

VII. Visualizing

A. "Am I thinking in visual terms?"

B. "Can I visualize the key aspects of my generalizations, abstractions, and relationships?"

C. "Can I describe my problem in visual language, using metaphors and similes?"

D. "Can I set up visual juxtapositions and sequences among the facts to represent the key relationships?"

E. "Do my visualizations help me see distinctions—that is, discriminate among the facts and identify them in relation to each other?"

F. "What analogies are suggested by my visualizations?"

G. "What are the similarities *and* dissimilarities involved in my visualized analogies?"

VIII. Manipulating Symbols

A. "How can I represent a complicated relationship by using a simplified symbol for it?"

B. "Which of my problem-solving material is available to me only in symbolic form?"

C. "Will the formulation of my problem be improved if I reduce the verbal symbolization to writing?"

D. "Is my problem itself due to an unconscious assumption that my symbols are identical with reality?"

E. "Do my symbols effectively point to the realities they are supposed to symbolize?"

F. "Which of the elements in my problem are symbols for reality and not the reality itself?"

G. "Do the symbols I have selected abstract and highlight the important characteristics of the reality with which I am dealing?"

H. "How can I diagram the problem?"

I. "What are the key relationships I wish to diagram?"

J. "What is the best symbolic representation for the type of relationships involved in my problem—lines, arrows, spheres, squares, etc.?"

K. "In what sequence should my diagram show the relationships?"

L. "What scale can I use to represent degrees of quality and quantity in the problem elements?"

M. "In building my model, what are the factors most relevant to my problem, and how can I isolate them so that I may concentrate on the crucial factors?"

N. "By what criteria can I test my model to see if it behaves in a way that will correspond with reality?"

IX. Typical Solutions

A. The Panoramic Method

1. "What are the basic alternatives possible in the situation?"
2. "What alternatives exist within each of the alternatives?"
3. "What data are relevant to each?"
4. "What are the probable consequences of each?"
5. "How can I maximize the favorable consequences and minimize the unfavorable ones?"
6. "Have I really listed all the possible alternatives?"
7. "How accurate are the predictions I am making about each alternative?"
8. "What are the personal values by which I am judging the consequences of each alternative?"

B. The Classification Method

1. "Into what class of problems does my problem fall?"
2. "What are the solutions usually applied to this class of problems?"
3. "In what respects does my problem conform to the other problems in this class?"
4. "In what respects does my problem differ from the other problems in this class?"
5. "Do circumstances or additional facts require that I reclassify my problem?"

C. The Critical Factor Method

1. "What element or elements in my problem must be changed or acted upon to achieve my objective?"
2. "Has my problem been adequately stated so that its formulation suggests what is likely to be the critical factor or factors?"

3. "What must I eliminate from the situation or add to the situation in order to achieve my goal?"
4. "In identifying the critical factor, will the history of the problem reveal its presence?"
5. "How long has the problem existed, when did it arise, and under what circumstances?"
6. "Did it generate any other problems, and was it the result of solving some other problem?"
7. "How much of a problem is it, and has it been more of a problem at some time and less of a problem at other times?"
8. "Who is affected by the problem, who was affected before, and who is no longer affected?"
9. "What has been the record of efforts to correct the problem?"
10. "Which of the factors in my problem are most closely related to my purpose?"
11. "In taking action to alter or eliminate the critical factor, is my remedy commensurate with the weight of the factor?"

D. The Method of Innovation
1. "Can I turn my premises upside down?"
2. "Suppose I deny my premises: what conclusions will follow?"
3. "Can I tear apart the components of my problem and rearrange them?"
4. "Can I change the characteristics of the components—size, shape, volume, timing, physical composition?"
5. "Can I reverse sequences?"
6. "Can I transpose cause and effect?"
7. "What would happen if I abandoned my basic beliefs about the problem?"
8. "What led people to accept the conventional premises, and how have conditions changed since then?"
9. "What if I carry my thinking to the extremes at

either end of the spectrum of available possibilities?"

10. "Suppose I ignore some of the elements in my problem and exaggerate the weight I give to others?"

11. "Suppose I didn't have this limiting factor in my problem: can I do something to alter that factor?"

E. The Adaptation Method

1. "In what respect is my problem like other problems that have been solved?"

2. "In what respect is my problem different from similar problems, and what adjustments can I make to compensate for the differences?"

3. "In what respect is my purpose different from the purpose of the problem-solver whose solution I am borrowing or adapting?"

4. "What is the general principle involved in the solution I am attempting to adapt?"

5. "What particular application must I make of the general principle?"

6. "Am I misusing my past experience by allowing it to force a rigid adherence to habitual practice and established patterns of thought?"

7. "Can I combine different elements in past experience to meet present needs?"

8. "Have I overlooked any past experience—my own or that of others—which is relevant to my purpose?"

9. "Am I rejecting relevant past experience because of an assumption that 'my problem is different'?"

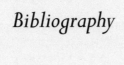

Bibliography

SELECTED BIBLIOGRAPHY

Psychology and Logic

Bross, Irwin D. J., *Design for Decision.* New York, Macmillan Co., 1953.

Bruner, Jerome S.; Goodnow, Jacqueline J.; and Austin, George A., *A Study of Thinking.* New York, John Wiley and Sons, 1956.

Chase, Stuart, *Guides to Straight Thinking.* New York, Harper and Brothers, 1956.

Dewey, John, *How We Think.* New York, D. C. Heath, 1933.

Dimnet, Ernest, *The Art of Thinking.* New York, Simon and Schuster, 1949.

Duncker, Karl, *On Problem-Solving.* Translated by Lees, Lynne S. Psychological Monographs, Vol. 58, No. 5. Washington, D.C., American Psychological Association, 1945.

Fromm, Erich, *The Forgotten Language.* New York, Grove Press, 1957.

Ghiselin, Brewster, ed., *The Creative Process.* New York, A Mentor Book, The New American Library, 1955.

James, William, *Psychology.* New York, Henry Holt and Co., 1905.

Köhler, W., *The Mentality of Apes.* London, Routledge & Kegan Paul, 1925.

Lewin, Kurt, *Resolving Social Conflicts.* New York, Harper and Brothers, 1948.

MacIver, R. M., ed., *New Horizons in Creative Thinking.* New York, Institute for Religious and Social Studies, distributed by Harper and Brothers, 1954.

Mill, John Stuart, *A System of Logic.* New York, Harper and Brothers, 1870.

Myerson, Abraham, *Speaking of Man.* New York, Alfred A. Knopf, 1950.

Pfeiffer, John, *The Human Brain.* New York, Harper and Brothers, 1955.

Stebbing, L. Susan, *Thinking to Some Purpose.* Harmondsworth, Middlesex, Penguin Books, 1939.

Stein, Morris I. and Heinze, Shirley J., *Creativity and the Individual.* Summaries of selected literature in psychology and psychiatry. Glencoe, Ill., Free Press of Glencoe, 1960.

Thomson, Robert, *The Psychology of Thinking.* Baltimore, Md., Penguin Books, 1959.

Tolman, E. C., *Purposive Behavior in Animals and Men.* New York, Century Co., 1932.

Vinacke, W. Edgar, *The Psychology of Thinking.* New York, McGraw-Hill Book Co., 1952.

Walter, W. Grey, *The Living Brain.* New York, W. W. Norton and Co., 1953.

Wechsler, David, *Range of Human Capacities.* Baltimore, Williams and Wilkins Co., 1952.

Wertheimer, Max, *Productive Thinking.* New York, Harper and Brothers, 1945.

Winkler, Franz E., *Man—The Bridge Between Two Worlds.* New York, Harper and Brothers, 1960.

Woodworth, Robert S., *Experimental Psychology.* New York, Henry Holt and Co., 1938.

Science and Philosophy

Barnett, Lincoln, *The Universe and Dr. Einstein.* New York, William Sloane Associates, 1948.

Beveridge, W. I. B., *The Art of Scientific Investigation.* New York, W. W. Norton and Co., 1957.

Butterfield, Herbert, *The Origins of Modern Science.* New York, Macmillan Co., 1960.

Calder, Ritchie, *Science in Our Lives.* New York, Signet Key Books, The New American Library, 1954.

Cassirer, Ernst, *An Essay on Man.* New Haven, Yale University Press, 1944.

Cohen, Morris Raphael and Nagel, Ernest, *An Introduction to Logic and Scientific Method.* New York, Harcourt Brace and Co., 1934.

Conant, James B., *Modern Science and Modern Man.* New York, Columbia University Press, 1952.

Conant, James B., *On Understanding Science.* New York, A Mentor Book, The New American Library, 1951.

Dewey, John, *The Quest for Certainty.* New York, Minton, Balch and Co., 1929.

Einstein, Albert and Infeld, Leopold, *The Evolution of Physics.* New York, Simon and Schuster, 1938.

Huxley, Julian, *Man in the Modern World.* New York, Harper and Brothers, 1944.

James, William, *The Philosophy of William James.* New York, Modern Library, 1925.

Newman, James R., "Einstein's Great Idea" in *Adventures of the Mind,* edited by Thruelson, Richard and Kobler, John. New York, Alfred A. Knopf, 1959.

Rapoport, Anatol, *Operational Philosophy.* New York, Harper and Brothers, 1953.

Reichenbach, Hans, *The Rise of Scientific Philosophy.* Berkeley, University of California Press, 1951.

Russell, Bertrand, *A History of Western Philosophy.* New York, Simon and Schuster, 1945.

Russell, Bertrand, *Human Knowledge.* New York, Simon and Schuster, 1948.

Santayana, George, *Winds of Doctrine.* New York, Charles Scribner's Sons, 1926.

Whitehead, Alfred North, *Adventures of Ideas.* New York, Macmillan Co., 1933.

Whitehead, Alfred North, *The Aims of Education.* New York, Macmillan Co., 1929.

Whitehead, Alfred North, *Essays in Science and Philosophy.* New York, Philosophical Library, 1948.

Wightman, W. P. D., *The Growth of Scientific Ideas.* New Haven, Yale University Press, 1953.

Young, J. Z., *Doubt and Certainty in Science.* Oxford, Clarendon Press, 1951.

Sociology and Anthropology

Childe, V. Gordon, *Man Makes Himself*. New York, A Mentor Book, The New American Library, 1951.

Coon, Carleton S., *The Story of Man*. New York, Alfred A. Knopf, 1954.

Howells, William, *Back of History*. Garden City, N.Y., Doubleday and Co., 1954.

Leighton, Alexander H., *Human Relations in a Changing World*. New York, E. P. Dutton and Co., 1949.

Mayo, Elton, *The Social Problems of an Industrial Civilization*. Boston, Graduate School of Business Administration, Harvard University, 1945.

Spicer, Edward H., ed., *Human Problems in Technological Change*. New York, Russell Sage Foundation, 1952.

Semantics and Linguistics

Johnson, Wendell, *People in Quandaries*. New York, Harper and Borthers, 1946.

Korzybski, Alfred, *Science and Sanity*. Lancaster, Penna., The International Non-Aristotelian Library Publishing Co., 1941.

Laird, Charlton, *The Miracle of Language*. New York, World Publishing Co., 1953.

Lee, Irving J., *Language Habits in Human Affairs*. New York, Harper and Brothers, 1941.

Lee, Irving J., ed., *The Language of Wisdom and Folly*. New York, Harper and Brothers, 1949.

Rapoport, Anatol, *Science and the Goals of Man*. New York, Harper and Brothers, 1950.

History and Biography

Churchill, Winston, *The Second World War*. Boston, Houghton, Mifflin Co., 1948.

Churchill, Winston, *The World Crisis*. New York, Scribner's Sons, 1923.

Durant, Will, *The Story of Civilization*. 8 Volumes. New York, Simon and Schuster, 1942-1963.

MacIver, R. M., ed., *Moments of Personal Discovery*. New York, The Institute for Religious and Social Studies, Harper and Brothers, 1952.

Muller, Herbert J., *The Uses of the Past*. New York, Oxford University Press, 1952.

Pratt, Fletcher, *Ordeal by Fire*. New York, William Sloane Associates, 1948.

Toynbee, Arnold, *A Study of History*. 10 Volumes. New York, Oxford University Press, 1933-1954.

Untermeyer, Louis, *Makers of the Modern World*. New York, Simon and Schuster, 1955.

Vallentin, Antonina, *The Drama of Albert Einstein*. Garden City, N.Y., Doubleday and Co., 1954.

Business

Amber, George H. and Amber, Paul S., *The Anatomy of Automation*. Englewood Cliffs, N.J., Prentice-Hall, Inc., 1962.

Drucker, Peter F., *The Practice of Management*. New York, Harper and Brothers, 1954.

Kibbee, Joel M.; Craft, Clifford J.; and Nanus, Burt, *Management Games. A new technique for executive development*. New York, Reinhold Publishing Corp., 1961.

Lemke, B. C. and Edwards, James Don, eds., *Administrative Control and Executive Action*. Columbus, Ohio, Charles E. Merrill Books, Inc., 1961.

Newman, William H., *Administrative Action*. Englewood Cliffs, N.J., Prentice-Hall, Inc., 1951.

Simon, Herbert A., *The New Science of Management Decision*. New York, Harper and Brothers, 1960.

Miscellaneous

Barzun, Jacques, *The House of Intellect*. New York, Harper and Brothers, 1959.

Donovan, Joseph W., *Modern Jury Trials*. New York, G. A. Jennings Co., Inc., 1924.

Highet, Gilbert, *Man's Unconquerable Mind*. New York, Columbia University Press, 1954.

Wellman, Francis L., *The Art of Cross-Examination*. New York, Macmillan Co., 1948.